An exhibition organized by the Commitee of the Exhibition of Living National
Treasures of Japan for the following museums in the United States:

— **Museum of Fine Arts, Boston**
  November 3, 1982 — January 2, 1983

— **The Art Institute of Chicago**
  January 29, 1983 — March 20, 1983

— **Japanese American Cultural and Community Center,**
  Los Angeles
  April 5, 1983 — May 1, 1983

Living National Treasures
of
Japan

**THE EXHIBITION
LIVING NATIONAL TREASURES OF JAPAN**

Made possible by grants from:
— The Japan Foundation
　　Commemorative Association for the Japan World Exposition 1970
— The Vehicle Racing Commemorative Foundation

Sponsored by:

— Mitsubishi Heavy Industries, Ltd.
— Mitsubishi Electric Corporation
— Mitsubishi Motors Corporation
— Mitsubishi Corporation
— The Mitsubishi Bank, Ltd.

Primary Sponsors of the Exhibition:
— The Japanese Ministry of Foreign Affairs
— The Japanese Agency for Cultural Affairs
— The Committee for the Exhibition of Living National Treasures of Japan
— Nippon Television Network Corporation
— The Yomiuri Shimbun
— Museum of Fine Arts, Boston

With cooperation of:
— The National Museum of Modern Art, Tokyo
— The National Museum of Modern Art, Kyoto

COLLABORATORS

Co-author:
Hiroshi HARADA, Vice Director Intangible Cutural Properties and
Folk Culture Division, pages *12 — 15*
Kunio MINAMI, Senior Cutural Properties Inspector, pages *16 — 18* and *36*
Tetsurô KITAMURA, Specialest for Professor, Kyoritsu Women's Unviersity, pages *18 — 24*
Makoto YAGIHASHI, Specialest for Cultural Properties Inspector, pages *25 — 29* and *35*
Mikio ÔTAKI Specialest for Cultural, Properties Inspector, pages *29 — 32*
Morihiro OGAWA, Fellow for Research in Japanese Arms and Armor, Museum of Fine
Arts, Boston, pages *3 2 — 35*

Co-translator:
Patoricia MASSY
Shigetaka KANEKO
Takehiro SHINDÔ

Layout and Design:
Ryûji HISAMA, Ôtsukakôgeisha, Tokyo
Shirô YOSHIKAWA Ôtskakôgeisha, Tokyo

Cover Design:
CARL ZAHN, Director of Publications, Museum of Fine Arts, Boston

Photographs:
Daizaburô YONEDA, Tokyo
Kazuyuki YAZAWA, Ôtsukakôgeisha, Tokyo

General Editor:
JAN FONTEIN, Director, Museum of Fine Arts, Boston

This catalogue was made possible through cooperation of The Vehicle Racing
Commemorative

Front cover design: K. Serizawa's two-fold screen, Plate No.99.

JAPANESE WORKING COMMITTEE

WATARU KONISHI
Director, Important Intangible Cultural Properties and Folk Culture Division
Agency for Cultural Affairs

KUNIO MINAMI
Senior Specialest for Cultural Properties Inspector, Agency for Cultural Affairs

MAKOTO YAGIHASHI
Specialest for Cultural properties Inspector, Agency for Cultural Affairs

MIKIO ÔTAKI
Specialest for Cultural Properties Inspector, Agency for Cultural Affairs

SEIZO HAYASHIYA
Curator, Craft Department, Tokyo National Museum

MITSUHIRO HASEBE
Curator, Craft Department, National Museum of Modern Art, Tokyo

TAKEO UCHIYAMA
Curator, The National Museum of Modern Art, Kyoto

MASAKI NAKANO
Professor, Tokyo National University of Fine Arts and Music

TETSURÔ KITAMURA
Professor, Kyôritsu Women's University

SUETARÔ KAWAKAMI
Acting Director, Cultural Promotions Headquarters, The Yomiuri Shimbun

UNITED STATES WORKING COMMITTEE

MORIHIRO OGAWA
Curator-in-Charge of the Exhibition, and Fellow for Research in Japanese Arms and
Armor, Museum of Fine Arts, Boston

LINDA THOMAS
Registrar, Museum of Fine Arts, Boston

YASUHIRO IGUCHI
Conservator, Museum of Fine Arts, Boston

JUDITH DOWNES,
Designer, Museum of Fine Arts, Boston

JACK V. SEWELL
Curator, Oriental Art, The Art Institute of Chicago

OSAMU UEBA
Associate Curator, Oriental Art, The Art Institute of Chicago

GERALD D. YOSHITOMI
Executive Director, Japanese American Cultural and Community Center, Los Angeles

MILES M. KUBO
Gallery Director, Japanese American Cultural and Community Center, Los Angeles

ADMINISTRATIVE OFFICE

Manager-in-Charge:
KAZUYUKI IKEDA
Nippon Television Network Corporation

Executive Manager:
MASAYA ASANO
Nippon Television Network Corporation

Executive Manager:
AKIKO ICHIHASHI
Nippon Television Network Corporation

Staff:
SHIGEO KUNO
Nippon Television Network Corporation

SABURÔ UENO
Nippon Television Network Corporation

SHUNSUKE MIYAO
Nippon Television Network Corporation

TSUNEMICHI YANO
Nippon Television Network Corporation

KENGO MORIUCHI
Nippon Television Network Corporation

Contents

	Page
Foreword, by Yosoji Kobayashi	10
Preface, by Jan Fontein	11
Japanese Fraditional Crafts and the Government Administration for Their Protection	12
A Summary of History and Current Status of Japanese Traditional Crafts	16
Plates	37
List of Exhibits	253
Introduction to the Artists	264
Glossary	278

The Japanese of the mid-nineteenth century were amazed by the outside world into which they thrust when they emerged from the "Shogun era" and three hundred years of isolation. In a determined attempt to catch up with the modern world the Japanese decided it would be necessary to make great changes within their country. Unfortunately, in their eagerness to modernize, the Japanese lost their appreciation for many of the traditions from which their culture had developed.

Concerned for the preservation of much of the traditional Japanese culture, scholars like Earnest F. Fenollosa and William S. Bigelow of the Museum of Fine Arts, Boston, established major collections of Japanese and other Asian arts. Just as the early foreign visitors in their great "black ships" opened up the Japanese people's eyes to the outside world, this appreciation for Japanese culture shown by organizations such as the Museum of Fine Arts, Boston, greatly impressed the Japanese and helped them to eventually reconsider their short-lived disregard for their traditional culture.

Later, when the battles of the World War II threatened the ancient capitols of Kyoto and Nara during the tragic break in friendly relations between the United States and Japan, the physical destruction of centuries of Japanese culture was again prevented with the decision to not subject these cities to bombing. The Japanese people will never forget that this noble decision was largely the result of the individual effort of the Boston Museum's former assistant curator Dr. Langdon Warner and the influence he exercised through his former students in the name of preserving the cultural heritage of Japan for the benefit of future generations.

I and my fellow countrymen have very deep feelings for these great men who so highly esteemed Japanese culture and we have the greatest sense of gratitude for the friendly relations between the United States and Japan which they helped promote through cultural exchange.

In the past I have the pleasure of working with the Museum of Fine Arts, Boston, on two separate occasions in the co-sponsorship of exhibitions which introduced the Museum's finest selections of western painting to the Japanese people. I am honored to again be associated with this pioneering museum in sponsoring an event so long-awaited by the Japanese people: an exhibition of rare and priceless Japanese paintings which have never been permitted to be loaned outside the Museum. When this exhibition opens in Tokyo and Kyoto from March of 1983 the process of US-Japanese cultural exchange will take another great stride.

It has been my great desire to somehow compensate the Museum of Fine Arts, Boston, for its immeasurable contributions to my country because cultural exchange is a mutual two-way process. This desire lead me to contribute to the restoration of the Japanese garden in the Museum of Fine Arts, Boston, and to establish the Matsutaro Shoriki Fund for the promotion of the study of Asian arts.

And now nothing gives me more pleasure than to be participating in the Japanese Living National Treasures Exhibition with the joint sponsorship of the Museum of Fine Arts, Boston, in taking the exhibition to Boston, Chicago and Los Angeles.

We Japanese have long preserved our traditional arts and crafts, with many of these cherished techniques having been handed down from parent to child and master to apprentice for over 1,000 years, Today, in modern Japan, recognition is given not only for the works of these arts and crafts, but also for the artisans and craftsmen who are practicing and preserving this invaluable part of our traditional culture. Out of our love for their work and the importance we feel they have for our culture, the most skilled of these individuals and groups are given the title "Living National Treasures".

The Japanese Living National Treasures Exhibition, with 241 contemporary representative works and demonstrations, is of unprecedented size and scale. Not even in Japan has there ever before been such a major exhibition of individuals and their works. It is our great desire with this extensive exhibition to give the American people the opportunity to now observe and enjoy this vital link with our past.

In closing I would like to express my deepest appreciation to the staffs at the Museum of Fine Arts, Boston, the Art Institute of Chicago and the Los Angeles Japanese-American Cultural and Community Center, the honorary and staff members of the Japanese Living Treasures Exhibition Committee, the sponsors and the other associate organizations for their tireless efforts in paving the way for this exhibition.

October 1982.

Yosoji Kobayashi

Yosoji Kobayashi
Chairman of the Board,
Nippon Television Network Corporation,
President, The Yomiuri Shinbun

The establishment by the Japanese Government of the Living National Treasure (Ningen Kokuhô) Award in 1955 is an act of enlightened cultural policy admired by people all over the world. The Museum of Fine Arts is proud, therefore, that it was asked to host the first exhibition in the United States that consists of works created by the traditional artists who were awarded this distinction.

In Japan exhibitions of the works of Ningen Kokuhô are held regularly and are enjoyed by many. Yet even there an exhibition of the scope and size of *Living National Treasures of Japan* has not been held before. By opening this exhibition in Boston on Japan's National Holiday *Bunka no Hi* (Culture Day), concurrently with the reopening of our renovated Asiatic galleries, we wish to demonstrate that the Museum's traditional respect for the ancient arts of the East is matched by its commitment to the arts of the present. That the exhibition and the Department of Asiatic Art open at the same time is, therefore, a tribute to the great masters of both the past and the present.

This exhibition was organized in cooperation with the Agency for Cultural Affairs (Bunkachô) in Tokyo, whose Commissioner-General Mr. Bunichiro Sano took a personal interest in this venture from the very beginning. Without the enthusiastic support of Mr. Yosoji Kobayashi, Chairman of the Board of Nippon Television Network and President of the Yomiuri Shimbun this project, sponsored by these two corporations, would never have been realized. It is a special pleasure to acknowledge the generous additional support received from the Japan Foundation, the Vehicle Racing Commemorative Foundation, Commemorative Association for the Japan World Exposition 1970, Mitsubishi Heavy Industries, Ltd, Mitsubishi Electric Corporation, Mitsubishi Motors Corporation, Mitsubishi Corporation and the Mitsubishi Bank, Ltd.

Japanese public collections, private collectors and several of the artists themselves generously lent to this exhibition. The fugitive colors of textiles and lacquers make it necessary to replace certain objects after one month of exhibition. We are especially grateful to the artists and owners of these pieces for their willingness to let these fragile masterpieces travel.

The exhibition comes from the quiet world of the dedicated men and women who have inherited and who uphold the great traditions of Japan's artistic past. As this aspect of Japan is only too often forgotten in the industrialized world of today, we hope that many will come to see this exhibition. After closing in Boston the exhibition will travel to the Art Institute of Chicago and to the Japanese American Cultural & Community Center in Los Angeles. To have this exhibition conclude its tour of the United States in the area where Japan's contribution to American culture began would seem to be particularly appropriate.

Jan Fontein
Director
Museum of Fine Arts, Boston

(1) The Development of Techniques of Japanese Applied Arts

Japanese handicraft arts can be divided according to their materials and manufacturing techniques into ceramics, textiles, lacquerware, wood work, bamboo work, metal work, paper, dolls and others. The techniques of these applied arts vary in their origin and history of development. They have come down to the present day through periods of prosperity and adversity and have survived Chinese, Korean and other foreign influences as well as changes in Japan's culture and social life.

Ancient forms of Japanese crafts can be seen in unearthed archaeological relics such as earthenware objects made during the Jômon period, thousands of years B.C. Lacquered bows, combs, bowls and other wooden artifacts, and *rantai shikki* (bamboo basketwork coated with lacquer) date back to the late and final Jômon period. Earthenware objects showing traces of knit or woven textures evidence the existence of textile techniques in this prehistoric era.

During the ensuing Yayoi period (300 B.C.–300 A.D.), bronze mirrors, bronze swords, bronze spears and other bronze objects were imported through exchange with China and Korea; bronzes imitating these, as well as the unique bell-shaped bronzes known as *dôtaku*, were manufactured in Japan. Iron was introduced at about the same time, and iron ploughs, sickles and other farm implements were produced in the late Yayoi period. Fabrics woven of vegetable textiles such as wisteria, *kôzo* (a type of paper mulberry), *choma* (ramie), and also silk began to appear.

Interchange with China and Korea became more frequent in the fourth to fifth and sixth centuries, and many technical experts came over to Japan. Metal work objects of this period include those buried with the dead in *kofun* (protohistoric tumuli) such as bronze mirrors, swords, armor, horse trappings, and various personal ornaments. These pieces reveal a variety of metal techniques, for example: metal casting; metal carving such as line engraving, openwork, inlay; forging for swords, also hammering and gilding — all on a relatively high technical level. Techniques of wheel throwing and firing introduced from Korea in this period served to motivate the development of ceramic crafts from the earlier earthenware to the Sué pottery.

The Asuka and Nara periods of the seventh and eighth centuries saw the introduction of Buddhist culture, which led to notable progress in various applied art crafts. Considerable improvement during the preceding era in the design of metal tools and the techniques of using them contributed to the progress.

Large works of metal casting such as Buddhist statues (exemplified by the Great Buddha of Tôdai-ji Temple), temple bells, and standing lanterns were produced in this period. *Keri-bori* (kicking incision), *nanako* (granulation), and other new techniques of metal carving were developed while shapes and kinds of metal work, as seen on Buddhist ritual objects, multiplied as never before. Examples of very precise and excellent crafts in the field of wood work are preserved in the Shôsô-in Repository of Imperial Treasures. They show that every conceivable kind of wood work technique was in use in this period; *sashi-mono* (joinery), *hiki-mono* (lathe work), *kuri-mono* (gouging), *hori-mono* (carving), and *mokuga* (marquetry). Bamboo work also reveals the early establishment of such basic techniques as plaiting for flower baskets, joining for boxes, and so on.

Lacquer art also progressed due to improved techniques, some introduced from China, for preparing the wooden and bamboo bases and applying gold filings, metal particles or plate, and other decorative materials. Lacquer art techniques of this period range over *kin-gin-e* (painting in gold and/or silver pigment), *makkinru* (depositing gold filings), *mitsuda-e* (litharge painting), *heidatsu* (also termed *hyômon*, embedding of sheet metal cutouts), *raden* (mother-of-pearl inlay), and so on. Used as their bases are wood, bamboo, leather (cowhide, etc.), and ramie cloth glued together in many layers.

In the field of textiles, new kinds of fabrics like *nishiki* (colorful patterned plain weave), *aya* (twill weave) and *ra* (gauze weave) and the techniques of weaving them were imported from China. Dyeing techniques of this period include *shibori-zome* (tie-dyeing), *rô-zome* (wax-resist dyeing) and *hasami-zome* (interposed dyeing, squeezing the cloth between two perforated or engraved wooden boards before dyeing). Ramie and silk fabrics were woven and their output increased, not only in the central region but in local districts also.

The craft of making paper, along with those of making pigments, carbon ink, and brushes, is said to have been introduced in 610 from Korea by the Buddhist priest Donchô. The

technique of papermaking reached a considerably high level in this period, as is evidenced by surviving specimens.

Sué pottery still was in the mainstream of ceramics. Three-colored and green-glazed wares were made during the eighth century under the influence of Chinese *san-ts'ai* (three-color ware) of the T'ang dynasty, but these disappeared after a short while.

As shown above, the major applied art crafts were founded during the Nara period (eighth century), and some of them actually reached a state of virtual perfection.

Applied art designs in the Heian period gradually found their way out of the T'ang style of the Nara period into a Japanese style which amply reflected native sensibility and aesthetic sense. Lacquer art, especially *chôdo* (household furnishings serving also as interior decorations) used in the homes of nobility and Buddhist ritual objects such as *sûtra* (Buddhist scripture) boxes, became richer and more subtly beautiful. Techniques were polished, too; *maki-e* especially, helped by combination with other techniques like *raden*, saw remarkable development.

Textile crafts succeeding those of the Nara period were Japanized in the environment of patrician society, giving birth to certain stereotyped decorative patterns, known as *yûsoku* patterns, reserved for use by the nobility. They were transmitted to the nobility and samurai society of the ensuing Kamakura period, and are now retained in the ceremonial costume of the Imperial Court.

Swords, too, changed from the *chokutô* (straight sword) of the Nara period to the beautifully curving blade termed *Nihon-tô* (Japanese sword). Armor also became ornate. The metal fittings, dyed leather, braided cords and other decorations display work of the highest technical level achieved up to that time.

Thus the Nara and Heian periods saw the flowering of the major crafts: metal work, lacquer art, wood and bamboo work, Japanese paper (*washi*), and so on.

In and after the Muromachi period, tea-ceremony kettles were manufactured in quantities because of the popularity of *cha-no-yu* (tea ceremony), and in metal art a special new type of casting was devised. Fine, elaborate crafts were used for ornamental metal fittings, personal ornaments, and so on in the Edo period.

In lacquer art works reflecting diversified *maki-e* techniques as well as new trends in shapes and designs began to appear. The techniques of *chôshitsu* (carved lacquer) and *chinkin* (hairline engraving filled in with gold) were born under Chinese influence in the late Muromachi period. Lacquer wares of individually characteristic technique and design were produced in local districts.

Washi (Japanese paper) of various qualities, for use not only in painting and writing but also in everyday life, were manufactured for particular purposes in all parts of the country.

In and after the Kamakura period, and notably in the pre-Modern age, the crafts which saw the most remarkable progress and change were ceramics and textiles.

Following the tradition of Sué pottery, ceramic centers in the provinces of Bizen, Tamba, Shigaraki, Echizen, Owari and Mikawa manufactured jars, bowls, and so on, beginning in the Nara or Heian period. Their activities continued to be focused on these everyday utensils until the Muromachi period. At the same time, the influence of Chinese ceramics of the Sung, Yüan and ensuing dynasties motivated the manufacture at Seto of glazed pottery and porcelain wares imitating the shapes and designs of Chinese celadon, pale white porcelain (*ch'ing-pai*), *temmoku* bowls, and so on. The vogue of the tea ceremony, which began in the Muromachi period and spread widely in the Momoyama period, inspired the making of *chatô* (tea-ceremony ceramics) such as Ki-seto (Yellow Seto), Seto-guro (Seto Black), Shino and Oribe at factories in Eastern Mino Province. Along with these Eastern Mino centers, those in Bizen, Iga, and Shigaraki began also to produce tea-ceremony pottery wares. These have formed one current of Japanese ceramic art continuing to the present time.

The many Korean potters who came over to Japan between the late sixteenth and early seventeenth centuries originally established their kilns in Hagi, Takatori, Agano, and other areas. Western Japan became one of the central regions for the Japanese ceramic industry. In the Arita area white porcelain, celadon, and blue and white porcelain wares were created; the technique of *iro-e* (overglaze enamel decoration) was established in the mid-seventeenth century, and Arita became a center for *iro-e* porcelain. Enameled porcelain was made also at Kutani in the present Ishikawa Prefecture, while enameled pottery originated in

Kyoto.

In the field of textiles, the techniques of embroidery and suri-haku (application of gold and/or silver leaf) progressed in the Muromachi and Momoyama periods. Tie-dyeing also thrived, but a variety termed tsujigahana disappeared after a short period of prosperity. Dyeing by means of stencils came into use at this time. The great demand for stencil dyeing (dyeing over stenciled resist) in the Edo period led to the development of crafts for making and using the stencils for dyeing. The technique of yûzen-zome, which made colorful freestyle designs possible, was created in the middle Edo period. Yûzen-dyed fabrics with regionally characteristic styles were produced in Kyoto and also in Kanazawa and Edo (Tokyo), and were widely favored.

Besides these, kasuri (ikat), shima (stripe) and other distinctive weaves began to thrive as local industries. Echigo jôfu and Yûki tsumugi, for example, succeeded weaving and dyeing crafts from olden times and have been loved by the general public. The cotton kasuri weave, which also flourished in the Edo period, was used widely in common life, thus leading to the development of the techniques of kasuri weaving and stencil dyeing.

Many contemporary artists, continuing these traditional crafts, show inventive tendencies. Toward the end of the Taishô era (1912–1926) the folk art movement arose, advocated by Muneyoshi YANAGI and his colleagues, who were inspired by the forms and designs of everyday household objects used by the common people and began to pattern works of applied arts after them. Shôji HAMADA, Keisuke SERIZAWA, and Tatsuaki KURODA are among such artists.

(2) The System of Protection of Applied Art Crafts and Its Present State

Japanese crafts until the Medieval period belonged to and developed under the patronage of the ruling classes, namely, the Imperial Court, the nobility, and the samurai class, as well as religious establishments (Shintô shrines and Buddhist temples). During and after the pre-Modern age, as a result of the demands of the commoners, crafts became diversified, and new techniques were invented.

After the end of the nineteenth century, as new European and American techniques were introduced, and manufacture was gradually mechanized, demand for traditional handcrafted products began to decrease. Especially after World War II, because of the rapid development of techniques and change in the manner of living, social and economic conditions necessary to their survival were lost to many traditional crafts; their decline or actual disappearance was feared. The Japanese government decided to take measures for protecting them as it had done for old works of art, old buildings and other tangible cultural properties.

Protection of cultural heritage in Japan began in 1871, when the Government proclaimed that important old works of art should be protected and that the names and possessors of such works should be reported to the nation. In 1897 the "Law for Preservation of Old Shrines and Temples" was enacted, and valuable works of architecture, painting, sculpture, applied arts, and so on, were registered by the Government. The "Law for Preservation of National Treasures," formulated in 1929, extended protection formerly limited to possessions of shrines and temples to buildings and works of fine and applied arts in general. Another law, enacted in 1919, protects historic sites, gardens, and other areas of high cultural value.

These various laws concerning the protection of cultural heritages were unified in 1950 in the "Law for Protection of Cultural Properties," and traditional crafts and performing arts were included as objects of protection. Intangible Cultural Properties are defined in the Law as "intangible cultural products materialized through such human behaviors as drama, music, dance and applied arts which have a high historical or artistic value." Between 1950 and 1953 only those Intangible Cultural

Properties which were feared to become lost were placed under protection. This rule was revised in 1954 to include those which are not for the present in danger of becoming lost but which are of especially high historical or artistic value; these were to be registered as Important Intangible Cultural Properties and would be protected nationally.

This protective system, in addition to registering particularly valuable crafts and performing arts, designates the persons or groups possessing the crafts and performing arts as their Holders. This is because Intangible Cultural Properties such as performing arts and applied art crafts have been transmitted from man to man and, unlike material art objects, are defined by human activities. Registration of Important Intangible Cultural Properties and nomination of their Holders, thus, are two parts of one and the same system. Those who are Holders of Important Intangible Cultural Properties are popularly known as "Living National Treasures."

Registration of Important Intangible Cultural Properties and nomination of their Holders (individuals or groups) come under the jurisdiction of the Minister of Education, who is advised by the Council for Protection of Cultural Properties concerning the suggested registration and nomination.

Currently, three criteria are used in selecting Important Intangible Cultural Properties for registration:
(1) Those which are of specially high artistic value.
(2) Those which hold a specially important position in the history of applied arts.
(3) Those which are of high artistic value or which hold an important position in the history of applied arts, and which at the same time have conspicuous local characteristics.

Selected as Holders of Important Intangible Cultural Properties are persons or groups highly trained and well versed in the registered Intangible Cultural Properties and capable of high artistic representation.

To date fifty-nine items (kinds) of crafts have been registered in conformity with this system and criteria, and seventy persons and eleven groups have been named as their Holders.

The registered crafts are as follows: In the field of ceramics, Shino, Bizen, Hagi, Enameled Porcelain, and Folk Art Pottery wares, totaling eleven items with ten persons and two groups nominated. In the field of textiles, twenty-two items, twenty-five persons and five groups for *Yûsoku* Weaves, *Yûzen* Dyeing, *Edo-komon, Kata-e-zome,* and so on. These include crafts showing conspicuous local characteristics such as *Shôai-zome, Ojiya-chijimi* and *Echigo-jôfu* which document the development and change in weaving and dyeing crafts.

The field of lacquer art covers six items including *Maki-e, Chinkin* and *Chôshitsu,* with eight persons and one group. The field of metal work covers *Rogata* Casting, Tea-ceremony Kettles, Temple Bell, Metal Carving, Japanese Sword, and so on, with ten items and seventeen persons. In addition there are ten items, ten persons and three groups pertaining to Wood and Bamboo Work, Dolls, Handmade Japanese Paper, and the like.

The Government has taken several measures for the protection of these Important Intangible Cultural Properties. For example, it provides the Holders of the registered crafts with an annual subsidy to defray expenses for training and improvement in their crafts and for educating their successors. It also provides grants to cover a part of the expenses of groups of Holders — prefectures, cities, towns, villages, etc. — and to assist in the raising of successors for their projects. For instance, annual grants are given for such activities to the institutes of lacquer crafts in Ishikawa and Kagawa Prefectures and to the Group Holders of the crafts of *Kurume-gasuri, Ojiya-chijimi, Bashôfu* and *Miyako-jôfu.*

As other measures of protection, the Government purchases the works of Holders of the crafts and keeps records of manufacturing processes by means of documents, photographs, films, and so on. Recording of techniques in films was begun in 1971. Finished to date are those of *Kakiemon, Iro Nabeshima, Maki-e, Chôshitsu, Yûsoku* Weave, *Ise Kata-gami, Echigo-jôfu,* Japanese Sword, Metal Carving, and Handmade Japanese Paper.

Aside from these, the Government annually sponsors or supports the "Exhibition of Living National Treasures," "Exhibition of Traditional Japanese Crafts," "Exhibition of Masterpieces of Traditional Crafts," "Exhibition of Newly Made Japanese Swords," and so on with a view to encouraging traditional crafts and enhancing the people's understanding and recognition of them.

CERAMICS

Japanese ceramic art is among the foremost in the world in the long span of its history, the exceeding variety of its materials and techniques, and the height of its artistic achievements. Its origin dates back to the earthenware of the Jômon period, several thousand years B.C., and since then it has developed in many directions through repeated acceptance or influence of alien techniques mainly from China and Korea.

Chief among the imported techniques are: fabricating with the potter's wheel and firing with *ana-gama* (cave kiln), introduced from the Korean peninsula about the mid-fifth century; technical influence on Ko (Old) Seto ware by Chinese celadon and iron-glazed wares imported in the thirteenth and fourteenth centuries; production of porcelain and blue and white wares by Korean potters who came over in the early seventeenth century; and the subsequent introduction of the Chinese technique of overglaze enamel decoration.

These techniques, which played an important part in the development of Japanese ceramics in their respective periods, were adapted to materials available in Japan and to the life mode and artistic sense of the Japanese people, until eventually new traditions were formed in this country.

Currently there are many ceramic centers in various areas of Japan whose wares are named for the localities where they originate. Many of these centers are following in the tradition of ceramic arts prior to the pre-Modern age.

Among these local centers, those which have the oldest tradition are Seto (Aichi Prefecture), Tokoname (Aichi Prefecture), Echizen (Fukui Prefecture), Shigaraki (Shiga Prefecture), Tamba (Hyôgo Prefecture), and Bizen (Okayama Prefecture). They originated in the late Heian or Kamakura period, succeeding the Sué and Haji potteries of earlier periods, to satisfy the demand for such everyday utensils as jars and bowls as well as objects for use in religious rituals. The wares, except that of Seto, were generally high-fired, hard, unglazed, grayish-brown wares, often partly covered with the natural glaze formed when ashes of the firing wood fell accidentally on the surface. Bizen ware, in particular, has never been glazed but is valued for the tasteful effect of its exposed body and the "kiln transmutation" that takes place during firing. Bizen ware is registered by the Japanese Government as an Important Intangible Cultural Property. Nominated as its Holders are the late Tôyô KANASHIGE (Catalog No. 27—30) and Kei FUJIWARA (Catalog No. 31—32).

Seto, favored with rich resources of good quality pottery clay, is the center where the body of the ware was first decorated by line-engraving, stamping, applying, and other methods, and covered with high-fired iron or ash glaze.

Eastern Mino (Gifu Prefecture), abutting Seto, began toward the end of the Muromachi period, and on into the Momoyama period when the tea ceremony became popular, to manufacture tea-ceremony pottery and table wares of such characteristic types as Shino, Ki-Seto (Yellow Seto), Seto-guro (Seto Black) and Oribe. Shino tea bowls amply covered with a white feldspathic glaze, powerful black lacquer Seto-guro tea bowls, and *Oribe* food vessels characterized by a rich variety of forms and distinctive deep green glaze are valued highly as ceramic wares rich in Japanese elegance. Tajimi, Toki, and neighboring areas have since developed as large ceramic centers in eastern Japan rivaling Seto. Many contemporary ceramic artists are active in this region.

In 1930 Toyozô ARAKAWA discovered a kiln site in the mountainous area of Ôgaya in Gifu Prefecture where Shino ware had been made in the Momoyama period. He reconstructed on the spot a kiln of the time and revived antique-style Shino (Catalog No. 1—2), Seto-guro (Catalog No. 3) and Yellow Seto (Catalog No. 4). He was nominated Holder of the Important Intangible Cultural Properties "Shino" and "Seto-guro" in 1955.

Ceramic industry in the Kyûshû district made remarkable progress thanks to the Korean potters who came to Japan after two Japanese expeditions to Korea in the late eleventh century The pottery wares which were developed in this way include Karatsu (Saga Prefecture), Agano (Fukuoka Prefecture), Takatori (Fukuoka Prefecture), Satsuma (Kagoshima Prefecture) and Hagi (Yamaguchi Prefecture). Under the patronage of the feudal lords ruling the respective areas, these centers made tea-ceremony objects and utensils for daily use. Thus they constitute one of the traditions on which present-day ceramics are based.

Karatsu is a ware which was widely developed in Hizen Province (the present Saga and Nagasaki Prefectures). Its naive, tasteful style in pottery such as tea bowls, *mizusashi* (water jars),

and flower vessels, is appreciated in the tea-ceremony realm. Muan NAKAZATO has worked since the 1930s to revive Old Karatsu, and was nominated in 1976 as Holder of Important Intangible Cultural Property "Karatsu Ware" (Catalog No. 35—36).

Hagi ware, too, has been loved as tea-ceremony pottery since the early pre-Modern age. Following the tradition of the Korean Yi dynasty, its technique has been maintained at Matsumoto, Hagi City, Yamaguchi Prefecture and Fukawa, Nagato City in the same prefecture. The late Kyûwa MIWA, heir to the official ware of the former Mori clan, cultivated a distinctive style in the warm, graceful tone and technique of white glaze. For this he was nominated in 1970 Holder of the Important Intangible Cultural Property "Hagi Ware" (Catalog No. 33—34).

The manufacture of porcelain in Japan began at the start of the seventeenth century, when Korean potters living in what is now Saga Prefecture discovered a mine of petuntze at Arita. The discovery led to the making of the first white porcelain and blue and white (white porcelain with blue underglaze decoration) in this country.

The major types of decoration on porcelain are *sometsuke* (blue and white) in which a design is painted, under the glaze, in *gosu* (cobalt oxide pigment), and *uwa-etsuke* or *iro-e* (overglaze enamel decoration) in which the decoration is painted in colors after glaze firing. Japanese *iro-e* porcelain is believed to have been first crafted at Arita using an imported Chinese overglaze enamel technique. Arita enameled porcelain thereafter was developed into the three perfect styles of Kakiemon, Ko (Old) Imari and Iro (Enameled) Nabeshima.

The enamel decoration of Kakiemon, together with its milk-white body known as *nigoshi-de,* saw stylistic perfection around the Genroku era (1688–1703). The *nigoshi-de* body declined after the late Edo period but has been revived in the modern age by Kakiemon SAKAIDA XII and his son XIII. The technique of Kakiemon ware (*nigoshi-de*) was registered in 1971 as an Important Intangible Cultural Property and the Kakiemon Ceramic Technique Preservation Society has been organized for its preservation.

Iro (Enameled) Nabeshima, the official ware of the former Nabeshima clan which ruled the Saga area during the feudal age, was made by highly trained craftsmen with strictly selected materials. It is the most elaborate of Japanese enameled porcelain wares. The official Nabeshima factory lasted until the end of the Edo period. After the ensuing Meiji era (1868–1912) the Imaemon IMAIZUMI family fell heir to the Iro Nabeshima techniques, from preparation of the body and glaze to glaze firing and overglaze enameling. The technique of Iro Nabeshima, as well as that of Kakiemon (*nigoshi-de*), was registered in 1971 as Important Intangible Cultural Property, for the preservation of which the Iro-Nabeshima Imaemon Ceramic Technique Preservation Society has been organized.

Another representative enameled porcelain of Japan, comparable to Kakiemon, Ko Imari and Iro Nabeshima, is Ko (Old) Kutani. Featuring a heavy, impressive style, this ware is thought to have been manufactured in Ishikawa Prefecture between the mid-seventeenth and early eighteenth centuries. The Terai and Komatsu areas in the prefecture constitute a center of Kutani ware, typically enameled porcelain. Many ceramic artists are currently active there.

Besides the Kakiemon (*nigoshi-de*) and Iro Nabeshima mentioned above (both of which are group designations), the enameled porcelain techniques registered as Important Intangible Cultural Properties had as individual Holders Kenkichi TOMIMOTO and Hajime KATÔ, in recognition of their creative work in bringing enameled porcelain to the realm of modern ceramic art. Both have died and there is no individual Holder in this field now.

The late Kenkichi TOMIMOTO was an artist who considered beauty of form and decoration as the major premise of *iro-e* technique. In his late years he lived in Kyoto, where he created a new ornate *iro-e* porcelain with gold and silver added to overglaze enamels (Catalog No. 10—11, 14).

The late Hajime KATÔ studied Chinese enameled porcelain wares of the Chin-ching era (1522–54) of the Ming dynasty, particularly the *ôji kôsai* (red enamel against yellow enamel background) and the *kinrande* (gilded enameled ware with gold and silver leaf applied over enamel colors), eventually succeeding in restoring these techniques. These are superb technical achievements which represent the many facets of his ceramic art (Catalog No. 16, 17, 20).

Yûzô KONDÔ, a pupil of Kenkichi TOMIMOTO, was nominated as the Holder of Important Intangible Cultural Pro-

perty in the field of *sometsuke* (blue and white porcelain). His *sometsuke* is not a stylized elaborate craft such as the underglaze blue decoration of Enameled Nabeshima; it is characterized by painterly designs done in strong brushwork on a white porcelain body.

Kyoto, where the late Kenkichi TOMIMOTO and Yûzô KONDÔ were active, has been a ceramic center since the pre-Modern age. Around the middle of the seventeenth century, when enameled porcelain was produced at Arita, Kyoto saw the birth of the technique of decorating pottery with graceful overglaze enamel colors. Thereafter, too, in the middle to late Edo period, many kilns were built and distinguished artists of *Kyô-yaki* (Kyoto pottery and porcelain) appeared one after another.

Kyoto is the place where various domestic and imported ceramic techniques such as celadon, *shinsha* (copper red glaze), and iron glaze came together and saw notable technical development. Even now many ceramic artists are displaying varied techniques, from copies of classical pieces to *avant-garde objets*. One of them is the late Munemaro ISHIGURO who moved to Kyoto in 1927 and lived there thereafter. He has left many excellent works in the Chinese Sung dynasty crafts of *kaki* (reddish brown) *temmoku*, *konoha* (leaf) *temmoku*, *Sôaka-e* (Sung enameled ware) and so on (Catalog No. 5, 6). He was nominated in 1955 Holder of Important Intangible Cultural Property "Iron-glaze Pottery."

Contrasting with the polished, rather urban styles of Kyoto are the naive everyday "peasant wares" of local factories in sequestered locations. It was Muneyoshi YANAGI (1889–1961) who discovered and advocated wholesome artless beauty in the products of such local kilns. The late Shôji HAMADA was one of the pottery artists who were influenced by him. He lived after 1924 at Mashiko, then only an insignificant ceramic center in Tochigi Prefecture, where he studied ceramic crafts that had long been employed at local Korean and Japanese kilns and reproduced them in works of his own creation (Catalog No. 21—25). He was nominated in 1955 Holder of Important Intangible Cultural Property "Folk-Art Pottery."

TEXTILES

Japan has been blessed with a large number of ancient traditions, many of which are still thriving today. In considering the reason for the survival of these traditions in relatively unaltered form, it is necessary to look at the geographical location and climate of Japan, the influence of which is particularly evident in the dyeing and weaving traditions that have been so intimately related to the lives and history of the Japanese people.

The Japanese archipelago is located on the eastern fringe of the Asian continent, separated from it by the Sea of Japan and stretching from the northeast to the southwest in an arc like configuration. Four large islands comprise the bulk of the archipelago. On the eastern side of this island nation lies the Pacific Ocean, making Japan the outer wall, as it were, of the Asian continent. To the east of the islands flows the broad Japan Current, which originates near Luson Island in the Philippines and continues up toward the Kantô region of Japan.

This main current, and the affluent that diverges near the northwest side of Amami Ôshima Island, turn into the Tsushima Straits and enter the Sea of Japan. Continuing in a northerly direction up along the western coast of the islands, part of the current passes through the Tsugaru Straits and the Sôga Straits before flowing southward again into the Pacific.

The islands of Japan lie in the middle latitudes of the Northern hemisphere. A large part of the country lies in the temperate zone, but Hokkaidô in the north is in the subarctic zone, and the Ryûkyû Islands to the south are in the subtropics. As a result, there are significant differences in climate from region to region and, though one cannot make an unqualified statement, it can be generally said that there are wide variations in temperature and abundant seasonal changes. In fact, the variety of seasonal flowers that can be found in Japan is very unusual for the temperate zone. Moreover, the amount of rain is high, leading to relatively warm temperatures and, with the exception of winter, a high level of humidity. The warm temperatures and high humidity of the sultry summer season are naturally unpleasant for human beings but ideal for plant life.

As a result of its geographical location, Japan was able to reap the benefits accompanying the penetration of eastern culture across the ocean from the continent which could advance no further. Likewise, Japan was the recipient of the culture brought

up from the south along the Japan Current. In this way, different peoples and different cultures, able to go no further, interacted in Japan to form a distinctive Japanese culture.

A major concern of this culture was how to comfortably adapt to the unbearably hot and humid summer of Japan. An architecture with raised floors and deep eaves to facilitate ventilation, as well as clothing designed for comfort, are two excellent examples of this process of adaptation. Moreover, the custom of changing clothing and even household furnishings evolved as a human response to the changes in season. The type of material used to make clothing also increased in due course. Neutral tints and comparatively quiet hues of the sense of color that was fostered by the natural environment of frequent fog and mist.

Surrounded on four sides by the ocean which forms a natural barriers and isolated from the rest of the world by government olicy until the Meiji Restoration in 1868, Japan developed into a homogenous nation. Despite even changes in political systems, the cultural ethos of the country has remained intact, and the preservation of many of our traditions must be viewed within this context.

In 1955 a system, still in effect today, was inaugurated to designate certain craft techniques as "Important Intangible Cultural Properties," and the specialists practicing such technical arts as "Holders of Important Intangible Cultural Properties" or "Living National Treasures." Dyeing and weaving are two of these crafts, and seventeen individuals and five groups have been selected as preservers or holders of these, for a total of twenty-two designations. With the death of six of these individuals, only eleven remain today. This exhibition, however, includes the works of all seventeen individuals.

Twelve types of dyeing and weaving have been designated as Important Intangible Cultural Properties: *ra, yûsoku, seigô Sendai-hira, kenjo Hakata-ori, tsumugi shima-ori, kasuri-ori, Ojiya-chijimi-ori, Echigo-jôfu, Yûki-tsumugi, Kurume-gasuri, Kijoka-no-bashôfu, and Miyako-jôfu.* This essay will present an overview of these various traditions.

Ra, or silk gauze, was brought to Japan from China around the seventh century. Produced in quantity even in Japan during the eighth century, it is a complex, loose weave and was prized for its diaphanous, lacelike delicacy. Unfortunately, however, the production of *ra,* with its detailed structure, required considerable

time and skill, and with the loss of government patronage following subsequent changes in political leadership, *ra* production declined. After the medieval period, only very simple pieces were woven, and by the early Meiji period *ra* had completely ceased to be produced. Heirô KITAGAWA, one of the individuals designated as Holder of an Important Intangible Cultural Property, has revived this art. Studying samples of ancient weaving in the Shôsô-in Repository in Nara, he succeeded in producing a facsimile of *ra* in the early Shôwa period. His efforts to resuscitate the art of patterned *ra,* by far the most difficult *ra* technique which disappeared by the seventh or eighth century, have been highly acclaimed.

Yûsoku is a general term used to describe the type of fabric woven during the eleventh and twelfth centuries for the garments and household furnishings of the nobility. An exceedingly large number of weaves were designed: *nishiki* (brocade), *futa-e orimono* (a two-ply weave), *uki-orimono* (a "floating" twill weave), *aya* (figured silk), *shijira-seigô* (*seigô* silk seersucker), *kome* (a weave with a rice kernel texture), *kenmonsha* (a transparent gauze weave), and *nerinuki* (in which degummed silk is used for the weft). The foundation for all of these weaves was introduced from China around the seventh and eighth centuries. Chinese-style dress and accessories were also introduced and gradually adapted to the Japanese climate, countryside, and lifestyle. Likewise, textures, patterns, and colors in weaving came to suit Japanese tastes and sensibility. The selection and depiction of tranquil designs as well as the preponderance of quiet colors are an expression of native inclinations and are the hallmark of *yûsoku* textiles.

Seigô Sendai-hira refers to the type of weave used for *hakama,* skirtlike trousers which were de rigueur ceremonial wear for men. It is a flat weave constructed with glossed *habutae* warp filled with moistened, untwisted raw silk woof. (*Habutae* silk is destinguished by two warps used as one.) During the seventeenth and eighteenth centuries, the woven goods of Sendai in Miyagi Prefecture in northeastern Japan enjoyed a solid reputation for quality and, as a result, the weaving techniques used for *hakama* came to be popularly known as *Sendai-hira.* Eisuke KÔDA , another artist designated as Holder of an Important Intangible Cultural Property, lived in Sendai and continued the *seigô-hira* tradition until his death in 1970. *Seigô-hira's* virtue lies in its wrinkle-resistant quality produced by exploiting the elasticity of

the silk threads. In other words, this type of weave responded beautifully to the custom in the Edo period (still observable today) of sitting on the floor with knees folded under one's legs.

Kenjô Hakata-ori used for *obi*, the sash worn over *kimono*, is another technique that saw phenomenal development in the Edo period. The term *kenjô*, which means "to present", is derived from the ten pieces of men's *obi* that were routinely presented every year to the shogun in Edo (present-day Tokyo) by the Kuroda clan in northern Kyûshû. These *obi* always bore a *dokko* (Buddhist ritual object) *hanabira* (ceremonial plate for flower petals) design, and, as a result, this pattern came to be called *kenjô-gara* and, later, the weaving associated with it, *kenjô*. In *Hakata-ori*, a thin, broad woof is wrapped around the fine warp, resulting in a stiff texture with ridges. The crest is woven with a *mon* warp prepared expressly for this design. This technique is frequently seen in Indonesian textiles and leads us to believe that the development of *Hakata-ori* was strongly influenced by South Asian culture. *Hakata-ori* was originally used only in making men's *obi*, but a change in fashion in the middle of the seventeenth century led to the custom of wearing *obi* over women's *kimono*. *Obi* then became an indispensable part of women's clothing, and the production of *Hakata-ori* prospered. Today Zenzaburô OGAWA, another individual desingated as Holder of an Important Intangible Cultural Property, uses an old-fashioned hand loom to produce this distinctive textile. He is the only person engaged in this art.

Tsumugi shima-ori, *kasuri-ori,* and *tsumugi* are all spun from the silk floss of used cocoons (such as those which moths have eaten their way out of after developing from chrysalises) or cocoons of inferior quality (such as those jointly produced by two silkworms). These textiles, in other words, originated from attempts to recycle waste products and belong to an extremely old tradition. *Tsumugi* is hand spun with silk floss prepared from evenly smoothed out cocoons. The width of the thread varies tremendously. It contains many knobs and is prized, more than beauty, for its lightness and warmth and its practicality for sturdy silk goods. These qualities were highly prized during the thirteenth and fourteenth centuries, and *tsumugi* increased in popularity, especially among the samurai who sought an unostentatious lifestyle. Another reason for the dramatic

increase in *tsumugi* production after the seventeenth century was the passage of sumptuary laws regarding clothing. The wearing of silk among farmers, for example, was completely banned. *Tsumugi,* on the other hand, was permitted for village heads and farming women. It did not resemble the extravagant silks worn by merchants and was preferred for its lightness, warmth, durability, and practicality. Stripes and splashed patterns came to be the most common motifs for they were most suited to this basic flat weave. Rikizô MUNEHIRO of Gujô in Gifu Prefecture in central Japan revived the old art of *tsumugi* weaving after World War II. In addition, he provided numerous ideas of his own to *kasuri* weaving and broke new ground in both *tsumugi* and *kasuri* textile design. His work is greatly admired.

Ojiya-chijimi and *Echigo-jôfu* are high-quality summer textiles, made from hemp, which became well-known after the seventeenth century. As elsewhere, hemp garments were the oldest clothing made in Japan, and hemp remained essential for garments worn by the general populace until the Edo period.

However, with the importation of brocade textiles in the sixteenth century, cotton cultivation grew. Production of brocade dramatically rose, and brocade came to be used whole-heartedly by the people. As a result, the demand for hemp saw a marked drop, but the virtues of this material — its porousness which assures ventilation and simplifies laundering, its cool touch, and its stiffness— made it an excellent choice for summer wear. Hemp threads were spun as finely as possible and then woven into thin, light pieces. Much thought also went into devising a bleaching technique that would give both the threads and the cloth a pure white color. With these adaptations, hemp once again became a high-quality product.

Jôfu referes to this high-quality hemp textile and was apparently used to designate the goods presented during the eighteenth century to *daimyô* and to the *bakufu* government. *Chijimi* refers to a textile which prevents moisture from clinging to one's skin through its rough surface woven with heavy strands of thread.

Ojiya and Tôkamachi are towns located in Niigata Prefecture (formerly called Echigo) on the Japan Sea coast. This region is heavily covered with snow, and during the long winter season women spin hemp and work at their looms at home while waiting

for the snow to melt. Winter humidity is perfect for weaving hemp which is vulnerable to an arid environment.

Yûki-tsumugi is produced in the farming towns near Yûki City in Ibaraki Prefecture in east central Japan. This region has been raising silk since antiquity and was engaged in the export of cocoons. In due time silk goods bearing the name of the district came to be woven with waste cocoons that could not be shipped. While the production of *tsumugi* as a sales commodity had already been flourishing by the fourteenth century, the relative proximity of Yûki to great urban city of Edo, with its many consumers, must also have been a factor in the later popularity of *Yûki-tsumugi*. Originally produced primarily for men's wear, the demand for *Yûki-tsumugi* for women's clothing grew after the Meiji period. In addition, the availability of *kasuri* splashed patterns as well as an improvement in the quality of the weave gave it even more appeal.

Kurume-gasuri is a type of splashed-pattern weaving made from cotton cloth that rapidly spread in popularity after the seventeenth century. According to oral tradition, *Kurume-gasuri* was invented by an energetic and studious young woman in 1799. Cotton goods for everyday wear responded to the needs of the people and spread throughout the country. Indigo dyeing proved to be superior for these due to its durability in dyeing and its resistance to sunshine and laundering. *Kasuri* at first used very simple dots and lines in a geometrical configuration, but before long a sophisticated level of warp and woof techniques was devised and it became possible to design painterly compositions. The fountainhead of all Japanese cotton *kasuri*, *Kurume-gasuri* is significant in the history of Japanese textiles as a weave conceived by the common people.

Kijoka-no-bashôfu is woven with fibers stripped from the leafstalks of a type of banana native to the Philippines, and is a textile common to regions in the west tropics such as the islands in the southwest Pacific and Ryûkyû Islands where the plant is cultivated. The stiff texture of the fibers used for both weft and warp prevents the fabric from clinging to the skin, resulting in garments that are cool and comfortable and respond well to a hot evnironment. Kijoka is located on the northern coast of Okinawa and is also known as Ôgimi. In the past, garments made from abaca cloth were vastly preferred by the people of Okinawa, but with the increase in variety of clothing in the modern period, and with the changes in lifestyle, came a rapid decrease in the time-consuming production of this type of weaving. Against this background, Toshiko TAIRA of Kijoka in 1946, even before the war had ended, took the initiative in reviving the art of abaca weaving, and even before her designation as Holder of an Important Intangible Cultural Property, Kijoka was practically the only place where abaca cloth was being prepared. The *kasuri* threads for this weave are dyed in indigo prepared from the local Ryûkyû indigo plant or the tecachi plant which grows wild in tropical areas.

Miyako-jôfu is linen produced on the island of Miyako to the south of Okinawa. According to oral tradition, *Miyako-jôfu* was first produced in the latter part of the sixteenth century. Textiles were the only suitable goods that could be offered in lieu of the annual tax by the people on this isolated island which produced very little otherwise, and indigo-dyed linen formed the bulk of goods presented to the Satsuma and Shimazu clans of southern Kyûshû. The woof for *Miyako-jôfu* is, as is also true of *Echigo-jôfu*, made with thread spun from ramie. In the past, the *kasuri* thread was strictly hand knotted, but today both this traditional method and machines are used together. After it is woven, *Miyako-jôfu* is treated with paste, and a gloss, similar to that of wax-treated textiles, produced by striking the surface with a mallet.

In the related arts, eleven designations have been made in the fields of *Edo-komon, Ise-katagami-goshu, Nagaita chûgata, Yûzen, Yûzen-yôji-nori, Katae-zome,* and *Shôai-zome.* With the death of four of the individuals, however only seven remain.

The term *Edo-komon* was devised in 1955 when this technique was selected as one of the Important Intangible Cultural Properties. *Komon* (small patterns) is a traditional technique used in the dyeing of *kamishimo* (ceremonial dress) worn by samurai in the Edo period. The term *kogara*, on the other hand, refers to the small-sized pieces that were stencil dyed. It was to clarify these two that the general term *komon* was invented. The origin of this dyeing technique using paper patterns with tiny designs is not certain, but *komon* came to be used from around the sixteenth century in the *kataginu* (a stiff sleeveless robe worn on ceremonial occasions), *katabira* (a hemp garment worn in the summer), and *dobuku* (a short coat worn over *kimono*) of the samurai. The rise in demand for these patterns in the Edo period was, in fact, accompanied by a phenomenal development of the technique.

The term *komon* derives from the distinctive stencils with patterns of tiny dots used in dyeing. Resist paste is evenly applied over the surface of the stencil perforated with infinitesimally minute dots, and the joints of the pattern then carefully matched, requiring a prodigious amount of skill. The preparation of the paste itself requires years of training. However, as important as the application of paste and the dyeing process are, still, the most important component of *komon* designs is the stencil. In this respect, Ise stencil-cutting and *komon* dyeing are intimately inter-related.

The paper for the stencil is first prepared by joining two to three sheets of *washi* made from mulberry bark with persimmon tannin. The techniques used in cutting the stencil are *kiri-bori* (augur cutting), *tsuki-bori* (pushed knife perforation), *hiki-bori* (pulled knife carving), and *dôgu-bori* (patterned cutter perforation). These are all specialized techniques, requiring a great deal of skill and talent, and those individuals designated as Holders of Important Intangible Cultural Properties have been recognized for their mastery of one of these many techniques.

The *kiri-bori* technique requires the use of a cylindrically-shaped augur, with a semi-circular point that is twisted with the fingertips to make microscopic circles. The most detailed stencils have as many as 900 holes cut into a 3.3 cm square. *Tsuki-bori* is done with a small, sharp knife that is only 1 mm thick. The blade is pushed away from the body to cut delicate painterly patterns. *Hiki-bori* is used for cutting stripes. A ruler is used to guide the blade of the knife as it is pulled toward the body. In extremely detailed stencils, more than twenty lines will have been cut in a 3.3 cm wide space. *Dôgu-bori* uses tools with points shaped into, for example, one cherry blossom petal or a small triangle to reproduce the same pattern on the stencil.

In addition to these techniques is another called *ito-ire* involving the insertion of thread between the sheets of stencil paper. This was devised to combat the danger, especially in the case of cutting lines, of the infinitesimally thin piece tearing or, when paste is being applied, of their moving. After the cutting has been completed, the stencil papers are separated and silk threads inserted in between to secure the pattern. The stencil papers are then once again pasted together with tannin. This is an absolutely necessary secondary technique when cutting lines. The paper used for these stencils is produced in Suzuka (formerly Shiroko) near Ise in Mie Prefecture

in south central Japan. Famous since the Edo period, Suzuka paper is sold throughout the country and today produces over half of the nation's supply.

Nagaita chûgata is the term used to describe a technique in which cloth is stretched over an approximately seven-meter long drying board. The stencil paper is then placed over it, and paste applied. The cloth is peeled off once it is dry, reversed, and placed back on the board. Then a reverse stencil is carefully applied with paste to the surface, making sure that the application perfectly matches that on the other side. Finally the cloth is dyed in indigo. The first half of the term, *nagaita,* literally means "long board" and refers to the drying board used for the cloth. The second half, *chûgata* or "medium-size," refers to the dimensions of the stencil paper, between 14–28.4 cm. Today the same term has come to refer to dyed *yukata* (a light summer *kimono*). The distinctiveness of *nagaita chûgata* lies in the application of paste on both sides of the cloth and the pure white color of the resisted areas.

Yûzen-zome, a lovely dyeing technique that is uniquely Japanese, was developed in the Edo period and has seen spectacular growth. The distinctiveness of *yûzen* lies in its piecemeal application of dye or color to sections of the cloth. The patterns, therefore, are extremely painterly and require both skill in dyeing and a superb sense of design. It is no wonder, then, that outstanding artists are scarce. Altogether, *yûzen* dyeing requires over twenty specialized skills, from the first rough sketch to completion. The division of labor begins early, with a team of specialists assisting the central figure of the artist who has conceived the design. *Yûzen-zome* originated in Kyoto and spread from there to Kanazawa in Ishikawa Prefecture in western Japan, and Tokyo. Each of these regions has developed its own distinctive tradition and produced individuals to whom recognition as Holders of Important Intangible Cultural Properties has been accorded.

Yûzen-yôji-nori is a type of paste application that developed with the increased esteem for intricate craftsmanship in the latter part of the Edo period. In this technique, paste is applied to the tip of a small stick that is as thin as a strand of hair. The areas of the cloth that are to be resisted are then treated with this tool.

Katae-zome is a new term devised when the stencil cutting of Keisuke SERIZAWA was recognized, in order to distinguish it from the general term *kata-zome* describing less complex patterns

which covers a broad field. *Katae-zome* utilizes stencils to produce painterly compositions, a large number of which can be produced in a short period. Furthermore, the striking designs created by the precise lines and sharp silhouettes, and the sheer beauty of repeated, identical configurations, are features that cannot be found in designs painted by hand. Through the works of SERIZAWA and the late Toshijirô INAGAKI, the distinctiveness of stencil dyeing has been fully cultivated to create a new world of painterly art in textile design. In addition, Yoshitarô KAMAKURA pieces, based on the gorgeous *bingata* dyed patterns of Okinawa, are distinguished by their superb mastery of both the ancient techniques and the essence of the beauty of *bingata.*

Shôai-zome is an unusual technique used to produce the indigo dye so essential to textile production by allowing the leaves to ferment at room temperature. This can be done only in the summertime and is a simple, yet highly esteemed, technique that has emerged out of the philosophy of self-sufficiency in farming communities. The late Ayano CHIBA was a model of this philosophy. Deeply admired and respected, she sowed her own hemp seeds, cultivated the plants, spun and wove the thread produced from them, and then dyed the cloth she wove with homemade indigo dye, taking upon herself the entire process until her death at 90.

Kara-kumi, the final category to be summarized here, is a type of braiding that originated after the eleventh century. The most complex among the many kinds of braiding, *kara-kumi* was used to make *hira-o,* a type of *obi* from which a sword would be suspended and an essential part of the *sokutai* court dress worn by noblemen on ceremonial occasions. The late Jyûsuke FUKAMI was the only person until his death who could make authentic *kara-kumi.* Fortunately, however, research has begun recently on reconstruction of this technique and the tradition of *kara-kumi* has been revived once again.

DOLLS

The history of doll-making is indeed very old, and dolls are a part of every culture. However, we would be hard put to find, if we were to look at individual countries, another tradition with the variety and level of fine craftsmanship that is still carried on today in Japan. Perhaps we may even go so far as to say that Japan is the country of dolls in the world.

In Japan today a number of dolls have been designated as cultural properties. Among these are the dolls of the classical *bunraku* puppet theatre, the *kugutsu* and *ayatsuri-ningyô* of the popular puppet theatre, and dolls used for floats which are an important source of ethnological information. These dolls, which are recognized for their exemplifcation of important industrial arts, were formerly an intimate part of everyday life and even today are cherished by collectors for their special appeal. They are, in short, the types of dolls admired and loved by many people.

Stone or metal has rarely been used in doll-making in Japan. Instead, wood, paper, and clay have been used abundantly to create a variety of dolls, each with distinctive characteristics. In particular, the adaptation of a number of techniques has produced a superior level of modelling. The inclusion of dolls as part of the applied crafts is due entirely to recognition of these achievements in craftsmanship.

Let us turn now to these techniques. Historically, the oldest dolls were made of clay. Produced between roughly 3000 B.C. and 300 B.C., *dogû* are the oldest extant examles. Human *haniwa* appear next in the chronological scheme. These are made of clay and were produced from around the mid–450s A.D. to aroung 600 A.D. Found primarily around the burial mounds of chieftains, the majority of *dogû* and *haniwa* are unglazed, although among them are a few with faces and bodies painted in vermilion.

The auther is inclined to doubt whether these sculpted humanlike figures can be strictly called dolls, but they are, in terms of the way in which they are made of unglazed bisque, identical to clay dolls being produced today, and thus perhaps may be called the precursor of clay dolls. Modelled figures were produced in great quantity around the eigth century but declined with the refinement of metal- and wood-working techniques. However, simple dolls which may be classified as toys were easy and cheap to make, and continue to be produced. These simple doll-making techniques had

spread throughout the country by the seventeenth and eighteenth centuries, with dolls from different regions acquiring distinctively local characteristics.

The majority of these clay dolls were made by preparing copies and adding colors to the unglazed product. Clay copies were made after an original, and, indeed, mass production is a feature of doll-making in the Edo period. This tradition can still be seen today in the majority of much loved locally-produced dolls.

Wood as a material for dolls has also been used since antiquity. There are numerous kinds of wooden dolls, which utilize an amalgamation of different techniques. One type uses wood as a ground to which color is added. Saga dolls and Nara dolls are two examples of this type. Saga dolls are distinguished by the use of thick applications of color, including gold, and elaborate patterns. Nara dolls, in contrast to the opulence of Saga dolls, display a straightforward modelling and bold carving techniques, in addition to a distinctive simplification of form.

In comparison with these vari-colored dolls are dolls treated with many layers of chalk (in liquid form made from pulverized seashells to which glue has been added) which, in the final step of production, are brushed to a sheen with horsetail (a kind of reed) stems, and whose faces and hair are painted in. Gosho dolls are an example of this type of doll. The outstanding feature of Gosho dolls in their perfectly white skin, the result of a technique using chalk that is one of several recorded processes under careful study now.

Besides the painted wooden dolls mentioned above, are dolls also made of wood but with swatches of exquisite fabric applied directly to the surface area. These kinds of dolls are called *kimekomi* dolls because of the way in which the areas to which swatches will be fitted are carefully prepared in advance. Kamo dolls and Yanagi dolls of the Edo period are examples of this type of doll. The *kimekomi* technique is the most frequently used technique seen today. Both the late Gôyô HIRATA and Ryûjo HORI are famous for their mastery of these techniques.

Ishô-ningyô, or costumed dolls, are made of wood painted with chalk and then dressed in clothing made from pieces of woven or dyed fabric. (Girls' Day dolls and other festival dolls comprise another category.) Depending upon the type of costume, a variety of subject matter could be depicted, and these dolls appealed to children as simple playthings or to adults as objects of connoisseur-

ship. With such a wide range of possibilities, this was by far the most popular type of doll in the Edo period. Furthermore, the increasing demand for *ishô-ningyô* stimulated the specialization of skills such that different people did the heads, hands and feet, and even the dressing of dolls. As a result, famous wigmakers, costuming experts, hairdressers, and the like appeared one after another. The late Gôyô HIRATA and Ryûjo HORI were designated as Living National Treasures for their specialized work with *ishô-ningyo* which themselves are designated as cultural properties.

Papier-maché dolls are produced through one or the other of the following two techniques. One technique is to prepare a copy from an original, as is the case with clay dolls, and to wrap paper around it. Another is to make a copy out of wood, glue layers of paper to the figure and, after it has dried, split the figure into two to remove the copy for repeated use, and then to wrap more paper around the figure before adding color with chalk or pigments. These types of dolls are called *hari-nuki* or *hari-ko* dolls. *Hari-ko* dolls are not as popular as clay dolls but are made in many local areas because they are light, sturdy, and relatively inexpensive to produce.

In addition to these wooden and clay dolls are dolls made of a clay-like substance produced by adding wheat starch glue to paulownia sawdust. Once dried, this material has the same sturdiness as wood but is lighter, is easy to model, and, furthermore, is suitable for mass production and therefore very inexpensive to manufacture. This material has been used since the mid-Edo period. This type of doll is called *tôso*. In place of the paulownia powder used for *tôso* dolls, mulberry fibers (which are used in making *washi* paper) may also be used. The fibers are cooked and starch is then carefully blended in. Over this foundation is wrapped layers of dyed *washi*, or ornaments may be added. This type of doll is called *shiso*. The late Juzô KAGOSHIMA devised and perfected these techniques from traditional *tôso* and *hari-ko* methods.

Another type of doll uses clay as a foundation but is glazed and then fired in a kiln. These ceramic dolls are primarily produced at the Seto and Imari kilns, but few outstanding specimens remain today, perhaps due to potters' interest in other art forms. There are also *nuigurumi* dolls sewn with layers of fabric fragments around a

figure made of cotton, but these employ such simple techniques that, again, there are few examples suitable for consideration as works of art. However, these are made by mothers for children and are much loved.

LACQUER WARE

Lacquered artifacts were manufactured and basic techniques of lacquering established in various parts of Japan as early as the prehistoric Jômon period. Lacquer was applied on various *kiji* (bases): wood, elaborately plaited bamboo stem, and earthenware, for example. The *kiji* was coated with *shitaji* (priming) of fine powder to smoothe the surface and facilitate adhesion of the lacquer. Red lacquer as well as black lacquer was in use. The refined aesthetic sense of the craftsmen is displayed in their work. No dirt or coarse brush markings mar the beautiful surface finish of the finest pieces. It is technically difficult to varnish smoothly with *ki-urushi* (raw lacquer taken from the *urushi* tree) alone. (A coat of *ki-urushi* alone results in an opaque amber varnish). Therefore red lacquer, for example, is prepared by mixing *bengara* (iron oxide), *shu* (mercury sulfide), or natural *shinsha* (cinnabar) in the lacquer and stirring carefully over a long period of time, a process which even now requires special skill. It is surprising to discover how good quality raw lacquer was collected in primitive times, how it was treated for effective varnish, how good brushes were made, and how black and red lacquer was prepared.

Lacquer juice is generated as sap in the *urushi* tree only when the tree is injured; it does not exist naturally in the plant. In the current method of collecting, small scars are cut in the tree in late spring, around June tenth. The sap does not immediately come forth. After four days larger, longer cuts are made horizontally over the previous ones. This process is repeated several times. Gradually the tree yields sap, but at first the sap contains much water. The normal method is to injure the tree and collect the sap every four days. However, if the sap is collected on a rainy day generation of the sap is disturbed, so that the four-day cycle is occasionally interrupted as natural conditions demand. The careful Japanese way is to injure the tree and immediately collect a small amount of sap from the scars; in that way, dirt does not get mixed in the sap and only good quality sap is obtained.

The densest and finest lacquer juice is obtained in August and September. The juice differs a little in quality according to the place where the *urushi* tree is growing. In Japan, lacquer from the northern part of Iwate Prefecture in the Tôhoku district (northeastern Japan) is the most adhesive, while that from the northern part of Ibaraki Prefecture in the Kantô district is highly transparent. Domestic production of lacquer is quite limited in quantity; the greater part of what is used is imported from China. For *uwa-nuri* (surface varnish), the final finish of high-class lacquerware or of works of art, however, the beautiful, glossy domestic lacquer is deemed indispensable.

Lacquer boasts of various properties which are absent from any other kind of varnish. It is remarkably durable, for instance, and remains unaffected by any chemical, though buried for thousands of years. In lacquerware manufacture it is important to know that lacquer juice hardens at specified temperatures and humidity. Other varnishes harden when they lose moisture. In the case of lacquer juice, the gummous substance contained in the juice absorbs oxygen from the air, causing the *urushi* to oxidize; the liquid, thus, is changed to a solid.

Domestic lacquer hardens at a temperature of 25° to 30° C. and humidity of 75 to 85 percent. Both the temperature and the humidity are considerably high. The lacquer does not harden easily in the Japanese winter climate, but does so rapidly in the sultry *tsuyu* (rainy season) and in the summer, making quick work possible. Japanese lacquer work technicians have in their studios large wooden cabinets of shelves called *urushi-buro* (*urushi* bath) where the interior atmosphere can be suitably controlled for such hardening. Since lacquer juice hardens in a few hours when heated at more than 100° C., it could be fused on armor and other metal objects in olden times. Even today it is fused on metal vases, pitchers, and the like.

As early as the Jômon period Japanese people manufactured lacquerware with full knowledge of the above-mentioned specific properties of lacquer juice. Even then the climatic conditions of Japan were suitable for lacquer art. Japanese lacquer techniques were carried on into the Yayoi and Kofun periods, and the art was employed for an increasingly wider range of artifacts. It was when Buddhism was introduced, however, that

works of the highest artistic value appeared.

The earliest surviving *densei* (preserved, as contrasted with buried and unearthed objects) example in the history of Japanese lacquer art is the Tamamushi Shrine owned by the Hôryû-ji Temple. It not only represents lacquer art of the Asuka period but is a composite of architecture, wood work, metal work, and painting of the time. Its decoration contains elements of cultures extending over the Korean peninsula, Chinese continent and even Greece, revealing that Japanese culture in those remote days had an international character. The Shôsô-in Imperial Treasures from the late Nara period (eighth century) also include many excellent works of lacquer art. Their decoration likewise embodies elements of various other cultures of the world.

One of the sword mountings among the Shôsô-in Treasures (sword mounting of *Kara-tachi* type decorated with gold, silver and mother-of-pearl) has a design of animals and other motifs drawn in liquid lacquer with rough *yasuri-fun* (gold filings) sprinkled over it, coated again with lacquer, and polished after dry with a piece of charcoal to bring the gold design to the surface. This technique, termed *makkinru* (gold powder scattering), was the forerunner of *maki-e* which was later to become the main current of Japanese lacquer art history. Besides this, the Shôsô-in Treasures display such crafts as *hyômon* (also termed *heidatsu,* embedding of cutouts of gold and/or silver plate), *raden* (nacre inlay, inlay of cutouts of beautiful glossy shell) and other techniques which, along with *maki-e,* became important elements of surface decoration in lacquer art in later times. The Treasures show that these techniques, still in frequent use today, had attained considerable development as long ago as the eighth century. They provide a glorious starting point for the history of Japanese lacquer art.

Lacquer art in the ensuing Heian period, like other fields of art, was freed from the influence of the Chinese style of the T'ang dynasty and a native classical style was established. (This was around the second half of the tenth century.) What played the pioneering role in this course of development was *maki-e* in which painterly free-style designs were presented in linear depiction with gold and silver *fun* (powder, filings) sprinkled over a liquid lacquer drawing. The *fun* used at first were rough *yasuri-fun* (raw filings), but gradually they became finer in grade,

and rounded and more regular in shape, making more precise decoration possible. *Hyômon* and *raden* on the Shôsô-in Treasures show designs of strong independent effect, but in the Heian period a decorative effect came to be added as part of *maki-e* art. The resulting designs, in which different techniques were brought together, were more complicated in expression and more idyllic in atmosphere.

A realistic, powerful style became dominant during the warriors' rule in the Medieval age. In the *fun,* too, there appeared in addition to the traditional *maru* (round) *fun* such new shapes as the flattened *hirame* (flat type) *fun* and *nashiji-fun* of diverse shapes. The basic crafts of *maki-e* were brought to perfection.

Maki-e art in the Edo period boasted of the skill in detail to manufacture fine objects for use by feudal lords. The *maki-e* works shown at exhibitions in various parts of the world as representative pieces of Japanese applied arts, or exported abroad as high quality goods in the Meiji period, were even more refined renditions of the techniques earlier reserved for the enjoyment of feudal lords. Distinguished technicians from various localities gathered in Tokyo, rivaling each other in workmanship, so that *maki-e* art in the Meiji and Taishô periods attained unprecedented technical perfection. Furthermore, excellent pieces of Chinese lacquerware of the Han dynasty were unearthed in Lolang in Korea and old cultural properties, including lacquerware, were repaired and restored. Techniques and designs of ancient Far Eastern lacquer art attracted renewed attention. All these factors strongly influenced modern lacquer art.

The manufacture of lacquerware in the Edo period was not limited to such large cities as Kyoto and Edo (the present Tokyo). With the encouragement of local feudal clans, lacquerware centers were established in various parts of the country to display distinctive local products. These local wares continued to be made and were even improved in the Meiji and ensuing periods of capitalism. *Wajima-nuri,* for example, made in Wajima City at the north end of Noto peninsula in Ishikawa Prefecture, is characterized by firm, beautiful varnish and by superb *maki-e* and *chinkin* decoration. The *chinkin* especially is of a high artistic level not to be seen in other localities.

Takamatsu City in Kagawa Prefecture, for another example,

gave birth to the distinguished artist Zôkoku TAMAKAJI (1805–69), who experimented with various new techniques, notably *kimma* and *chôshitsu*. Lacquer artists in Takamatsu have ever since worked in the tradition of Zôkoku to modernize his art.

Creative activities were not so brisk in the field of surface varnish, for *maki-e* decoration was in the mainstream of Japanese lacquer art. Artists in this field are becoming more numerous now, however. *Kyûshitsu* (lacquer varnish) artists, in addition to being skilled in varnish, have to master and excel in the respective crafts of preparing the *kiji* and fashioning the forms. *Magewa* (bent wood work), for example, is in itself an excellent method of making firm *kiji*, but a new method of *magewa* has been devised by which the hoops are set one over another to constitute a *kiji* as an entirety. Also, *kanshitsu*, which is hemp cloth applied to a frame and solidified with lacquer, though time-consuming, permits free modeling and is strong and is therefore tried by many of today's artists.

As stated above, many Japanese lacquer crafts originated in China, but have been Japanized and perfected both in technique and in design, while not a few have already disappeared in China.

Artifacts made in lacquer crafts include food vessels, *chôdo* (furniture and sundry interior furnishings), and other objects used in everyday Japanese life. Lacquerware has thus found its way deep into Japanese experience, and its graceful art has had a great influence on the people's appreciation of beauty. The elegant bulges and curves of lacquered bowls and boxes, the texture of lacquer varnish showing warm gloss, the *maki-e* designs in delicate gold drawing, are typical of Japanese beauty. Artists and craftsmen of lacquerware manufacture, which requires many years and hundreds of processes for the completion of a single piece, are confronted by many difficult conditions in our present time, yet there are many who are eagerly engaged in it.

WOOD & BAMBOO CRAFTS

Artifacts in wood and bamboo showing elaborate craftsmanship were made in Japan as early as the prehistoric Jômon and Yayoi periods. Wooden food vessels engraved with fine ornaments and objects plaited in a complex manner from bamboo stem have been unearthed in various parts of Japan.

Iron tools came into use in the protohistoric Kofun period. Numerous axes, hatchets, knives, awls, saws, as well as whetstones, tongs, and anvils have been discovered in fifth-century tombs.

Building upon the foundation of these crafts Buddhism introduced in and after the mid-sixth century, brought works and technicians of highly advanced wood and bamboo work who contributed to the extensive progress of the crafts in Japan.

Widely known as the earliest speciments of wood work in this country are, among others, the Tamamushi Shrine and Lady Tachibana's Shrine owned by the Hôryû-ji Temple and the Cabinet of Red-lacquered Zelkova Wood in the Shôsô-in Repository of Imperial Treasures. The Tamamushi Shrine especially, decorated as it is with lacquer and splendid metal fittings, is a composite of wood work, lacquer art, metal work, and painting.

The Shôsô-in Treasures include fine works of *sashi-mono, hiki-mono, mage-mono,* and *hori-mono* which are the basic crafts in wood work. They are the fountainhead of Japanese artistry in wood. Wood work artists of the present day learn much from the designs and techniques of Shôsô-in Treasures.

Sashi-mono is the craft of fabricating *chôdo* (furniture and other household furnishings) by combining boards, or boards and square bars, of wood. The pieces of wood are joined in such a way that the object is beautifully balanced in form and warp-proof over a long period of time. An object so made, without iron nails, can be preserved over centuries.

Hiki-mono (lathe work) is wood work turned on a lathe to form circular shapes for making bowls, trays, and the like. *Hiki-mono* works may be left plain in order to display the beautiful grains of wood, or may serve as a base for lacquerware. Methods have been developed not only for fashioning circular or rounded shapes but also for decorating the surface with engraved lines.

Kuri-mono (scooping) is wood scooped or roughly carved into a

desired shape with an adz or other tools, and finished off with a small plane. Unlike *hiki-mono*, which is confined to round, regular shapes, *kuri-mono* permits any shapes desired. It is used for making bowls and other receptacles.

Mage-mono (bent work) is fabricated by bending a thin strip of wood into a hoop. Uncut long strip with the grain running all the way from one end to the other can be fashioned into very strong, durable shapes.

Hori-mono (carving) is employed not only in sculptural works such as Buddhist statues and Gigakuplay masks, but also in relief carving on the surface or openwork on the sides and of containers in various forms. The technique can be used for a rich variety of purposes.

Mokuga (marquetry) is another wood work craft of surface decoration typical of Shôsô-in Treasures. *Mokuga* combines small pieces of *shitan* (red sandalwood), *kokutan* (ebony), *tsuge* (boxwood) and other kinds of wood with beautifully colored, non-wood materials such as ivory and deerhorn, which are inlaid on a wooden box, for example, in designs of flowers, birds, geometric patterns and other motifs. The craft is frequently used by contemporary artists who favor its clear-cut presentation of exotic Central Asian romanticism.

In bamboo work likewise, technically and artistically advanced pieces were produced after the introduction of Buddhism. The earliest existing *densei* example in Japan is the bamboo cabinet (registered as a National Treasure) formerly owned by the Hôryû-ji Temple. Bamboo work objects are also well represented among the Shôsô-in Treasures. The Shôsô-in Treasures include objects retaining the pipe shape of bamboo, such as the *ôteki* (horizontal flute), *shakuhachi* (vertical flute), and writing-brush handles, others of plaited bamboo like boxes and baskets, and still others, such as *Kyôchitsu* (*sutra*-scroll wrappers), made by splitting the bamboo stem into fine strips, staining in colors, and knitting with threads.

As the *cha-no-yu* (tea ceremony) became fashionable in the Medieval age, subtle, simple beauty became one of the ideals. Wood work and bamboo work renewed favor because of the natural beauty of the materials. Imported wood, such as *kokutan* from China and Southeast Asia, had earlier been highly valued, but now *kuwa* (mulberry) and other domestic wood became the major materials. Bamboo work, too, turned from the elaborate

Chinese-style crafts of intricately plaiting finely split strips of bamboo, often in imitation of solid metal shapes, to Japanese-style crafts in which bamboo was used simply in its natural cylindrical form, as exemplified by *tsutsu hana-ike* (cylindrical flower vase of bamboo).

Instinct for artistic creation emerged among wood and bamboo craftsmen after the Meiji era. Competitive exhibitions were organized in applied arts as in other fields. Noteworthy especially was the creation in 1927 of the Applied Arts Department in the Teiten, the largest art exhibition in this country. Works in wood and bamboo were admitted to the exhibition after examination, giving an important stimulus to experts in the fields that had tended to be neglected by the general public. By stressing the ability of individual artists the competitive exhibitions greatly influenced these formerly conservative fields where *oyakata* (masters, teachers), supported by the *iemoto* (school head) system, had enjoyed strong authority.

Oyakata who lacked technical ability, or who did have ability but lacked a creative sense of designing, gradually lost their influence.

While the works shown at the governmental exhibitions tended to be pieces appreciated for their high technical and artistic merits, at the end of 1920 a folk-art movement among non-governmental artists started under the leadership of Muneyoshi YANAGI. This movement, with its aim to discover naive, forceful and pure beauty in daily-use articles which had been earlier neglected, was a great encouragement for craftsmen of wood and bamboo work. Both governmental exhibitions and the non-governmental folk-art movement have exerted an important influence on modern artists.

Of the two artists nominated as Holders of Important Intangible Cultural Properties in the field of wood work, Kôdô HIMI was recognized for his works shown at the governmental Nitten exhibitions and the exhibitions of Traditional Japanese Crafts. While having wood work objects in the Shôsô-in as his ideals, he has established an intellectual, noble style in which simple, modest decoration effectively finishes off the forms and designs.

The other, Tatsuaki KURODA, launched his creative activities with the folk-art movement which he began in Kyoto together with Muneyoshi YANAGI. Incorporating the impressive, powerful, plastic forms of local folk-art products in wood work, he has created pieces featuring forceful carving and construction

which stand out in the history of Japanese wood work. His works are rich in variety, ranging from small boxes to large furniture and interior ornaments such as tables, chairs, and cabinets. His contribution is also remarkable in enhancing the field of activities for wood work artists.

The two Holders of Important Intangible Cultural Properties in the field of bamboo work were active both at Nitten exhibitions and at exhibitions of Traditional Japanese Crafts. The late Shôunsai SHÔNO is one of the meritorious artists who brought bamboo work into prominence as modern art in the Shôwa era (1926-   ).

It was during the Taishô era (1912—26) that bamboo work was fully established as a creative art activity in modern Japan. Active as a pioneer in the Taishô era was Rôkansai IIZUKA (1890—1956), father of Shôkansai IIZUKA, the other Holder of the craft. His activities gave birth to many new crafts of bamboo plaiting. Shôkansai IIZUKA, inheriting the techniques of his father and also learning from classical works such as the Shôsô-in Treasures, has added smart, elegant designs.

As shown above, modern Japanese wood and bamboo works are of various sorts. What they have in common, however, is that all the artists try to appeal directly with the beautiful and strong characteristics of native plants.

METALWORK

Since ancient times, gold, silver, copper, tin, and iron were thought to be representative Japanese metals. Called *gokin* (five metals), they were noted for their fusibility, malleability, and hardness, and were used to make Buddhist ritual objects, arms and armor, personal ornaments, and other requisites for daily living. The history of metal crafts started in the Yayoi period (300 B.C.–300 A.D.), during which time new culture, influenced by interchanges with the Continent, evolved mainly in the northern Kyûshû district. First to be imported were bronze swords, spears, halberds and mirrors, and iron axes. In the second half of this period, as is evidenced by unearthed stone molds, imitations of these objects were produced in Japan. Metal work is believed to have advanced independently in this epoch in the Kinki district, where bell-shaped bronzes called *dôtaku* are mainly dis-

covered. Bronze mirrors, apparently copied after imported Chinese ones, appeared in the Kofun period (fourth to seventh centuries); there are as well mirrors whose designs were conceived by the Japanese. Unearthed also from *kofun* (protohistoric tombs) of the period are crowns, hats, earrings with pendant ornaments, bracelets, finger rings, belt clasps, waist pendants, ornamental shoes, horse trappings, and so on, which prove that basic metal work techniques had been established in the country at that time.

Buddhism was introduced to Japan in the Asuka period (538–645). Buddhist temples were built and Buddhist statues were frequently made. Metal work was used in Buddhist arts, as were other crafts. New techniques were imported, for example, by visiting *roban hakase* (experts in bronze pagoda spires) from the Korean kingdom of Paekche. Many excellent examples have survived from the Asuka and Hakuhô (538–571) periods, for example the crowns of the Guze Kannon and Kudara Kannon statues in the Hôryû-ji Temple, the gilt bronze openwork *kanjô-ban* (Buddhist ritual banner) formerly in the Hôryû-ji, and the Sartra Casket fixed in the foundation stone in the central pillar of the pagoda at the temple. Hammered metal works include the long-handled incense burners with the handles terminating in magpie-tail shape made of *chûjaku* (natural brass) whose origin and history are unknown, and repoussé Buddhist images hammered out or carved in relief on bronze plates, a technique which flourished in these and the following late Nara periods. Metal casting is typified by the bronze temple bells at the Myôshin-ji in Kyoto and the Kanzeon-ji in Fukuoka. The Tempyô period (710–794) was a peak period for metal crafts, represented by the Great Buddha of Nara at Tôdai-ji measuring 16 m. in height, on which over twelve years of work and 443,000 kg. of copper material were lavished. Typical also are the cast bronze octagonal lantern and its fire chamber made at the time of the construction of the temple, the bronze bell, and the bronze *Kan'yoku-ban* (ablution basin) used in that temple at the ritual of "ablution of the newborn Buddha". The bronze coin Wadô Kaichin was issued in the year Wadô 1 (708), a fact showing that there was mass production of cast metal coins at that time. The spread of cremation fostered the making of cinerary urns, and the establishment of the *Ritsuryô* (statute) system brought about the casting of governmental seals and other official and private

bronze seals. Metal work in the Tempyô period is represented among others by Shôsô-in Imperial Treasures which include a wide variety of costume ornaments, *chôdo* (furniture and other interior furnishings), food and liquid vessels, pastime articles, musical instruments, objects for annual functions, arms and armor, Buddhist artifacts, and even carpentry and other tools. Gold, silver, *hakudô* ("white bronze," copper alloy with a high percentage of tin), *shakudô* (niellolike copper alloy), *chûjaku*, *sawari* (brasslike alloy of copper, tin, and lead or silver) and iron are used in them, and all conceivable kinds of metal work crafts, including filigree and surface polish, are employed.

The Heian period (794–1185) saw the absorption of the Chinese culture of the late T'ang dynasty which was introduced by Nittô Hakke (eight priests visiting T'ang China) such as Saichô and Kûkai, while interruption of the custom of sending ambassadors to T'ang motivated purely Japanese-style works. For example, there appeared Fujiwara period mirrors (Haguro mirrors) with designs free from the symmetry of T'ang-style compositions, and Buddhist ritual objects of graceful forms and decoration reflecting the taste of patricians of the time. These were modified copies of *mikkyô hôgu* (objects for use in esoteric Buddhist rituals) imported from China. Other masterpieces include the bronze temple bells at the Jingo-ji, Eizan-ji and Byôdô-in Temples, the *keman* (pendant plaques symbolizing chaplets of flowers) at the Chûson-ji, and relief images of the Buddhist god Zaô Gongen, all displaying the characteristics of metal art of the time.

The Kamakura period (1185–1392) was a period in which the samurai (warrior) class took leadership. In the still more Japanized culture of this period, elegant grace gave way to a heavy, impressive style rich in three-dimensional effect. Japanese-style designs adopted for Buddhist ritual implements and mirrors, and the *wa-shô* (Japanese bell) form established for temple bells, became norms to be followed in later periods. The bells at the Kenchô-ji and Enkaku-ji are typical examples. While line engraving was a feature of metal carving in the Heian period, high and low reliefs became dominant, the former being typified by *kakebotoke* (high-relief Buddhist images on bronze plaques), *keko* (flower baskets for use in the Buddhist flower-scattering ritual) and *shari-tô* (stupa-shaped sarira caskets). Ornamental

metal parts on armor like those on the *ô-yoroi* (full armor) owned by the Kasuga Taisha and Kushibiki Hachiman-gû Shrines are typical low relief.

Admiration of aristocratic culture and interest in exoticism existed side by side during the Muromachi period (1392–1573); influential also was the spirit of *cha-no-yu* (tea ceremony) which held the simplicity and quietude of Zen (Contemplative, Intuitive) Buddhism in high regard. The vogue of tea ceremony brought about the separation of the *cha-gama* (tea-ceremony kettle) from kettles merely for boiling water, thus leading to the birth of kettle manufacture at Ashiya near the estuary of Onga River in Kyûshû and at Temmyô, Sano, in the Kantô district. Ashiya kettles are in *shin* (standard, formal) form, with a *kuri-guchi* (flaring lip of the mouth), goblin-mask *kantsuki* (supports for ring handles), and *ha* (flange above the base). They are dignified in form and elegant in decoration. Temmyô kettles have *koshiki-guchi* (straight upright mouth), and their surface is rough and rich in rustic effect. In the field of metal carving, excellent examples are noted on the mountings of swords such as the *Koshi-gatana* with oak and owl design owned by the Kasuga Taisha and the *Koshi-gatana* with peony design owned by the Aso Jinja. Active also in this field was Yûjô GOTÔ who established for later artists the norm of sword mounting. Iron *tsuba* (sword guards) made by armorers of the period include many splendid pieces.

The Momoyama (1573–1615) was a period in which Buddhism was oppressed, internal warfare continued, and the *wabi* (simple, quiet) style of tea ceremony was established. Notable works of metal art in this period are armor, sword furniture, and tea-ceremony kettles. Kettles suiting the taste of tea masters were made at the *kama-za* (kettle factory) at Sanjô in Kyoto, where the distinguished kettle maker Dôjin NISHIMURA appeared and where his pupil, Yojirô TSUJI, produced kettles of *shiribari* and *amidadô* types to the taste of the great tea master Sen no Rikyû. Myôju UMETADA, pioneer of *shintô* (new swords) and a sword furniture artist, was skilled also in making *tsuba* (sword guards) and was responsible for a novel style in *hira* (flat) inlay work. Matashichi HAYASHI, in the service of the Hosokawa clan ruling the Higo (Kumamoto) district, created a distinctive style of Higo inlay. Noteworthy in other fields of metal art were architectural fittings whose designs show characteristics of

the period.

Chônin (merchant-class people, bourgeoisie) were among the supporters of culture in the Edo period (1615–1868). With the growth of cities and development of social economics, construction of Buddhist temples and Shintô shrines became widespread, increasing the demand for large-scale works of metal casting. At the same time small elegant objects in *rôgata* (lost wax) casting, such as water droppers, brush stands, *yatate* (portable brush-and-ink cases) and other articles for the writer's desk, as well as *netsuke* (catches for medicine cases or tobacco pouches worn on the waist) came into wide favor. In addition to these, *ekagami* (long-handled mirrors) were popular among people of the commonalty and were mass-produced by means of *fumikaeshi* (recasting in matrixes taken from the originals), so that mirrors of coarse designs, techniques and materials were widely circulated. The Gotô family specialized in sword furniture of traditional, dignified *ie-bori* (carvings for shogunate) style, while Sômin YOKOYA, Toshinaga NARA, Jôi SUGIURA and other artists of *machi-bori* (metal carvers not employed by The shogunate) made sword furniture of novel designs intended primarily for artistic appreciation. *Kazari-shoku* (specialists in elaborate precious-metal carving) were busy with the manufacture of *kanzashi* (ornamental hairpins), tiny bells and other personal ornaments, smoking pipes, and metal fittings for chests of drawers, folding screens, *mikoshi* (sacred palanquins), *dashi* (festival floats), and so on. Their technical skill was best displayed in women's hair ornaments, which tended to become increasingly ornate.

In 1876 the new constitutional government established in the Meiji era issued a decree abolishing the wearing of swords on the person. Having no work, sword furniture artists switched to making personal ornaments and other cultural objects, but the Government, with its policy for the encouragement of industry, provided a means of survival for metal work artists. Japanese metal crafts were displayed at the 1873 Vienna World Exposition and won many awards. Systematic education in metal art was begun at the Tokyo Fine Arts School in 1890. The following year the system of Teishitsu Gigei In (Court Artists) was instituted for the encouragement of arts. The metal carving artist Natsuo KANÔ, and subsequently Shômin UNNO and others, were honored with the title of Court Artist. Along with Natsuo in *katakiri-bori* carving and Shômin in brilliant *zôgan* (inlay), there was Ippu KASHIMA, who distinguished himself in the field of metal carving with designs in *sumi-e* (ink painting) style. From the end of the Meiji era on, graduates from the Tokyo Fine Arts School, while studying classical works, were influenced by Western handicraft arts. Chief among them were Kakuya OKABE, Kamezô SHIMIZU, Hozuma KATORI and Nobuo TSUDA. The cast metal artist Hozuma KATORI, gave lectures at his alma mater on the history of Japanese metal art and wrote books on the subject, giving guidance in this way to metal art circles of the time. He was followed by such eminent artists as Senroku KITAHARA, Kiyoshi UNNO, Toyochika TAKAMURA, and Shôdô SASAKI, who worked nobly for the preservation of the tradition and techniques of Japanese metal art.

Among the traditional crafts of metal work some have disappeared or have undergone changes according to social and economic conditions of the times. Fortunately, however, the major crafts have been preserved to the present day, and are kept alive by artists engaged in exhibition activities, their assistants and co-workers, and by their families and successors. The technicians live mainly in large and middle-sized cities and their environs, or in areas where the traditional metal crafts are local industries. The techniques and their processes are always subject to demand, quality of materials, trends of exhibitions, and other such factors which lead them in simpler, more convenient directions. For example, the emergence of new machines which facilitate easy, inexpensive manufacture of imitative articles has had an immediate effect on the quantity and shape of working tools and implements and the materials and processes of their manufacture, causing the original craftsmanship to be lost sight of. The only conceivable way to maintain this tradition in the contemporary world is to create artistically excellent, serious works which can vie with modern products, but this imposes a considerable burden on the artists. The Government, therefore, valuing the cultural worth of the traditional crafts and hoping to transmit them rightly, endeavors to protect them by means of the system of registering Important Intangible Cultural Properties in conformity with the Law for Protection of Cultural Properties. Existing crafts so protected in the field of metal art are: *Chûkin* (metal casting), fabricating by pouring molten metal into a matrix;

Tankin (metal beating), utilizing the malleability of metals to fabricate by beating with a metal or wooden hammer; *Chôkin* (metal carving), decorating a metal surface by carving with chisels of various kinds; Surface Treatments such as gilding, coloring, and polishing; Preparation of Materials; *Kazari* (highly manipulated, specialized decorative metal-work methods), and so on.

The first registration of Important Intangible Cultural Properties in the field of metal art took place in 1955; simultaneously nominated as their Holders were the late Iraku UOZUKI for his craft of casting *Dora* (gongs) in *sawari* (copper alloy with a high percentage of tin) and finishing off by hammering for profound tone and resonance; and the late Kiyoshi UNNO for his *Chôkin* (metal carving) along the line of Mito metal work. Thereafter, *Chûkin* by the late Toyochika TAKAMURA was so registered in 1950; *Rôgata* (lost wax) Casting by the late Shôdô SASAKI in 1960; the Tea-ceremony Kettle by the late Tetsushi NAGANO, employing the *sôgata* method of casting and using *wazuku* (domestic pig iron), in 1963; the Higo Inlay and Openwork by the late Mitsumasa YONEMITSU, a craft of *tsuba* making peculiar to the Higo district (the present Kumamoto Prefecture). In 1977, Masahiko KATORI's craft of making *Bonshô* (temple bells), taking the sound effect into consideration when casting large-sized works, was registered; so was Shiro SEKIYA's *Tankin* (metal hammer work) combining the techniques of hammering and soldering. Tea-ceremony Kettles was registered again in 1978 with Ikkei KAKUTANI as its Holder. *Chôkin* also was registered again the same year, with Shirô NAITÔ, former professor at the Tokyo University of Arts, as its Holder; the following year Ikkoku KASHIMA, specializing in *nunome zôgan,* was nominated Holder of the same craft. The artists who have been nominated Holders of Important Intangible Cultural Properties are responsible for the "refinement of techniques and education of successors" under annual government subsidy.

In addition to the Important Intangible Cultural Properties, the Government protects traditional metal work crafts by means of recording and making technical samples. To date ten crafts have been so protected: in the field of metal carving, *Nunome Zôgan,* Higo Openwork and Higo Inlay, and Kaga Inlay; in metal hammering, Hammerwork Coppers of Tsubame; in casting, Tea-ceremony Kettles, *Rôgata* (lost wax) Casting, Nambu Tea-ceremony Kettles and Nambu Iron Pots, and Polishing of Cast Mirrors; included also are Akita Silver Wire Work and *Nagashi-komi Zôgan* and *Rôzuke Sukashi-iri Tetsufukuro-uchi* (a composite of metal carving and metal hammer work).

SWORDS

Japanese swords can be classified into two major types: *chokutô* with straight blades and *wantô* with curving blades.

The *chokutô* was originally introduced from China and the Korean peninsula, presumably in the third or fourth century, but it is unclear how far back it can be dated. The majority of existing *chokutô* are finds unearthed from *kofun* (protohistoric tombs, fourth century or later). Specimens of *densei* (preserved in the society, as contrasted with unearthed) are the Heishi Shorin Ken and Shichisei Ken owned by the Shitennô-ji Temple and a few others, as well as over fifty examples kept in the Shôsô-in Repository of Imperial Treasures. *Chokutô* blade forms can be classified into *hira-zukuri, kata-kiriha-zukuri* and *kissaki-moroha-zukuri,* the latter two being probable derivations from the first. *Chokutô* and other swords shaped prior to the birth of *wantô* or *shinogi-zukuri* form, now termed *Nippon-tô* (or *Nihontô:* Japanese swords), are referred to as *jôko-tô* (archaic swords).

The development from the *chokutô* to the *wantô* was due to the fact that, while the former was used for thrusting, the latter was more suitable for cutting. This was probably because fighting was done more often on horseback than on foot. The *Nippon-tô* was brought to perfection in the period of transition from the early Historic age, governed by the Imperial family and the nobility, to the Medieval age in which the newly risen warrior class came into power, that is between the middle tenth and early eleventh centuries.

Japanese swords are divided, by the characteristics of the periods in which they were made, into *kotô* (old swords) of the Heian to late Muromachi periods; *shintô* (new swords) of the Momoyama and ensuing periods when imported European *namban-tetsu* (iron brought by the "southern barbarians") came to be used; *shinshintô* (very new swords) between the late Edo period and the 1876 decree prohibiting the wearing of swords; and

gendaitô (modern swords) thereafter to the present time.

Japanese swords recently classed in terms of the blade length are: *tachi,* longer than 60 cm. and bearing *mei* (inscription on the tang) on the *haki-omote* (the side which becomes the outside when the sword is hung from the waist with the cutting edge downward); *katana,* longer than 60 cm. and bearing the *mei* on the *sashi-omote* (the outside when the sword is worn thrust through the girdle with the cutting edge upward); *wakizashi,* between 30 and 60 cm.; and *tantô,* shorter than 30 cm.

The *tachi* was worn hung from the girdle from the Heian period to about the early Muromachi period; it was convenient for equestrian fight. The *katana,* worn thrust through the girdle, was better suited for fighting on foot; suitable for group fighting, it replaced the *tachi* in the middle Muromachi period, and thereafter became the major type of Japanese sword. Surviving examples of the *wakizashi* include a few from the Nambokuchô period but the majority are from the early Muromachi and later periods. The *wakizashi* was paired with the *katana* (*dai-shô,* "large and small") and worn thrust through the girdle. As for the *tantô,* existing specimens from the Heian and early Kamakura periods are very few. Most are from the middle and late Kamakura period and afterwards and were used in everyday self-defense and in close fight on the battlefield.

The material of Japanese swords is iron sand, from which steel is obtained by heating in reducing atmosphere at a relatively low temperature. The steel is heated at a temperature higher than 1,200° C. and hammered, folded, and hammered again many times over in order to remove impurities such as sulphur and phosphor. The result is *kawa-gane* (skin steel). The soft *shin-gane* (core steel) is wrapped in this hard *kawa-gane,* so that the finished blade cuts well but does not break or bend.

The *kawa-gane* is hammered after folding it horizontally, vertically, or both. The manner of folding and hammering results in different *kitae-hada* (blade patterns) such as *itame, mokume,* and *masame.*

After the blade is hammered into shape it is coated all over with *yakiba-zuchi* (tempered-edge clay), consisting mainly of a mixture of fire clay and carbon powder on which *midare-ba, sugu-ha, notare-ba,* and other *hamon* (edge patterns) are drawn. This process is termed *tsuchi-dori* (clay treatment). After this *tsuchi-dori*

the blade is dried, heated in the furnace, and put into water for *yaki-ire* (quenching). The cutting edge is further hardened by rapid cooling, while the *ji* (ground part), covered with the clay, remains relatively soft, creating a sharp yet elastic blade. *Sori* (curvature) of the blade results from differences in heat transmission in the blade.

The forged blade is polished to adjust the form and thickness and to bring forth the hue of the steel and the blade pattern on the *ji.* Polishing (*kenma*) is the important, indispensable finishing touch on the sword as a work of art in steel. The *sori,* which permits perpendicular cutting when the sword is used, lessens the shock of the cut, and produces the blade best suited for cutting. The *shinogi-zukuri,* with a ridge running along the blade lengthwise, is more effective in cutting than the *hira-zukuri* and *kiriha-zukuri;* a sharp-angled cross section gives the blade better balance and lightens its weight.

The major characteristics of Japanese swords lie in (1) the beautiful curves resulting from the *sori* and the *shinogi-zukuri* construction; (2) the elaborate *jihada* (ground pattern on the blade face) created by the combination of *shin-gane* and *kawa-gane* and by repeated folding and hammering; and (3) the rich variety of *hamon* effected by *tsuchi-dori* and *yaki-ire.*

Demand for swords decreased after the decree abolishing the wearing of swords. Most swordsmiths had to give up their occupation. However the Sino-Japanese war which broke out in 1904 revived the demand, and sword makers resumed their activity. Sadakazu GASSAN in 1906, and subsequently Kanenori MIYAMOTO, were nominated Teishitsu Gigei-in (Court Artists). Sword manufacture again thrived after the middle of the Meiji period, but at the close of World War II, Japanese swords were all confiscated by the Occupation Forces as weapons. The Allied Forces order was later amended to allow Japanese of good will to retain valuable antique swords, after examination. It became possible once more to own swords of artistic value, but the swords confiscated in the interim are believed to number about three million.

The making of swords was prohibited after 1945 by the Weapons Manufacture Prohibition Decree. It was the worst crisis in the history of Japanese swords as well as for sword makers. Sword manufacture was about to die out. Thanks to the

efforts of many concerned persons, it became possible in 1953 to make swords with the approval of the National Commission for Protection of Cultural Properties (the present Agency for Cultural Affairs). In the following year, 1954, the Society for Preservation of Japanese Art Swords held an exhibition for the display of sword making craft. Japanese sword makers thus recovered a means of exhibiting their works.

In 1955 Sadatsugu TAKAHASHI, who studied under Sadakazu GASSAN and Sadakatsu GASSAN and who excelled in Bizen style, Sôshû style, and blade sculpture (decoration engraved on the blade face), was designated Holder of Important Intangible Cultural Property. In 1963 Yukihira MIYAIRI, good at Mino and Sôshû style, and in 1971 Sadaichi GASSAN, representative of the Gassan family continuing from Sadayoshi GASSAN, Sadakazu to Sadakatsu and specializing in the family tradition of *ayasugi-hada*-style, Sôshû style, and blade sculpture, were likewise designated. Also named in 1981 was Masamine SUMITANI who features the florid Bizen style and who has achieved notable results in reproducing archaic swords. In the field of *kemma* (polishing), the craft was registered as an Important Intangible Cultural Property in 1975, whereupon Nisshû HON'AMI and Mitsutaka ONO were designated Holders.

Japanese swordsmiths have experienced several threatening crises but have overcome them each time. Currently there are 263 sword makers, and as many as 3530 blades were made during the year 1981. The use of swords as weapons has come to an end, but swords are still being made, and will continue to be made, as household treasures of the Japanese people and for occasions celebrating childbirth and other festive events.

TÔSÔGU (SWORD FURNITURE)

Tôsôgu are metal work pieces used in sword mounting. They include such objects as the *tsuba* (guard) for protecting the hand and for balancing the weight of the blade; *kozuka,* a knife worn in the scabbard, specifically its decorated handle; *kôgai,* a sort of skewer for adjusting the hair, also worn in the scabbard; *menuki* for decoration of the hilt and for preventing a slip of the hand; *fuchi* and *kashira* (caps on the base and top of the hilt) for strengthening both ends of the hilt; and so on.

Sword furniture pieces now regarded as objects of artistic

appreciation are mostly those made for *uchigatana wakizashi* and *tantô-goshirae* during the Momoyama and Edo periods. They include pieces made of gold, silver, *shakudô* (niellolike copper alloy), copper, *shibuichi* (silver alloy), brass, iron, and so forth, having the surface finished off in *tsuchime* (texture resembling hammer markings); *ishime* (roughened surface with fine chisel markings resembling stone work); *nanako* (fish roe, a granulated ground produced by covering the area with a series of minute dots); and *migaki-ji,* polished, mirror-smooth surface.

The carving includes such varied methods as *taka-bori* (relief), retaining the design in raised relief; *sukidashi-bori,* with the background engraved and the design retained on surface level; *ke-bori* and *katakiri-bori,* varieties of line engraving; and the like. They are often embellished further by *zôgan* (inlay) or *iro-e* (covering parts of the design with inlay of metals and alloys of several colors).

Tsuba (guards) prior to the early sixteenth century were mostly simple iron guards, almost always without *mei* (inscription). The Momoyama period in the late sixteenth century saw the appearance of inscribed and decorated *tsuba* by Myôju UMETADA, Kaneie, Matashichi HAYASHI, and other masters.

Manufacture of *kodôgu* (sword furniture excepting *tsuba*) was monopolized by the Gotô family which served the Ashikaga, Toyotomi, and Tokugawa shoguns. The pieces made by this family, called *ie-bori* (carvings for shogunate), were used for formal sword mountings. Prior to the early seventeenth century the Gotô family specialized exclusively in *kodôgu* and never made *tsuba.* They adhered to certain stereotyped forms and style, which naturally tended to lack variety and taste. Sômin YOKOYA, who appeared in the eighteenth century, broke through the convention. After him metal work artists other than those of the Gotô school, called *machi-bori* (metal carvers not employed by the shogunate), used diverse metals and alloys such as gold, silver, and *shakudô* in combination to work out ornate, gorgeous pieces which were very popular among newly wealthy merchants.

Matashichi HAYASHI was an artist in the service of the Hosokawa clan ruling the Kumamoto fief. He made *tsuba* of well-hammered iron, decorated with openwork and gold inlay in florid designs of cherry, arabesque, and other motifs. Rakuju KAMIYOSHI, active at the end of the Edo period, followed in his style and almost equaled him in workmanship.

The tradition of Rakuju was inherited by Yasuhira TANABE and his son Kichitarô. Mitsumasa YONEMITSU entered the studio of Kichitarô at the age of fifteen and trained himself in the crafts of Higo *zôgan* (inlay) such as *nunome* (fabric-mesh pattern) *zôgan*, *hira* (flat) *zôgan*, and *horikomi* (engraved) *zôgan*. He was nominated Holder of Important Intangible Cultural Property in 1965 as the only expert who has maintained the techniques of traditional Higo *zôgan* since the Momoyama period. Demand for sword furniture has also decreased due to the decree abolishing the wearing of swords. The Higo *zôgan* craft with its floridity and firmness is now used for *obidome* (girdle clasps), tiepins, and other personal ornaments.

TESUKI WASHI (HANDMADE JAPANESE PAPER)

Individual Designation
(1) *Gampi-shi*: Eishirô ABE
Group Designation
(2) Association of *Sekishû Hanshi*: Sekishû Hanshi Technical Experts
(3) *Honmino-shi*: Society for Honmino-shi of Preservation
(4) *Hosokawa-shi*: Association of Hosokawa-shi Technical Experts
Individual Designation Cancelled
(5) *Echizen-Hôsho*: Ichibei IWANO

The oldest documentary record on *washi* (Japanese paper) is an article in the *Nihon Shoki*, an official history of Japan compiled in 720, where it is stated that the Korean Buddhist priest Donchô from the Koguryo dynasty, who came to Japan in 610, knew how to make paper. It is supposed that the craft of papermaking, invented in China probably in a period not much earlier than the reign of Empress Suiko (592—628), was introduced to Japan through the Korean peninsula.

The typical materials for Japanese handmade paper are *kôzo*, *gampi* and *mitsumata*. In each case the raw material is the bast fiber left after removing the surface *kuro-kawa* (black bark). The properties of this bast fiber show themselves in the finished paper and become the characteristics of the paper.

The process of Japanese papermaking consists roughly of boiling, beating, screening, and drying. Bast fiber, which is tolerant against alkali, is boiled in a solution of wood ash, lime, or soda ash in order to remove impurities. Then, because the bast fiber collects in bundles, it is beaten to separate the strands. When *neri*, a mucilaginous substance taken from the root of *tororo-aoi* (*Hibiscus Manihot, L.*), is added to the water, the turbulence subsides gentler, and the fiber floats in the water for a long period of time, so that screening is easily carried out. Furthermore, the *neri* facilitates the passing of pulp through the screen laced with small splintered pieces of bamboo; while the pulp is shaken slowly and thoroughly on the screen, the fiber can at the same time be well entwined. The mucilage changes only the quality of the water; it does not affect the paper at all. *Neri* is not the adhesive *nori* (paste), as is often supposed. After a time it disappears. Thus Japanese paper, as a rule, consists purely of intertwined fiber.

Except for a very slight amount of stone powder added for special purposes, it is formed with natural bast fiber. *Washi* therefore not only has tensile strength, but is so durable that it can be preserved unaltered in quality for more than a thousand years.

The fiber of the *kôzo* (*Broussonetia Kazinoki, Sieb.*) is especially long, averaging 1 cm. in length. It is strong and readily tangles. *Kôzo* paper is therefore, far more tolerant against crumpling and bending than *yôshi* ("Western paper," machine-made paper).

One of the characteristics of *washi* is that it is usable for a rich variety of purposes: not only for writing with ink and brush but as an architectural material for spreading on *fusuma* and *shôji* (sliding doors and screens), as crease-resistant material suitable for making *kimono* dresses and *obi* sashes, for various underlinings, and so forth. Despite its thin texture, *washi* does not tear readily, a quality which makes it widely usable. Particularly strong is *kôzo* paper, which predominates among currently manufactured *washi*.

The *Sekishû Hanshi*, *Honmino-shi*, and *Hosokawa-shi*, now registered as Important Intangible Cultural Properties, and the *Echizen Hôsho*, so registered formerly, are all *kôzo* paper. In principle, these varieties are, made of *kôzo* obtained locally. When local *kôzo* becomes unavailable, the manufacturers try to find another fiber similar in quality to the local one. The characteristics of *kôzo* fiber differ according to the locality where it is produced, and papers are known by their local characteristics.

The materials used for *gampi-shi* are of several kinds, notably the *gampi* (*Diplomorpha sikokiana, Honda*) and *ao-gampi* (*Wikstroemiaretusa, A. Gray*). Their fiber is shorter than that of the *kôzo*, namely about

0.3 cm., but is both transparent and glossy. The resulting *gampi* paper is often called Eastern parchment. Its compact texture does not deteriorate in humid environments, and is immune to vermin.

The *kôzo* can be cultivated, but the *gampi* must be collected from trees growing wild. Because of the shortage of material, *gampi-shi* manufacturers are now very few.

The fiber of *mitsumata* (*Edgeworthia chrysantha, Lindi.*) averages about 0.4 cm. in length. It is inevitably less strong but has a warm gloss. *Mitsumata* paper is soft and smooth, has elegant gloss, and like *gampi* paper, is not affected by vermin. It permits a smooth, pleasant movement when writing with a brush. It is favored for use in *kana* calligraphy, but its manufacturers are decreasing in number. Designation as an Important Intangible Cultural Property has not yet taken place in the field of *mitsumata* paper.

OTHER APPLIED ARTS

Included also among the applied arts are gem and stone work, ivory carving, cloisonné, glass, *Kirikane*, and so forth. Among these the Government has taken measures for recording as Intangible Cultural Properties cloisonné and *kirikane*, the latter having been registered as an Important Intangible Cultural Property.

The crafts of carving and polishing gems, jade and other precious and semi-precious stones are represented by rock crystal, agate and other works which have been transmitted since the Edo period in Kôfu, Yamanashi Prefecture, Obama in Fukui Prefecture, and so on. The processing of stones to make inkstones is said to have begun in Japan during the Kamakura period. Widely known among others are the Akama Inkstone in Yamaguchi Prefecture and the Amehata Inkstone in Yamanashi Prefecture.

Ivory carving in Japan is represented by works of *bachiru* preserved in the Shôsô-in Repository of Imperial Treasures. *Bachiru* is ivory stained in red, green, or blue, decorated with ornamental patterns in fine *hane-bori* (kicking incision) line engraving. The technique has been revived and is practised Nara.

Shippô (cloisonné or champlevé) is made by fusing a vitreous substance to a base of copper, silver, or other metals. The craft is supposed to have been imported from Korea during the seventh century, but it did not see general development until the end of the Edo period. It attained rapid technical perfection during the Meiji period thanks to the German expert Wagner's improvement of cloisonné enamel. The present centers of the traditional technique are Nagoya City and Shippô Town in Aichi Prefecture.

Glass, too, is believed to have been manufactured as early as the protohistoric Kofun period in Japan for the making of *magatama, sashi-dama* and other beads for lacing. It is thought, however, that the first receptacles of blown glass were manufactured in the early Edo period at Nagasaki in imitation of European craft. Cut glass was made in Edo (Tokyo) and Satsuma (Kagoshima) from the latter half to the very end of Edo period. The materials, implements, and crafts of the Edo period underwent extensive changes in and after the Meiji period, influenced by modern Western techniques. There is some possibility, however, that the old blown glass and cut glass techniques will win renewed recognition as traditional handicraft arts, in the wider sense of the term, thanks to glass works shown at recent exhibitions of Traditional Japanese Crafts.

Kirikane (cut gold), originally employed for decorating of Buddhist statues and paintings, is gold and/or silver leaf previously cut into fine threadlike strips or triangular or square bits and applied to a base.

The craft was brought over from the Continent along with the introduction of Buddhist culture, and saw unique development in Japan in and after the Nara period. Its patterns became rich in variety and its technique reached the height of development in the Fujiwara and Kamakura periods, but gradually declined after the middle Muromachi period. Of late this *kirikane* technique has come to be used on works of applied arts. Ornamental boxes (Catalog No. 235), tea-ceremony objects, folding screens (Catalog No. 236), and the like successfully show the artistic effect and subtle texture of fine *kirikane* work. Considered a valuable craft in the history of Japanese applied arts, the technique was registered in 1956 as an Important Intangible Cultural Property. The late Baitei SAIDA was designated Holder of the technique but died shortly after.

1 — Toyozô ARAKAWA   Tea Bowl, *Shino* ware.   1953.

2 — Toyozô ARAKAWA   Covered Water Jar, with a pair of loops, *Nezumi* ("mouse gray") *Shino* ware.   Around 1950.

3 — Toyozô ARAKAWA   Tea Bowl, *Setoguro* (''black *Seto*'') ware.   1959.

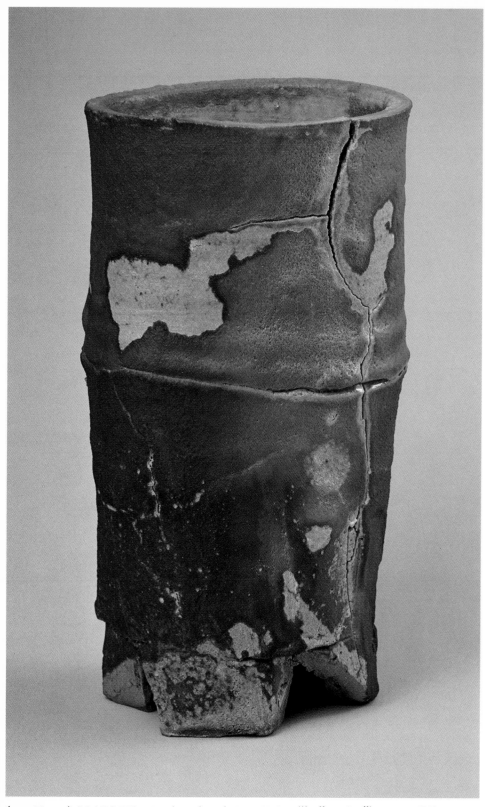

4 — Toyozô ARAKAWA   Bamboo-shaped Vase, *Ki-Seto* ("yellow *Seto*") ware.   1960.

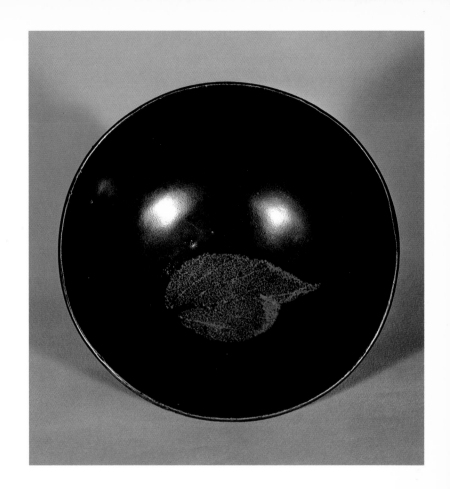

5 — Munemaro ISHIGURO
Tea Bowl, *Konoha* ("tree-leaf") *Temmoku* ware.   Around 1955.

6 — Munemaro ISHIGURO   Vase, *kaki* (persimmon color) glaze.   Around 1940.

7 — Munemaro ISHIGURO   Bowl, black glaze with a design of birds in brown dots.   1958.

8 — Munemaro ISHIGURO   Vase, white glaze with a colored design of persimmons.   1959.

9 — Kenkichi TOMIMOTO   Large Bowl, enameled porcelain with red *Sarasa* (printed textile) pattern.   1949.

10 — Kenkichi TOMIMOTO
  Vase, enameled porcelain with gold and silver colors framing panels of *sometsuke* (blue-and-white) landscapes.   1957.

11 — Kenkichi TOMIMOTO   Covered Vase, red-enameled porcelain with gold and silver fern-leaf pattern.   1958.

12 — Kenkichi TOMIMOTO   Five Dishes, porcelain with different *sometsuke* (blue-and-white) designs.   1960.

13 — Kenkichi TOMIMOTO   Two Wine Bottles, enameled porcelain with *Sarasa* (printed textile) pattern.   1939.

14 — Kenkichi TOMIMOTO   Octagonal Box, enameled porcelain with gold and silver fern-leaf pattern.   1958.

15 — Hajime KATÔ   Dodecagonal Bowl, enamelled porcelain with a design of *kumagaiso* (Lady's Slipper).   1944.

16 — Hajime KATÔ
  Covered Round Box, green-enameled porcelain with *kinrande* (gold color) design of *Hôsôge* (Heavenly Flower).   1958.

17 — Hajime KATÔ   Covered Jar, enameled porcelain with red and *kinrande* (gold color) floral pattern on yellowish ground.   1960.

18 — Hajime KATÔ   Large Plate, enameled porcelain with heron and willow design.   1961.

19 — Hajime KATÔ   Five Dishes, enameled porcelain with floral pattern.   1961.

20 — Hajime KATÔ   Six Stemmed Wine Cups, enameled porcelain with *kinrande* (gold color) chrysanthemum design.   1967.

21 — Shôji HAMADA   Large Bowl, *ame* (black candy) glaze with a white and blue cross.   1957.

22 — Shôji HAMADA   Large Bowl, white glaze with cursive drawing in black.   1960.

23 — Shôji HAMADA   Large Bowl, *kaki* (persimmon color) glaze with iron-colored circular design.   1962.

24 — Shôji HAMADA   Large Bowl, *namako* ("trepang's gray") glaze with black cursive drawing.   1962.

25 — Shôji HAMADA   Square Plate, *kaki* (persimmon color) glaze with reddish design.   1972.

26 — Shôji HAMADA   Square Bottle, salt glaze with white splashes.   1971.

27 — Tôyô KANASHIGE   Large Bowl, *Bizen* ware with *hidasuki* ("fire marks").   1960.

28 — Tôyô KANASHIGE   Covered Water Pot, *Bizen* ware.   1963.

29 — Tôyô KANASHIGE   Square Plate, *Bizen* ware.   1953.

30 — Tôyô KANASHIGE   Set of Five *Mukôzuke* (Serving dishes), *Bizen* ware.   1964.

31 — Kei FUJIWARA   Cylindrical Flower Vase, *Bizen* ware.   1963.

32 — Kei FUJIWARA   Large Bottle-Shaped Vase, *Bizen* ware.   1971.

33 — Kyûwa MIWA   Tea Bowl, *Hagi* ware.   1966.

34 — Kyûwa MIWA   *Mizusashi* (water container), *Hagi* ware.   1972.

35 — Muan NAKAZATO   Jar, *Ki-Garatsu* ("yellow *Karatsu*") ware.   1967.

36 — Muan NAKAZATO   Tea Bowl, *Karatsu* ware.   1968.

37 — Yûzô KONDÔ   Jar, porcelain with *sometsuke* (blue-and-white) pomegranate design.   1957.

38 — Yûzô KONDÔ   Jar, porcelain with *sometsuke* (blue-and-white) grapevine design.   1964.

39 — Imaemon IMAIZUMI XII.　　Large Plate, *Iro-Nabeshima* porcelain with *utsugi* (deutzia) design.　　1965.

40 — Imaemon IMAIZUMI XIII Large Bowl, *Iro-Nabeshima* porcelain with *karukaya* (Japanese pampas grass) design.   1969.

41 — Kakiemon SAKAIDA XII.   Covered Container, *nigoshide* (milk white) porcelain with floral design.   1957.

42 — Kakiemon SAKAIDA XIII.   Large Bowl, *nigoshide* (milk white) porcelain with floral design.   1975.

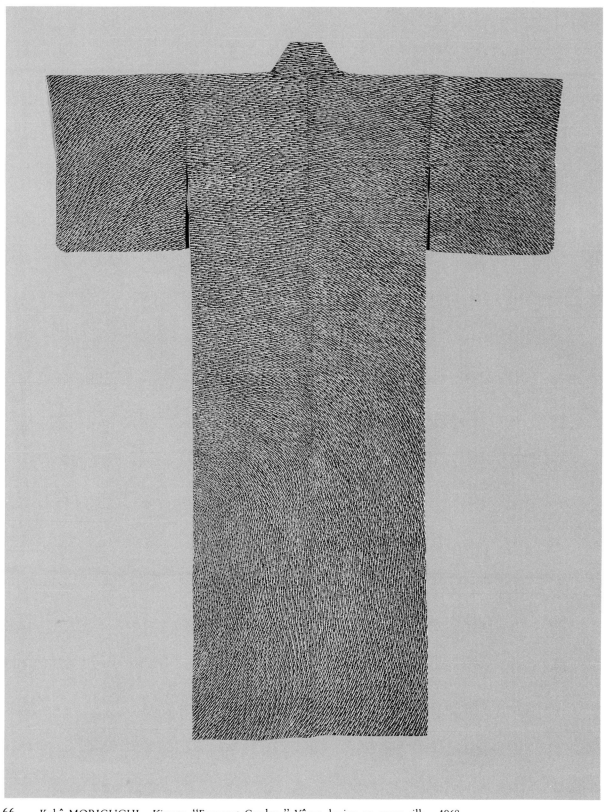

66 — Kakô MORIGUCHI   *Kimono*, "Fragrant Garden." *Yûzen* dyeing on crepe silk.   1968.

67 — Kakô MORIGUCHI   *Kimono*, "Plum Blossoms." *Yûzen* dyeing on crepe silk.   1972.

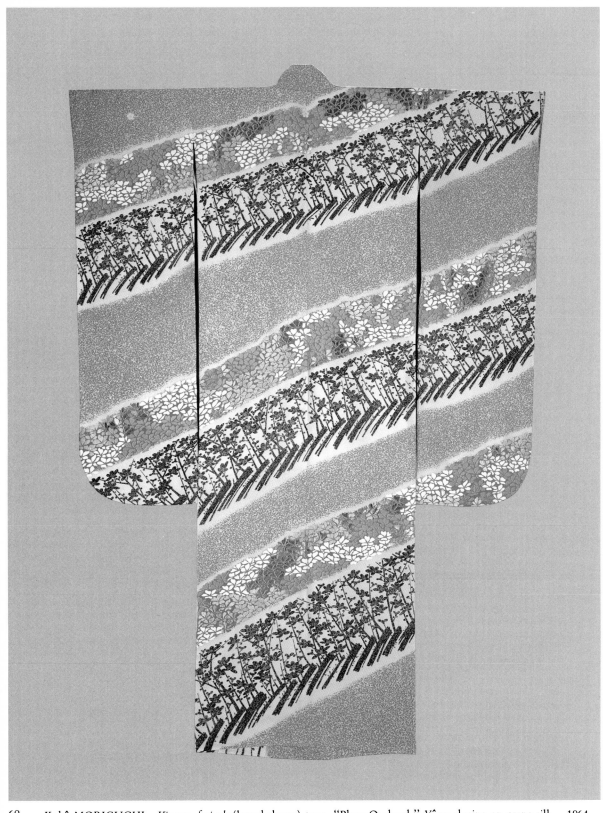

68 — Kakô MORIGUCHI   *Kimono, furisode* (broad sleeve) type, "Plum Orchard." *Yûzen* dyeing on crepe silk.   1964.

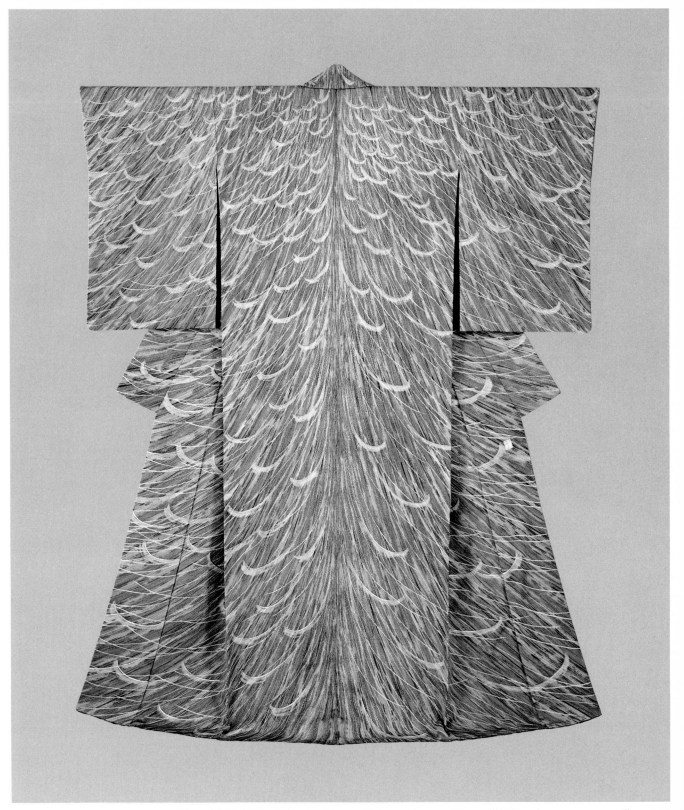

69 — Kakô MORIGUCHI *Kimono,* "Chrysanthemum Flower." *Yûzen* dyeing on crepe silk. 1960.

70 — Kakô MORIGUCHI   *Kimono*, "Fragrance of Four Seasons." *Yûzen* dyeing on crepe silk.   1959.

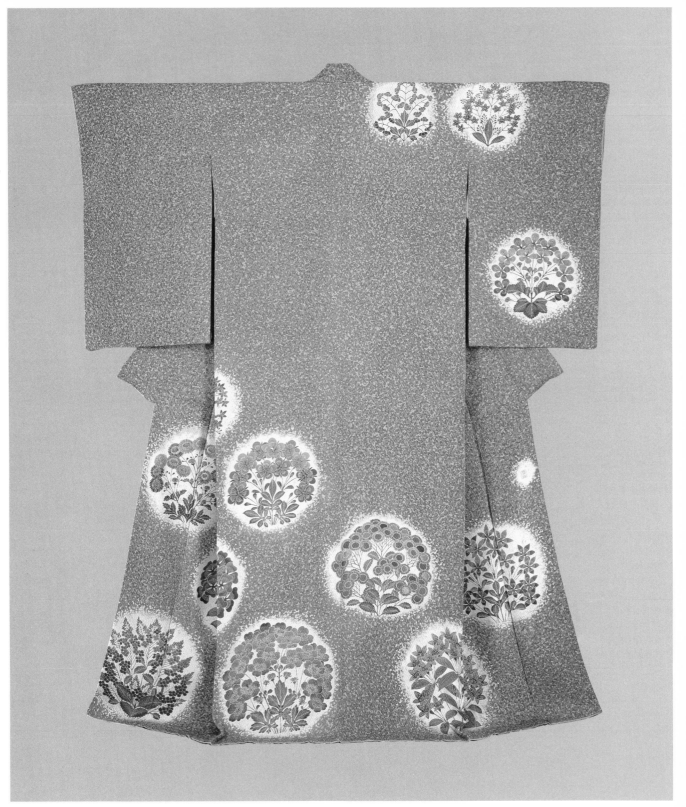

71 — Kakô MORIGUCHI   *Kimono*, "Image of Fragrance." *Yûzen* dyeing on crepe silk.   1959.

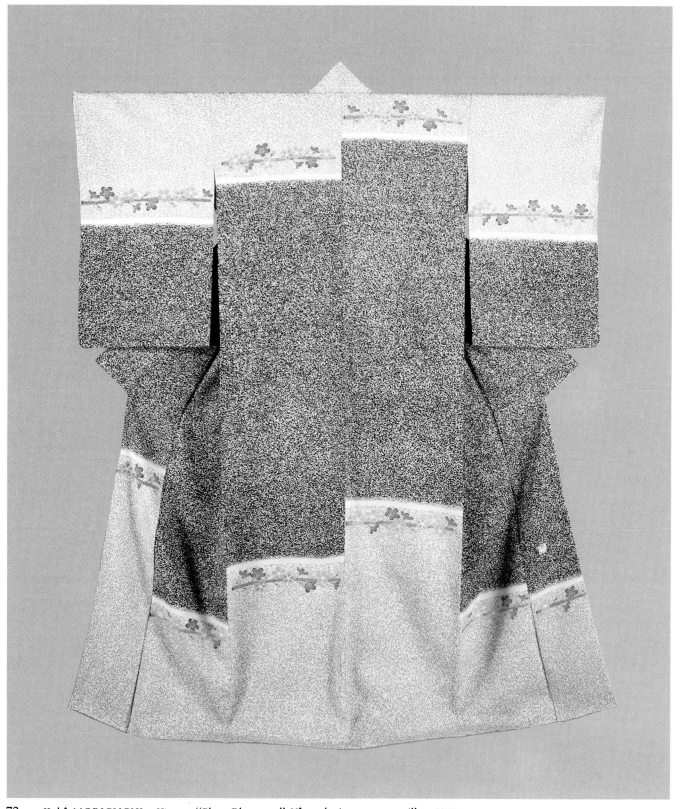

72 — Kakô MORIGUCHI   *Kimono*, "Plum Blossoms." *Yûzen* dyeing on crepe silk.   1973.

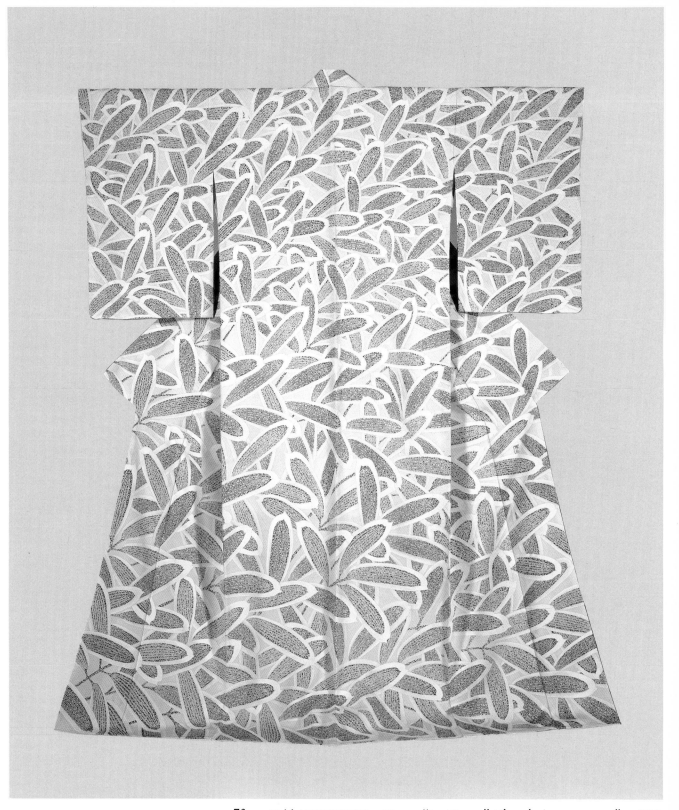

73 — Kakô MORIGUCHI *Kimono, "Last Snow." Yûzen* dyeing on crepe silk. 1969.

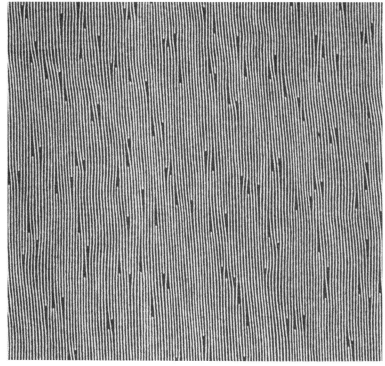

74 — Kôsuke KOMIYA
Kimono, Edo komon "Yorokejima (tottering stripe)."
Stencil dyeing on crepe silk.   1958.

75 — Kôsuke KOMIYA
Kimono, Edo komon "Goku Ichimatsu (fine checkered pattern)."
Stencil dyeing on crepe silk.   1958.

76 — Kôsuke KOMIYA
Kimono Material, *Edo komon "Waridakejima* (split bamboo stripe)."
Stencil dyeing on crepe silk.   1958.

77 — Yasutaka KOMIYA
Kimono, Edo komon "Daishô Shimazu (Shimazu's Large and Small Dots)."
Stencil dyeing on crepe silk.   1982.

78 — Yasutaka KOMIYA   *Kimono, Edo komon "Karamatsu* (Chinese pine)."
Stencil dyeing on crepe silk.   1982.

79 — Yasutaka KOMIYA
Kimono, Edo komon "Series of Fans." Stencil dyeing on crepe silk.
1969.

80 — Sadakichi MATSUBARA *Yukata* Garment, with stripe design. Stencil dyeing on cotton. 1954.

81 — Sadakichi MATSUBARA
Yukata Material, with design of bamboo and checkered pattern. Stencil dyeing on cotton. 1955.

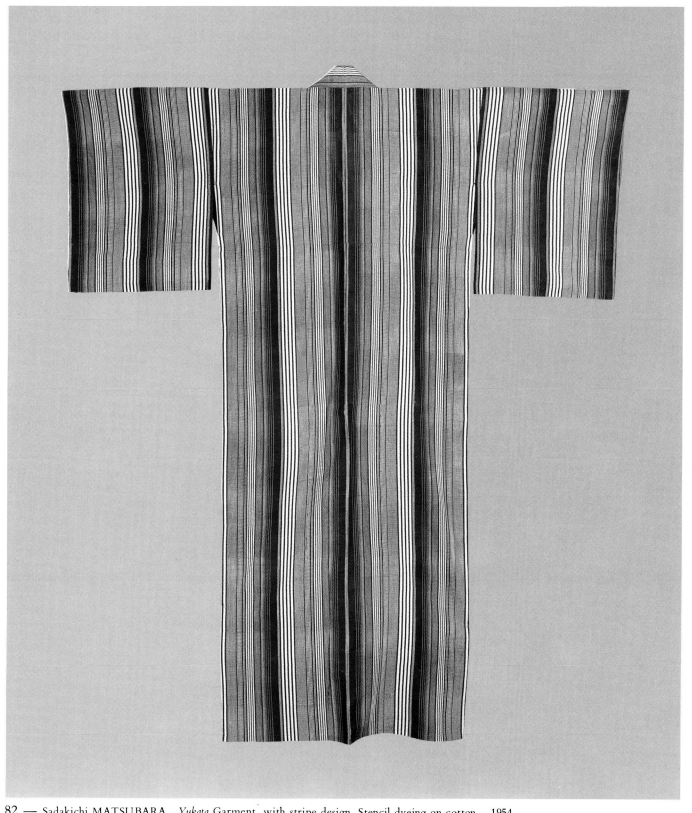

82 — Sadakichi MATSUBARA *Yukata* Garment, with stripe design. Stencil dyeing on cotton. 1954.

83 — Kôtarô SHIMIZU   *Yukata* Garment, "Bamboo." Stencil dyeing on cotton.   1965.

84 — Kôtarô SHIMIZU   *Yukata* Garment, "Clamshells." Stencil dyeing on cotton.   1952.

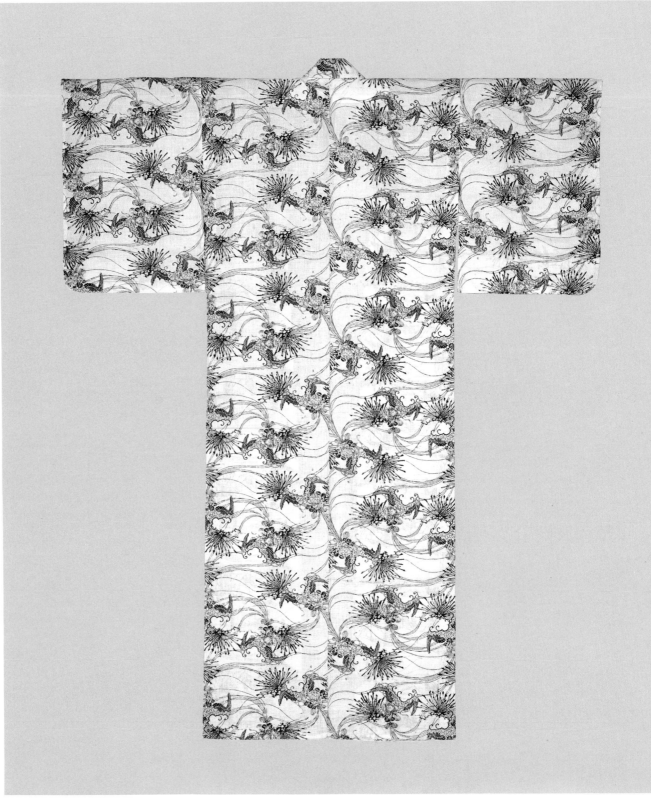

85 — Kôtarô SHIMIZU   *Yukata* Garment, "Chrysanthemums." Stencil dyeing on cotton.   1952.

86 — Hidekichi NAKAJIMA *Ise* Stencil, "*Goku Ichimatsu* (fine checkered pattern)." 1956.

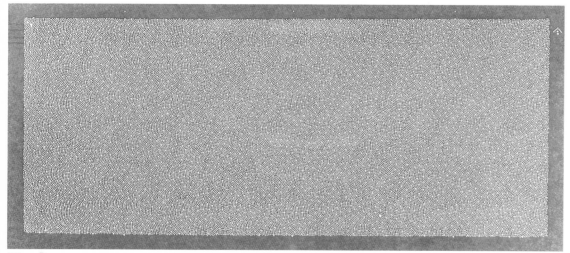

87 — Baiken ROKUTANI *Ise* Stencil, "*Daishô Shimazu* (Shimazu's Large and Small Dots)." 1958.

88 — Baiken ROKUTANI *Ise* Stencil, "*Karamatsu* (Chinese pine)." 1958.

89 — Yoshimatsu NAMBU *Ise* Stencil, "Dragon." 1960.

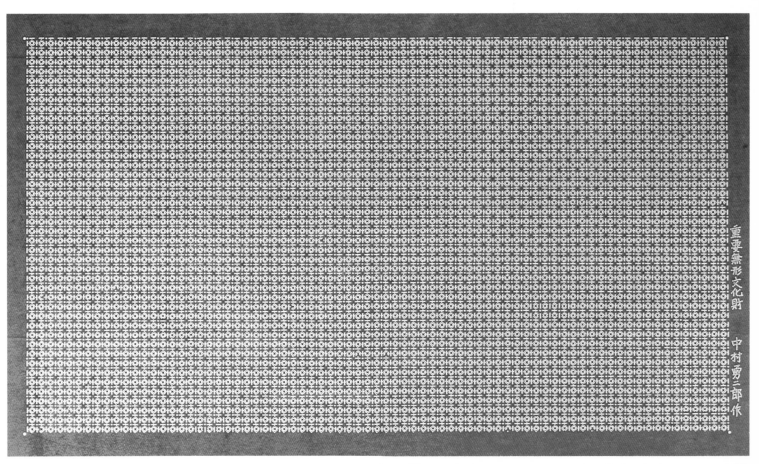

重要無形文化財　中村勇三郎作

90 — Yûjirô NAKAMURA *Ise* Stencil, fine lattice pattern. 1965.

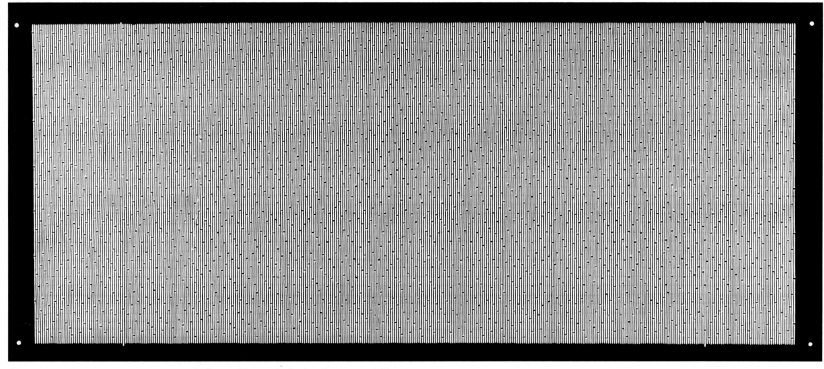

91 — Hiroshi KODAMA   *Ise* Stencil, "*Waridakejima* (split bamboo stripe)."   1957.

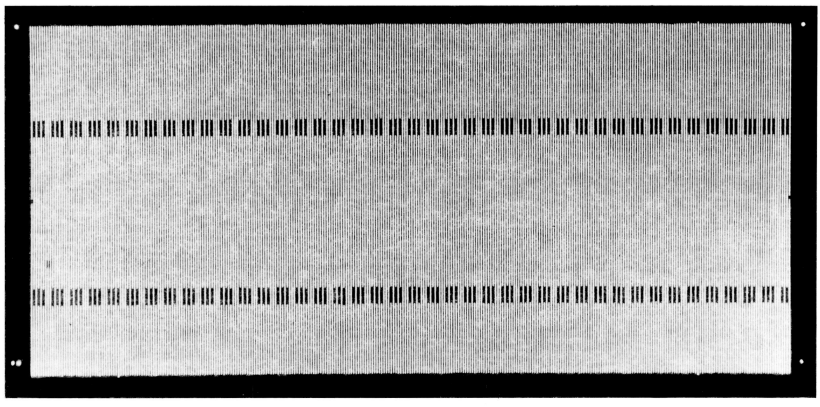

92 — Hiroshi KODAMA   *Ise* Stencil, ruled triple lines. Threaded by Mie Jônoguchi.   1982.

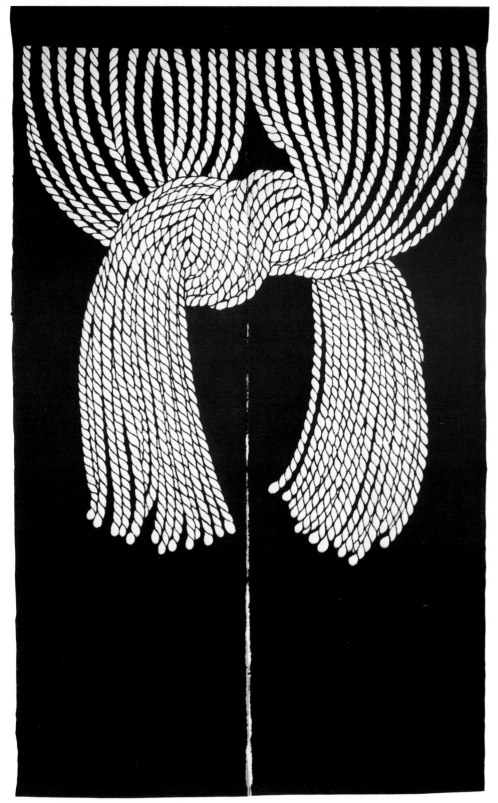

94 — Keisuke SERIZAWA

Noren (doorway curtain), with design of *nawa-noren* (rope curtain). Stencil dyeing on cotton. 1955.

93 — Keisuke SERIZAWA   Six-fold Screen, Japanese syllabary, each graph framed by a circle. Stencil dyeing on *tsumugi* weave silk.   1963.

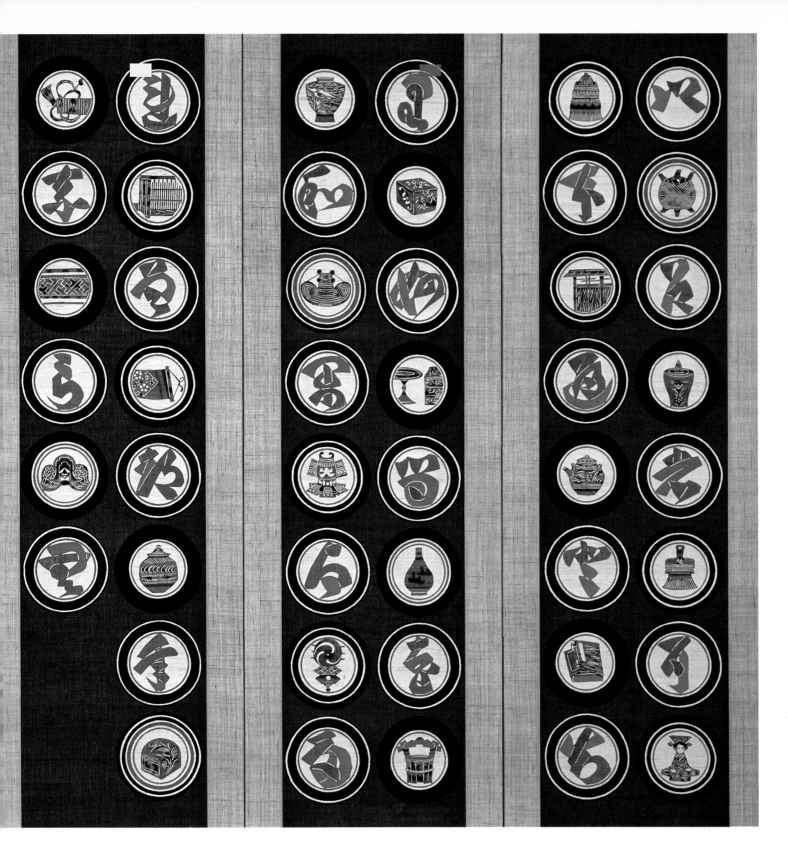

95 — Keisuke SERIZAWA   *Kimono*, with design of Japanese syllabary. Stencil dyeing on cotton.   1961.

96 — Keisuke SERIZAWA   Two-fold Screen, with design of Japanese syllabary in six columns. Stencil dyeing on linen.   1973.

97 — Keisuke SERIZAWA
  Noren (doorway curtain), with design of the character "*Kaze* (wind)." Stencil dyeing on cotton.   1957.

98 — Keisuke SERIZAWA
Kimono, with design of diagonal lattice and gold hand drawing. Stencil dyeing on *tsumugi* weave silk.   1972.

99 — Keisuke SERIZAWA
Two-Fold Screen, with design of Japanese syllabary in six columns. Stencil dyeing on cotton. 1973.

100 —Keisuke SERIZAWA   *Noren* (doorway curtain), with design of the character "*Hana* (flower)." Stencil dyeing on *tsumugi* weave silk.   1960.

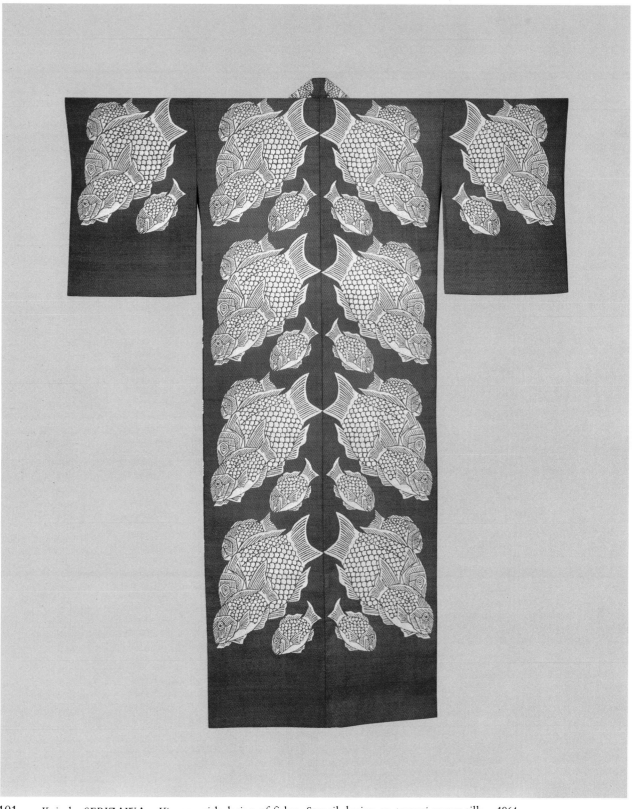

101 — Keisuke SERIZAWA   *Kimono*, with design of fishes. Stencil dyeing on *tsumugi* weave silk.   1964.

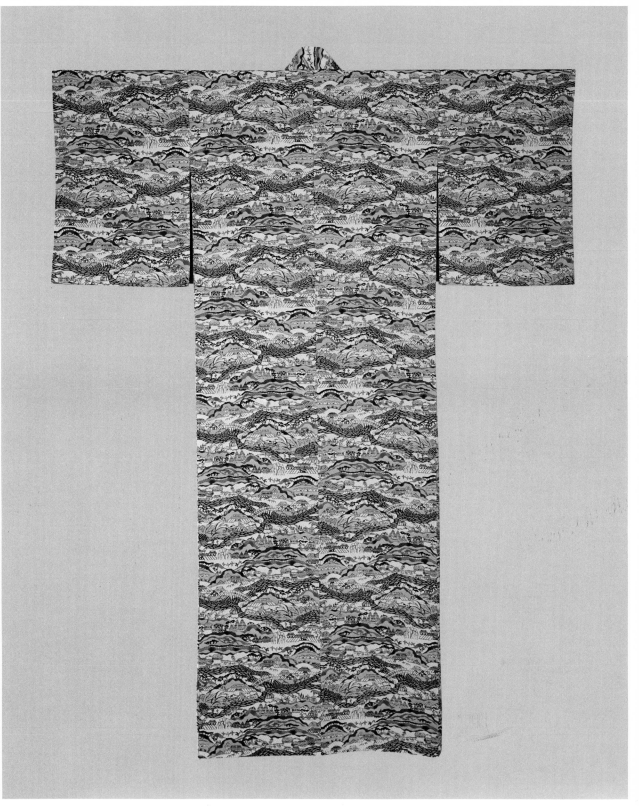

102 — Keisuke SERIZAWA   *Kimono*, "Ogawa Paper Mills Village." Stencil dyeing on crepe silk.   1943.

103 — Keisuke SERIZAWA   Two-fold Screen, with design of the four seasons. Stencil dyeing of *tsumugi* weave silk.   1960.

104 — Keisuke SERIZAWA   *Noren* (doorway curtain), with design of waterfall. Stencil dyeing on *tsumugi* weave silk.   1962.

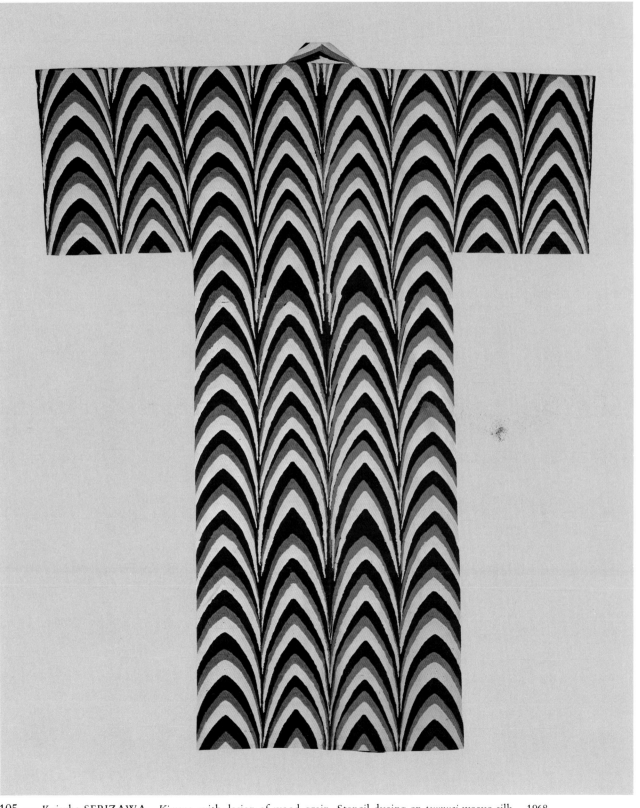

105 — Keisuke SERIZAWA *Kimono*, with design of wood-grain. Stencil dyeing on *tsumugi* weave silk. 1968.

106 — Toshijirô INAGAKI   Two-fold Screen, with design of wild grasses. Stencil dyeing on *tsumugi* weave silk.   1959.

107 — Toshijirô INAGAKI Wall-hanging, "Waving Heads of Wheat Plants." Stencil dyeing on cotton. 1961.

108 — Toshijirô INAGAKI   Wall-hanging, with design of the festival scene at Tôji Temple, Kyoto. Stencil dyeing on cotton.   1952.

109 —Toshijirô INAGAKI
  Kimono, with design of wild grasses, bamboo and *hitta* (knot-dyeing) pattern. Stencil dyeing on crepe silk.   1955.

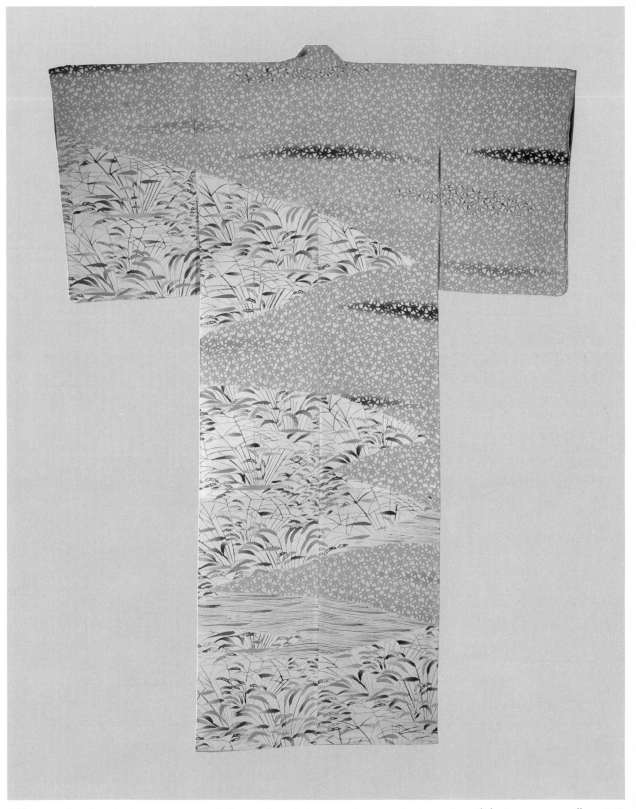

111 — Toshijirô INAGAKI *Kimono*, with design of maple-leaves and autumnal grasses. Stencil dyeing on crepe silk. 1958.

110 — Two-fold Screen, "Interior of Sanjûsangendô Temple." Stencil dyeing on paper. 1953.

112 — Toshijirô INAGAKI
Wall-hanging, "Standing Tiger." Stencil dyeing on cotton. 1960.

114 — Toshijiro INAGAKI
Wall-hanging, "Crouching Tiger." Stencil dyeing on cotton. 1960.

113 — Toshijirô INAGAKI   *Kimono*, with design of iris flowers and water. Stencil dyeing on crepe silk.   1958.

115 — Toshijirô INAGAKI *Kimono*, "Moss Garden." Stencil dyeing on *ro* (gauze) silk. 1956.

116 — Yoshitarô KAMAKURA   *Kimono*, with design of mountain landscape. Stencil dyeing on linen.   1975.

117 — Yoshitarô KAMAKURA   *Kimono*, with design of bamboo leaves. Stencil dyeing on linen.   1968.

118 — Yoshitarô KAMAKURA   *Kimono*, with design of dragonflies and reeds. Stencil dyeing on linen.   1980.

119 — Yoshitarô KAMAKURA   *Kimono*, "Pine, Bamboo and Plum-blossoms." Stencil dyeing on *tsumugi* silk.   1981.

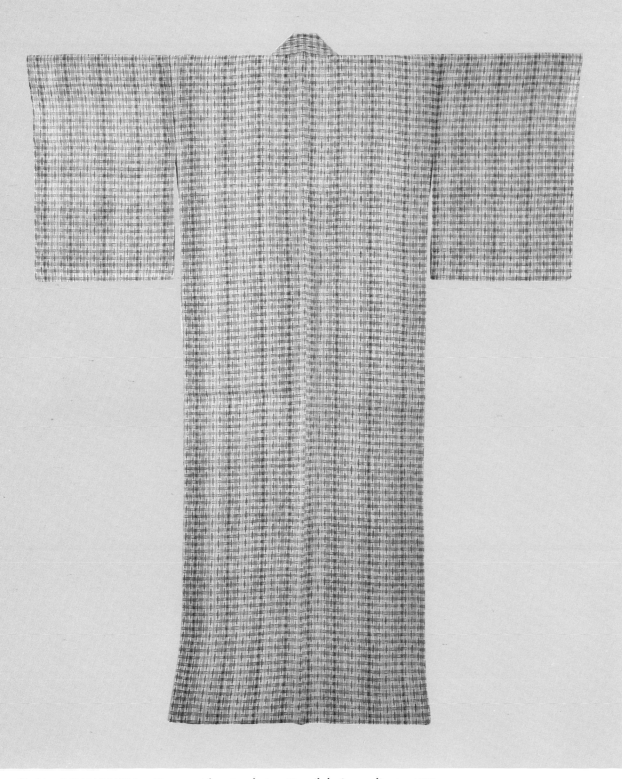

120 — Yoshitarô. KAMAKURA *Kimono*, with stripe design. Stencil dyeing on linen. 1969.

121 — Ayano CHIBA *Kimono* material, indigo-dyed linen. 1956.

122 — Ayano CHIBA *Kimono* material, indigo-dyed linen. 1960.

123 —Heirô KITAGAWA
Futae-orimono (double-woven) type silk, with circular butterfly
and hollyhock motifs on yellow ground.   1979.

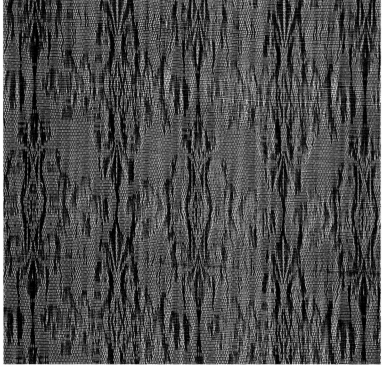

124 —Heirô KITAGAWA
Jôdai ra (ancient gauze) type silk, with vine-scroll
on *hanada* (pale blue) ground.   1959.

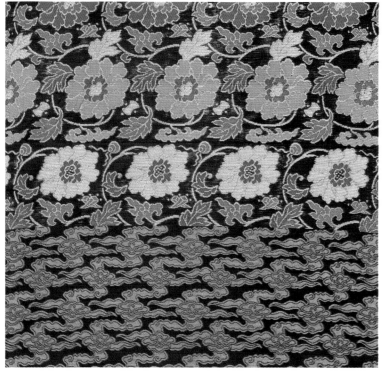

125 —Heirô KITAGAWA
Rakin (gauze with gold weft) type ilk, with motifs
of peony scroll and mushroom-shaped cloud.   1959.

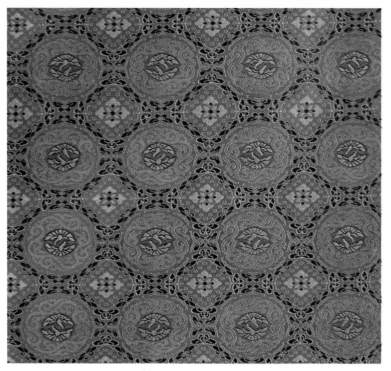

126 —Heirô KITAGAWA
Nishiki (brocade) type silk, with butterfly
and bird motifs on reddish ground.   1959.

127 —Heirô KITAGAWA
Green *Jôdai Horara* (ancient gauze) type silk.   1959.

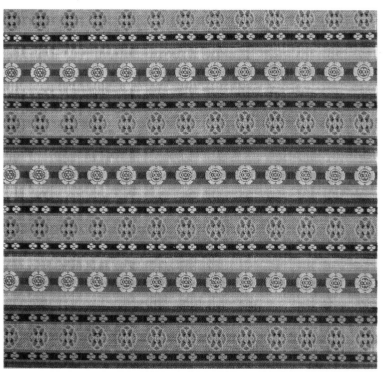

128 —Heirô KITAGAWA
Nishiki (brocade) type silk, with motif of *karabana ungen*
(Chinese flowers in gradations of color).   1959.

129 — Heirô KITAGAWA   Black *Ra* (gauze) type silk.   1959.

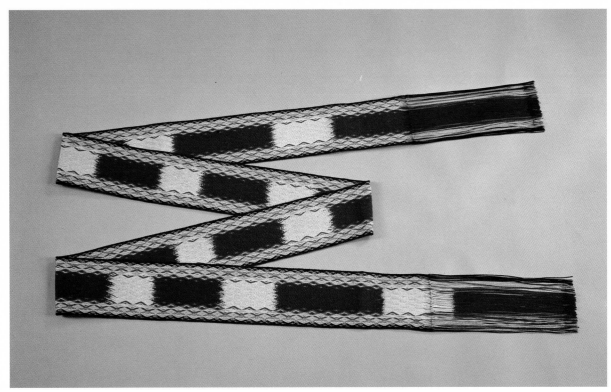

130 — Jûsuke FUKAMI   Sword Belt, *kumihimo* (braid) plaited in different colors.   1956.

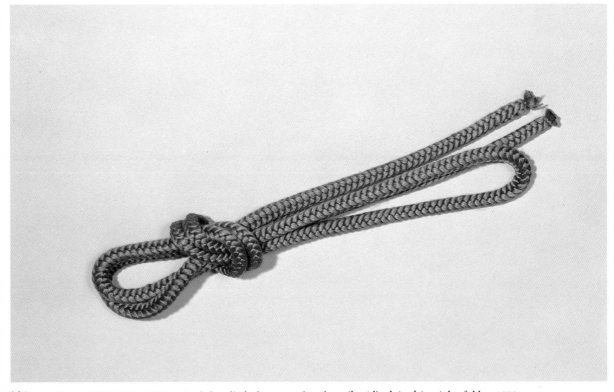

131 — Jûsuke FUKAMI   *Obijime* (sash band), light green *kumihimo* (braid) plaited in eight-fold.   1972.

132 —Jûsuke FUKAMI
Belt, *kumihimo* (braid) as reproduction of 8th century piece kept in the Imperial Repository Shôsôin.   1930.

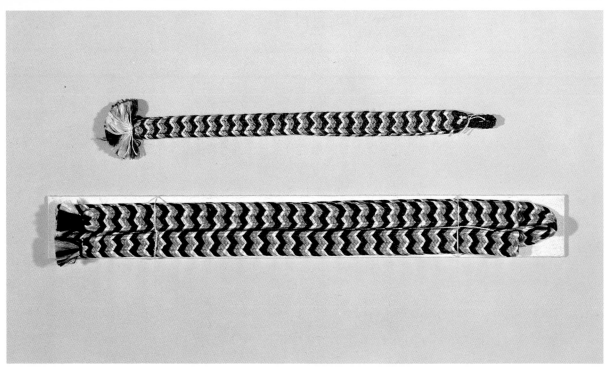

133-134 — Jûsuke FUKAMI
Obijime (sash band) and *Haorihimo* (braid for *haori* coat), reproduction of armor braid from Sanage Jinja Shrine. 1955.

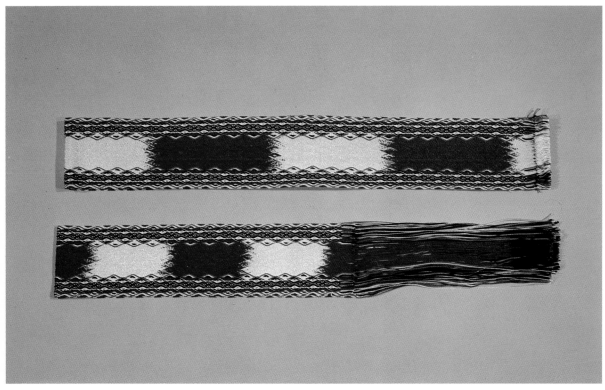

135 — Jûsuke FUKAMI   Sword Belt, *kumihimo* (braid) plaited in different colors.   1972.

137 — Eisuke KÔDA   *Hakama* (*kimono* trousers). *Seigô Sendaihira* type.   1968.

136 —Eisuke KÔDA *Hakama* (*kimono* trousers) material, "Phoenix's Elegance."
    Seigô Sendaihira type.   1958.

138 —Eisuke KÔDA *Hakama* (*kimono* trousers) material, "Immortal's Waterfall."
    Seigô Sendaihira type.   1958.

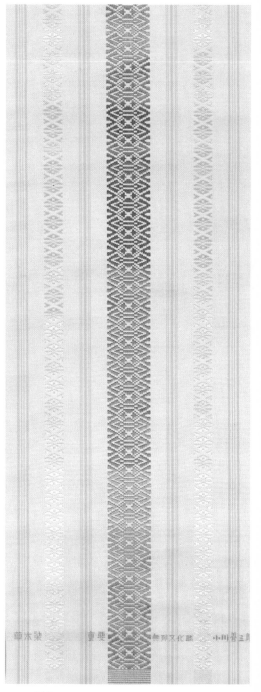

139 — Zenzaburô OGAWA
Kenjô Hakata-obi, Hakata type sash of
tough silk.   1964.

140 — Zenzaburô OGAWA
Kenjô Hakata-obi, Hakata type sash of
tough silk.   1973.

141 — Zenzaburô OGAWA
Kenjô Hakata-obi, Hakata type sash of
tough silk.   1982.

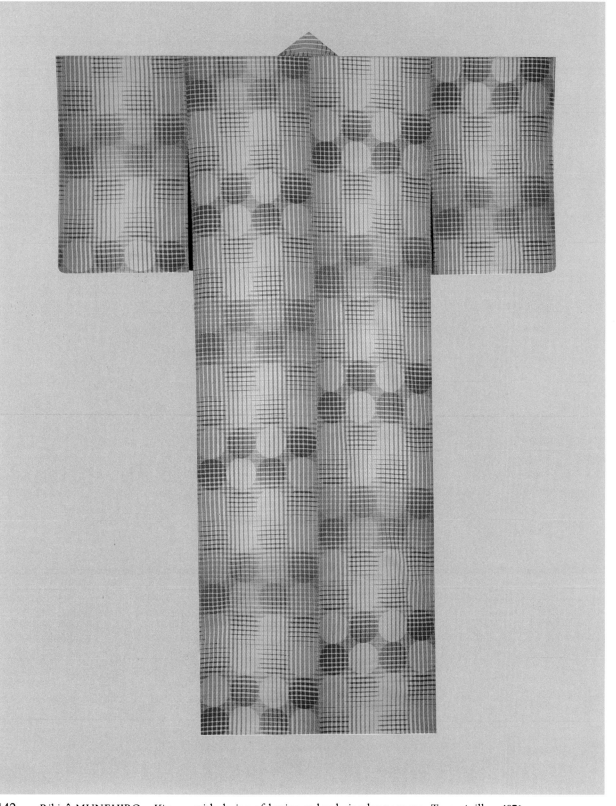

142 — Rikizô MUNEHIRO   *Kimono*, with design of lattice and red circular patterns. *Tsumugi* silk.   1976.

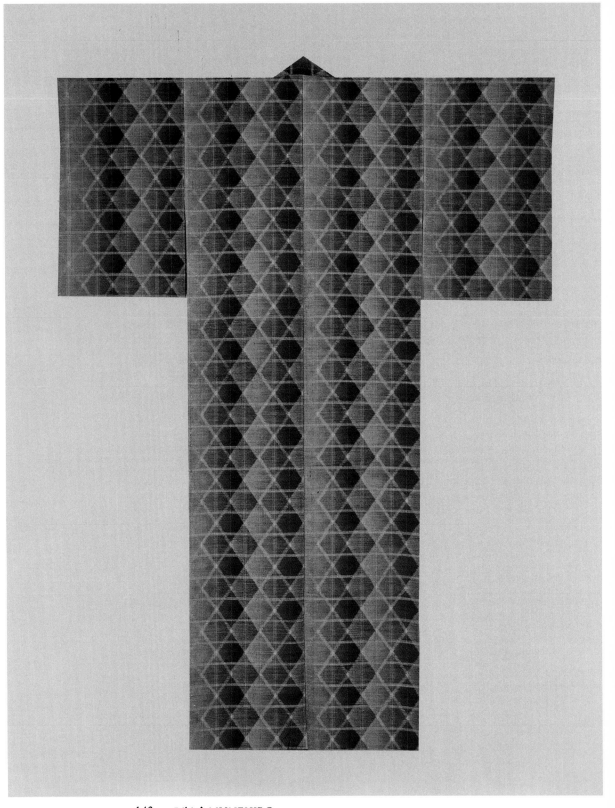

143 —Rikizô MUNEHIRO
Kimono, with design of gradating indigo-dyed bamboo plait pattern. *Tsumugi* silk.   1981.

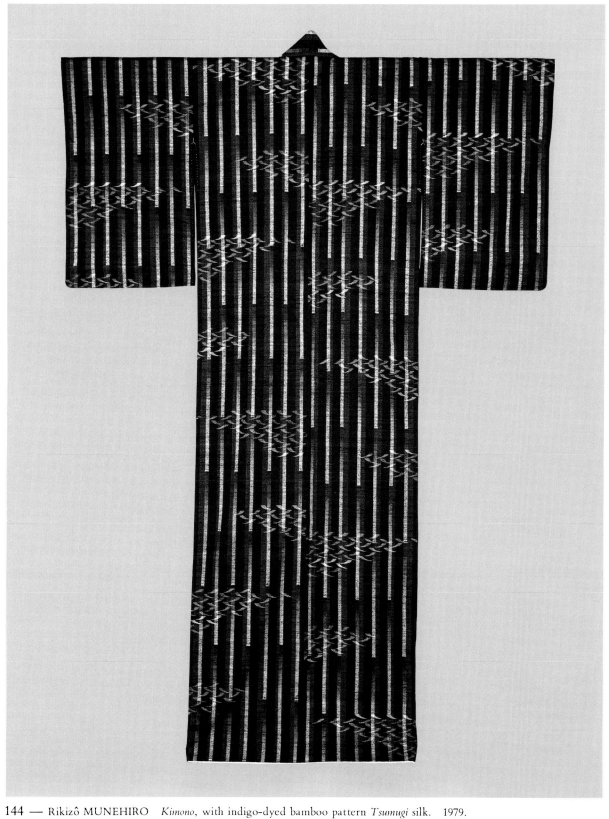

144 — Rikizô MUNEHIRO   *Kimono*, with indigo-dyed bamboo pattern *Tsumugi* silk.   1979.

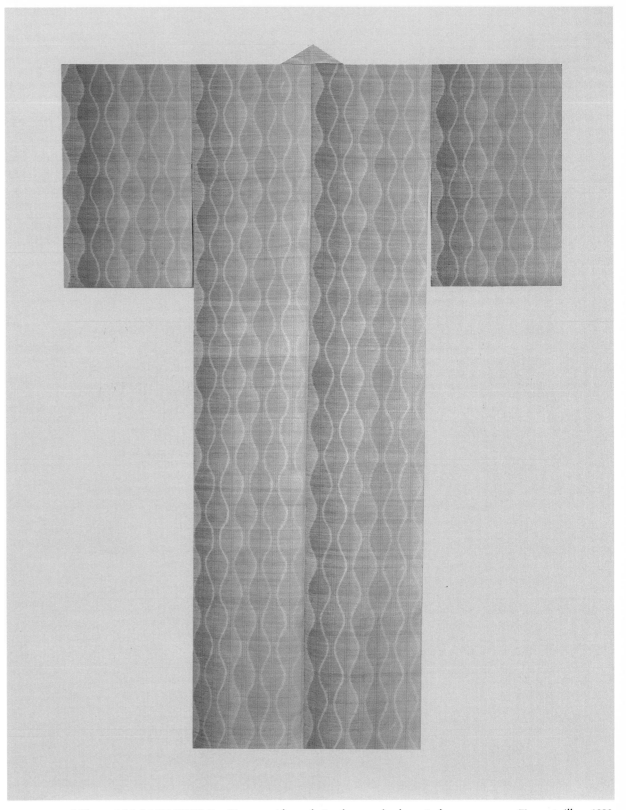

145 — Rikizô MUNEHIRO   *Kimono*, with gradating brown-dyed vertical wave pattern. *Tsumugi* silk.   1980.

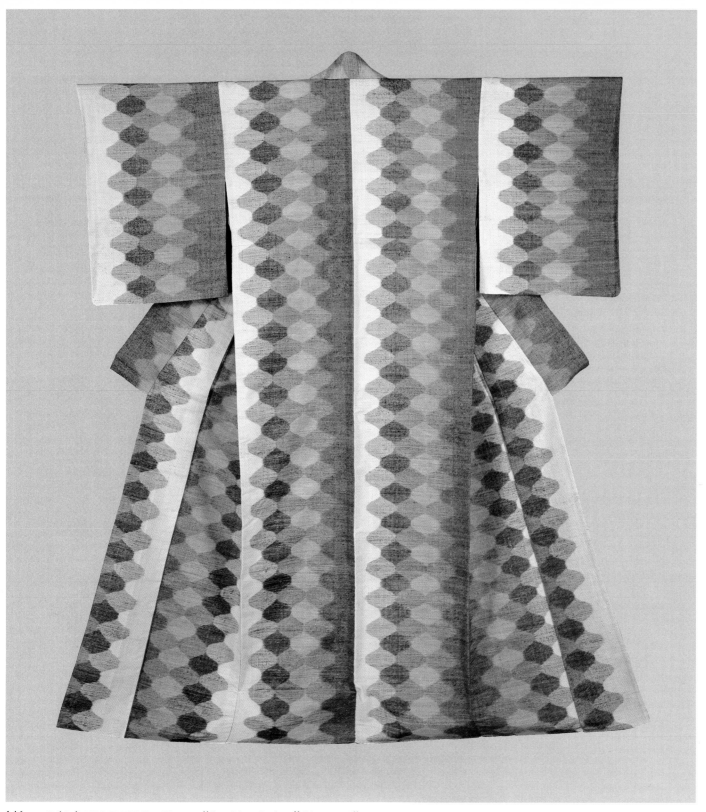

146 — Rikizô MUNEHIRO *Kimono*, "Awaiting Spring." *Tsumugi* silk. 1968.

147 — *Kimono*, with chrysanthemum cross pattern
on indigo ground. *Echigo Jôfu* linen.   1958.

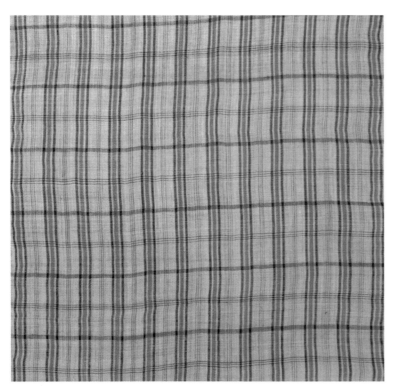

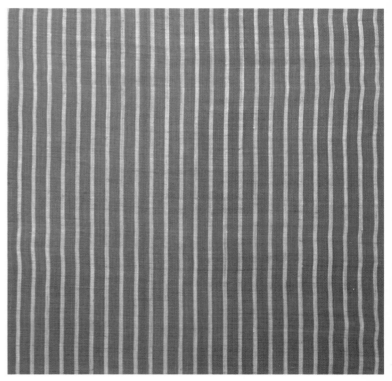

148 — *Kimono*, with brown and indigo lattice pattern on white and
brown ground. *Ojiya Chijimi* crepe linen.   1958.

149 — *Kimono*, with gray stripe on indigo
ground. *Echigo Jôfu* linen.   1958.

150 — *Kimono*, with *daimyôjima* ("*daimyô* stripe") pattern. *Yûki Tsumugi* silk.   1957.

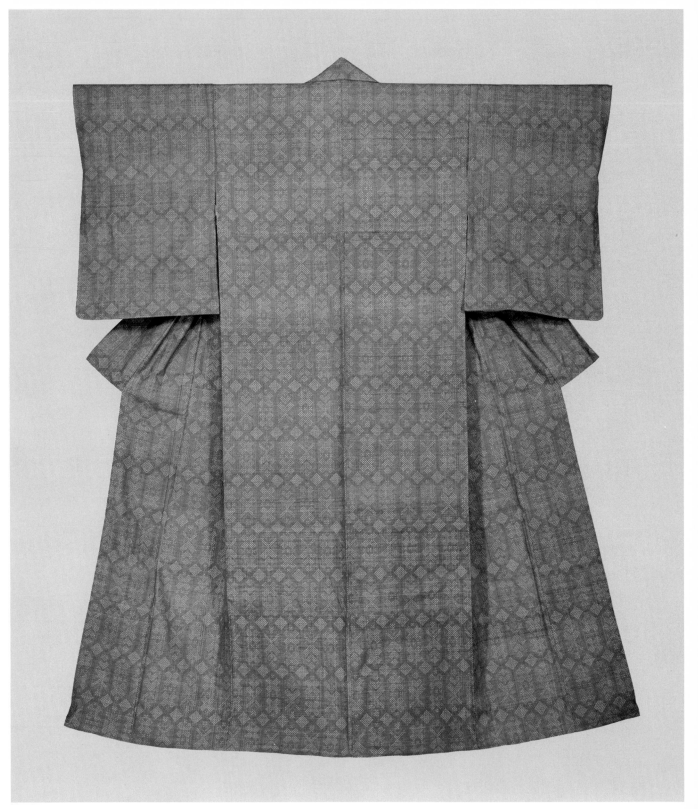

151 — *Kimono*, with *ka-gasuri* (mosquito splashes) in tortoise shell pattern. *Yûki Tsumugi* silk.   1957.

152 — *Kimono*, "Pine Trees and Fence." *Yûki Tsumugi* silk.   1976.

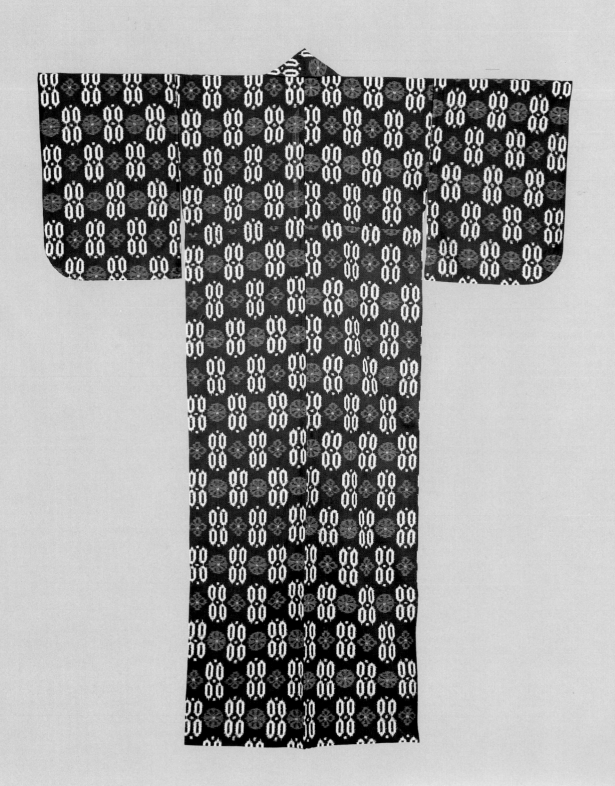

153 — *Kimono, Kurume Gasuri* cotton. 1958.

154 — *Kimono, Kurume Gasuri* cotton. 1958.

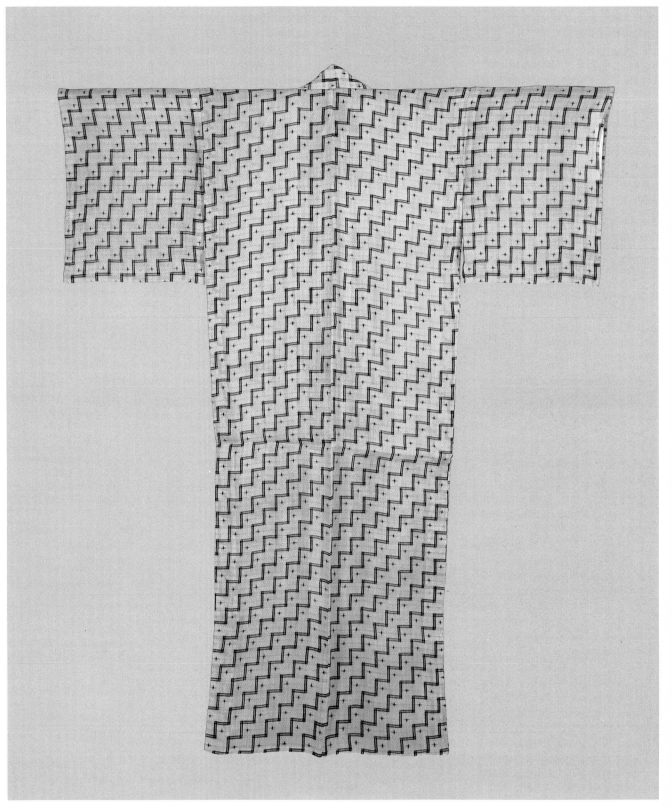

155 — *Kimono, "Kwaiya Banjô." Bashôfu* (banana-leaf fiber cloth). 1970.

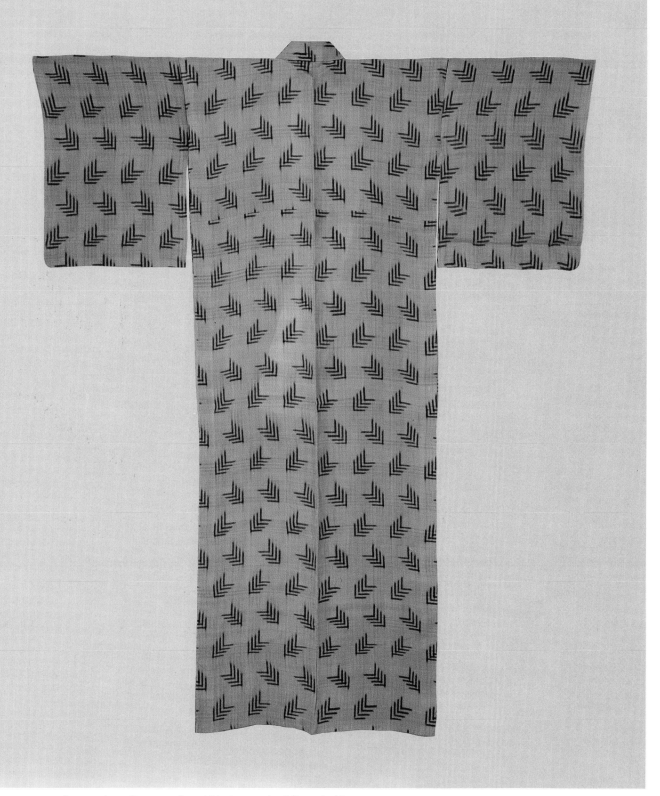

156 — *Kimono,* "*Sotetsu* (cycad) Leaves." *Bashôfu* (banana-leaf fiber cloth).   1978.

157 — *Kimono. Bashôfu* (banana-leaf fiber cloth).   1980.

158 —*Kimono* Material, with floral *kagasuri*
    ("mosquito splashes") pattern. *Miyako Jôfu* linen.   1977.

159 —*Kimono* Material, with *kagasuri*
    ("mosquito splashes") pattern. *Miyako Jôfu linen.*   1977.

160 — Gôyô HIRATA   Dressed Doll, "Clear Fountain."   1961.

161 — Gôyô HIRATA   Dressed Doll, "Leisurely Time."   1959.

162 — Ryûjo HORI   Dressed Doll, "Serenity."   1957.

163 — Ryûjo HORI   Dressed Doll, "Sign."   1954.

164 — Ryûjo HORI   Dressed Doll, "Pledge."   Around 1980.

165 — Juzô KAGOSHIMA   Doll, "Souvenir from Ômori." Papier maché.   1958.

166 — Juzô KAGOSHIMA   Dolls, "*Enju-bina* (Longevity Couple)." Papier maché.   1959.

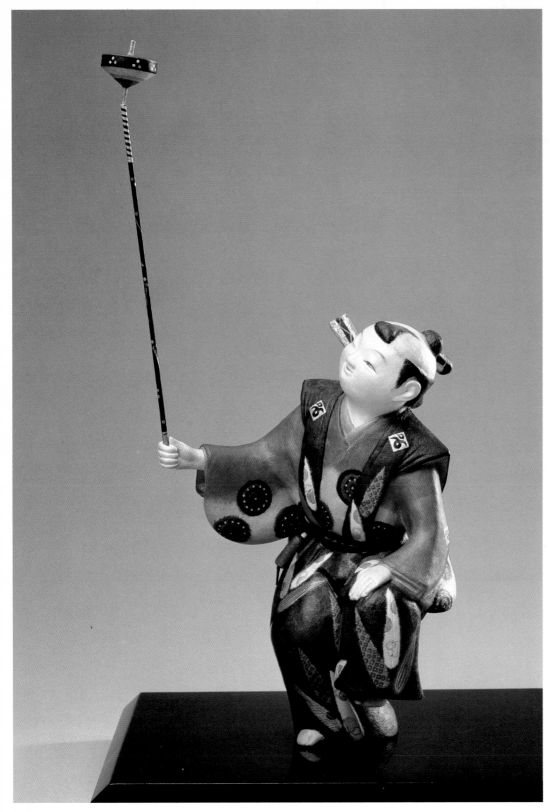

167 — Juzô KAGOSHIMA   Doll, "Playing with a Top." Papier maché.   1954.

168 — Shôzan TAKANO   Box for Calligraphy Paper, with a design of a lion. *Makie* (gold lacquar.)   1927.

169 —Shôzan TAKANO   Incense Case, with design of Paulownia emblem.
Makie (gold lacquer).   Around 1940.

170 —Shôzan TAKANO   Insence Case, with wave design.
Makie (gold lacquer).   Around 1940.

171 —Shôzan TAKANO   Insence Case, with peony design.
Makie (gold lacquer).   Around 1940.

172 — Shôzan TAKANO Portable Book Case, with animal and bird design. *Makie* (gold lacquer). 1931.

173 — Shôzan TAKANO   Box for Cosmetics, with design of squirrels and Japanese medlar. *Makie* (gold lacquer) on plain wood.   1940.

174 — Shôzan TAKANO Box for Cosmetics, with quail design. *Makie* (gold lacquer) on *kanshitsu* (dry-lacquer). 1965.

175 — Gonroku MATSUDA Box for Cosmetics, with design of animals, birds and flowers. *Makie* (gold lacquer). 1919.

176 — Gonroku MATSUDA   Box for Ink Stone, with a crane design. *Makie* (gold lacquer) and egg-shell.   1950.

177 — Gonroku MATSUDA   Box for Cosmetics, with design of black pine and oak leaves. *Makie* (gold lacquer).   1956.

178 — Gonroku MATSUDA   Decorative Box, with design of bamboo grove. *Makie* (gold lacquer).   1965.

179 — Gonroku MATSUDA   Six Covered Bowls, with design of plum blossoms. *Makie* (gold lacquer).   1967.

180 — Gonroku MATSUDA   Tea Caddy, with design of crane and tortoise. *Makie* (gold lacquer).   1944.

181 —Gonroku MATSUDA
    Tea Caddy, with design of wave and cherry blossoms. *Raden* (mother-of-pearl) inlaid *makie* (gold lacquer) on zelkova wood.   1977.

182 — Shôgyo ÔBA   Decorative Box, with design of melon and bird. *Hyomon.*   1981.

183 — Taihô MAE   Small Container, with design of a cat. *Chinkin.*   1962.

184 — Joshin ISOI   Octagonal Incense Tray, with design of dragon and phoenix. *Kimma*.   1955.

185 — Joshin ISOI Circular Incense Tray, with design of flowers and butterflies. *Kimma.* 1956.

186 — Joshin ISOI Box for Brushes, with acacia design. *Kimma.* 1957.

187 — Kôdô OTOMARU   Box for Cosmetic, with design of the moon and rabbit. Carved lacquer on wood.   1953.

188 — Kôdô OTOMARU   Octagonal Candy Box, carved lacquer on wood.   1955.

189 — Kôdô OTOMARU   Box for Calligraphy Paper and Box for *Tanzaku* (poetry paper), with design of intertwining wild thyme. Carved lacquer on wood.   1955.

190 — Kôdô OTOMARU   Candy Box, with flower design. Carved lacquer on wood.   1960.

191 —Kôdô OTOMARU   Incense Case, carved lacquer on wood
with silver inlay.   1963.

192 — Yûsai AKAJI   Tray. Red and black lacquer on *magewa* (bent chip) work.   1960.

193 — Yûsai AKAJI *Jikirô* (covered food container). Green and black lacquer on *magewa* (bent chip) work.   1975.

194 — Mashiki MASUMURA   Covered Box. *Kanshitsu* (dry-lacquer).   1978.

195 — Mashiki MASUMURA   Tray of Lobed Shape. *Kanshitsu* (dry-lacquer).   1981.

196 — Dinner Set, *Wajima-nuri* lacquer ware. Red lacquer on wood. Around 1925.

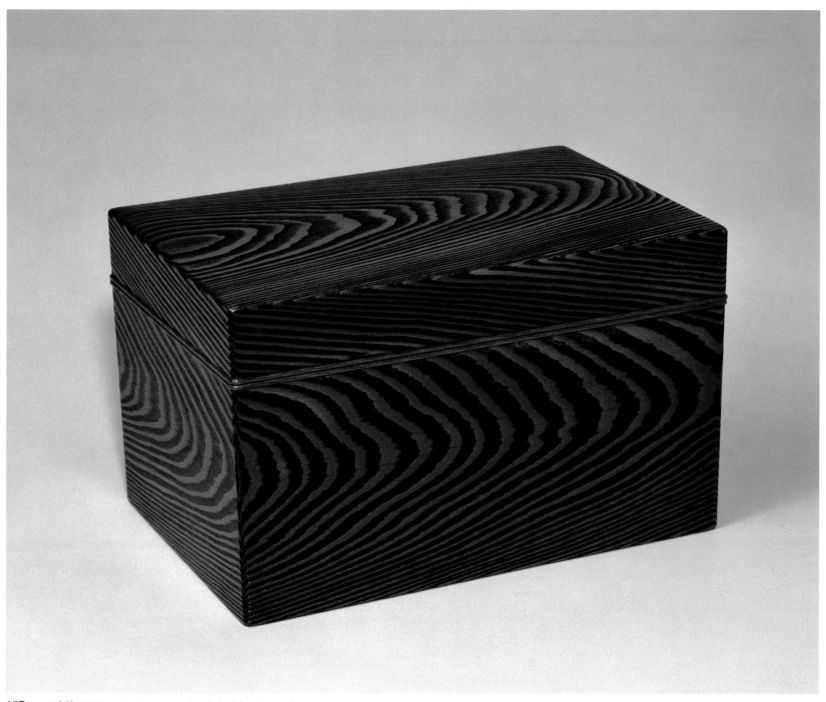

197 — Kôdô HIMI   Tea Box. Sand-polished larch wood.   1964.

198 — Kôdô HIMI   Low Table. Mulberry wood.   1974.

199 — Tatsuaki KURODA   Box for Cosmetics. Lacquer on Japanese horse chestnut.   1970.

200 — Shôunsai SHÔNO   Flower Basket. Purple bamboo.   1968.

201 — Shôunsai SHÔNO   Flower Basket, "*Kusudama* (Decoration ball)." Largely plaited purple bamboo.   1970.

202 — Shôunsai SHÔNO   Flower Basket, copying an old type. *Matsuba-ami* (pine-needle plait) type.   1974.

203 — Shôkansai IIZUKA   Decorative Box, with lozenge pattern. *Sashiami*-type plait.   1974.

204 — Shôkansai IIZUKA   Octagonal Basket, with lozenge pattern. *Sashiami*-type plait.   1980.

205 — Shôkansai IIZUKA   Flower Basket. Double plaited.   1977.

206 — Iraku UOZUMI   *Dora* (gong). *Sahari* (brass) ware.   1952.

207 — Shôdô SASAKI *Hiten* (Flying angel). Bronze, lost wax casting. 1934.

208 — Shôdô SASAKI   Deer. Bronze, lost wax casting.   1959.

209 — Tetsushi NAGANO   Tea Kettle, with wave pattern.   1965.

210 — Ikkei KAKUTANI   Tea Kettle, with fan design.   1979.

211 —Toyochika TAKAMURA   Flower Vase, with cloth-thread pattern.
Oborogin (silver and copper alloy).   1962.

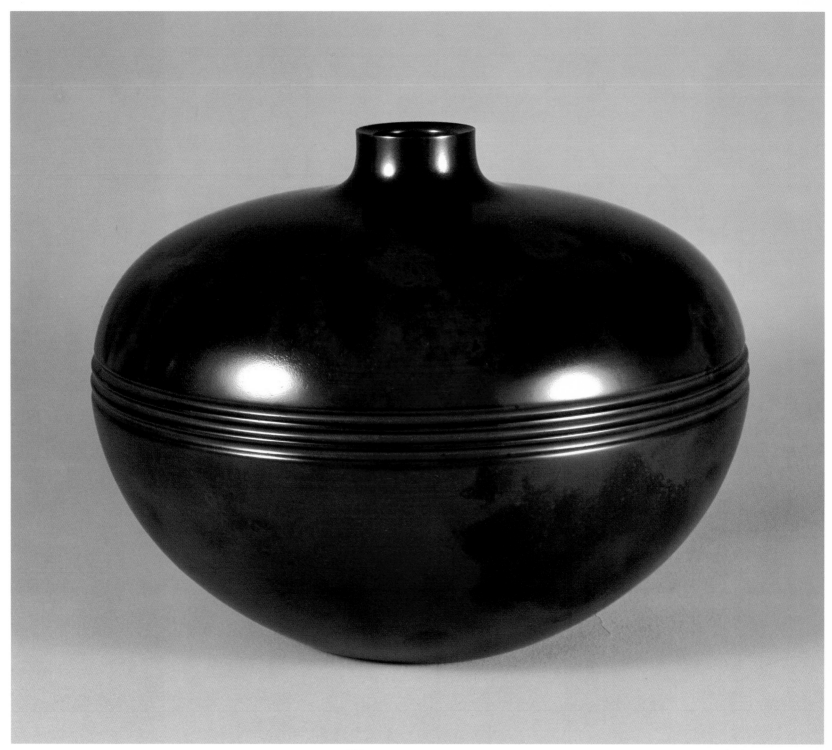

212 — Toyochika TAKAMURA   Vase, with design of horizontal lines. Reddish bronze.   1965.

213 — Masahiko KATORI   Bell. Bronze.   1982.

214 — Masahiko KATORI   Bell, with design of *hiten* (flying angels).   1982.

215 — Kiyoshi UNNO   Covered Box, with design of parrots and grapevine. Carved metalwork.   1928.

216 — Kiyoshi UNNO   Box, with design of two birds.   1931.

217 — Shirô NAITÔ   Silver Vase, with design of willow-tree.   1964.

218 — Shirô NAITÔ   Silver Plate of Hexagonal Shape, with openwork.   1981.

219 — Ikkoku KASHIMA *Mizusashi* (water jar), with design of flowers. *Zôgan* (inlay) work. 1977.

220 — Ikkoku KASHIMA   Flower Vase, with design of willow and stream. *Oborogin* (silver and copper alloy) ware.   1979.

221 — Shirô SEKIYA   Plate. Marbleized *shakudô* (gold and copper alloy) ware.   1972.

222 — Shirô SEKIYA   Bottle, with design of hammered lines. Silver and *shakudô*.   1974.

223 — Mitsumasa YONEMITSU   *Tsuba* (sword-guard) of Octagonal Melon Shape, with inlaid floral scroll.   1963.

224 — Mitsumasa YONEMITSU *Tsuba* (sword-guard) of Octagonal Flower Shape, with openwork and gold inlay. 1969.

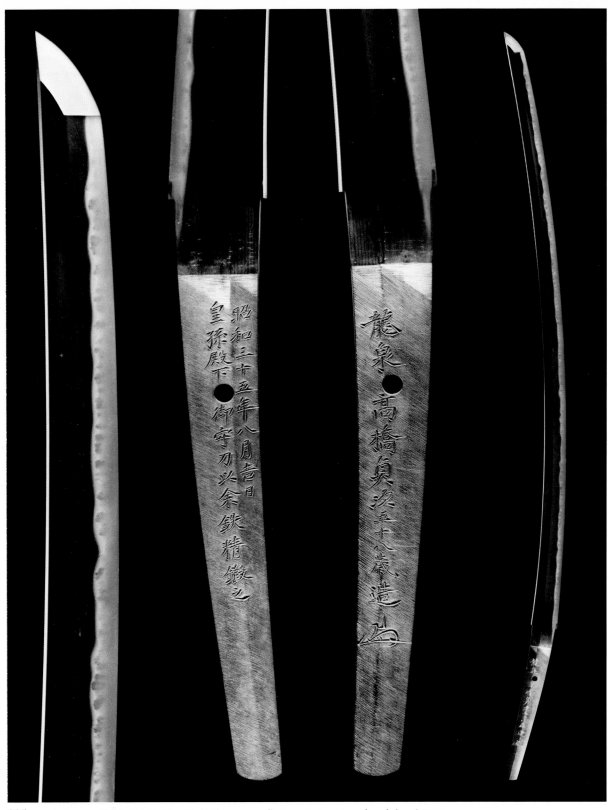

225 — Sadatsugu TAKAHASHI   *Tachi* (long sword). Inscription signed and dated 1960.

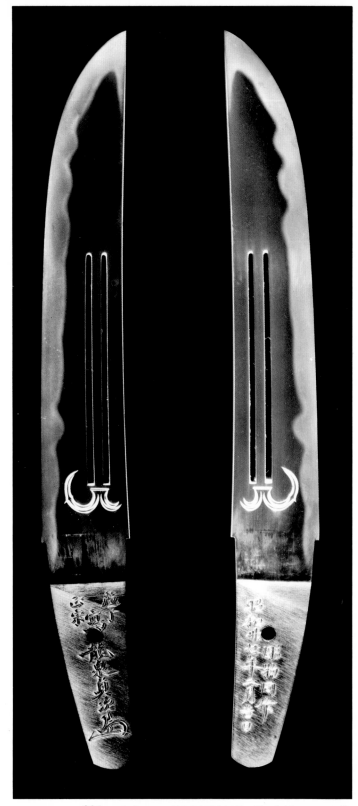

226 —Sadatsugu TAKAHASHI   *Tantô* (short sword).
Inscriptions signed and dated 1962.

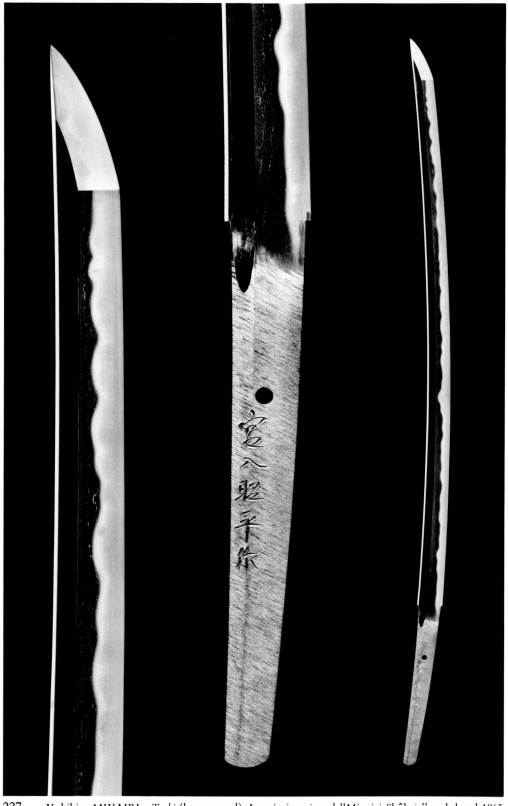

227 — Yukihira MIYAIRI   *Tachi* (long sword). Inscription signed "Miyairi Shôhei," and dated 1965.

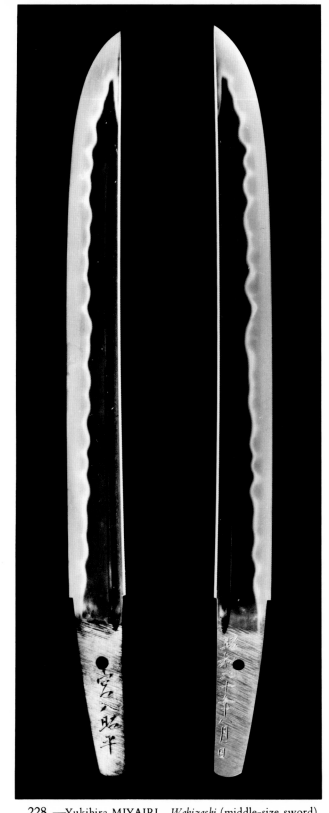

228 —Yukihira MIYAIRI   *Wakizashi* (middle-size sword).
Inscription signed "Miyairi Shôhei," and dated 1965.

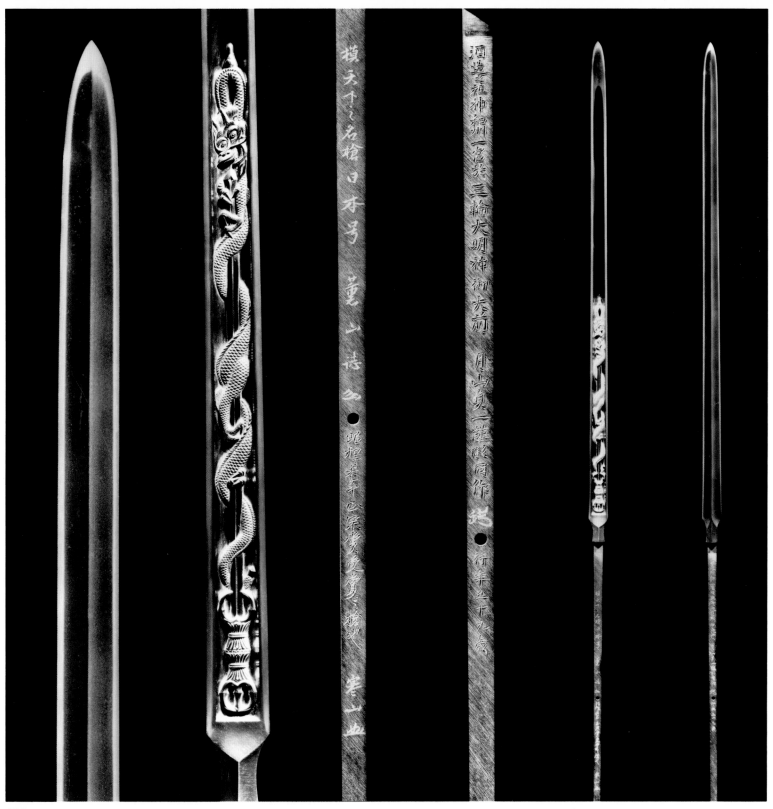

229 — Sadaichi GASSAN *Yari* (spear). *Yamato* style. Inscription signed and dated 1966.

230 — Sadaichi GASSAN   *Katana* (sword). *Sôshu* style. Inscription signed and dated 1977.

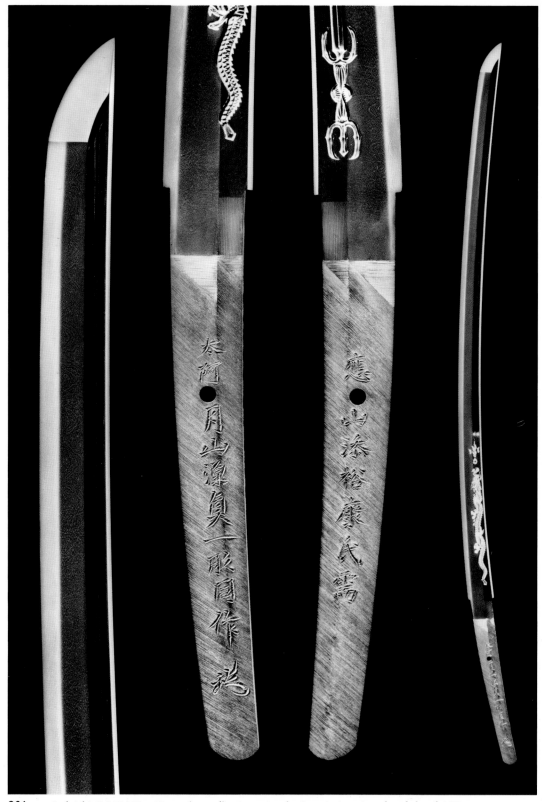

231 — Sadaichi GASSAN   *Katana* (sword). *Ayasugi* style. Inscription signed and dated 1979.

232 — Masamine SUMITANI *Yari* (spear). Inscription signed and dated 1973.

233 — Masamine SUMITANI *Tachi* (long sword). Inscription signed and datd 1973.

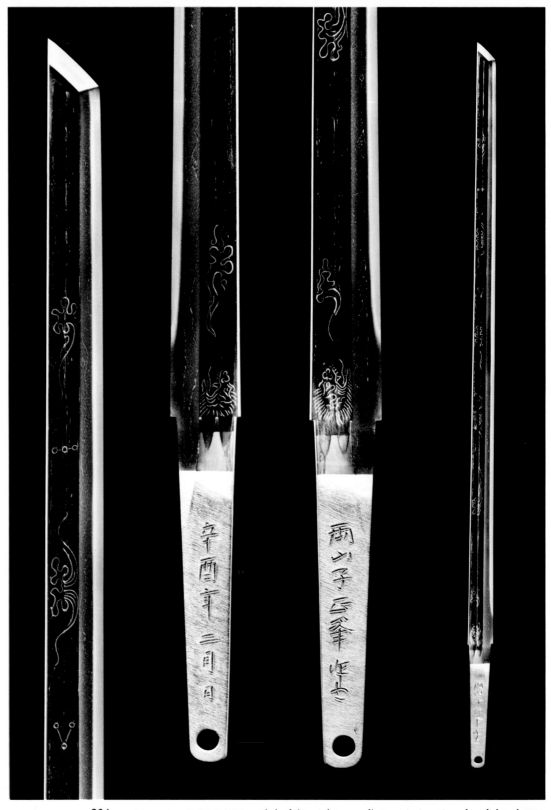

234 — Masamine SUMITANI   *Chokutô* (straight sword). Inscription signed and dated 1981.

235 — Baitei SAIDA   Decorative Box, with design of overlapping lozenge pattern. *Kirikane* (gold-leaf cutwork).   1965.

236 — Baitei SAIDA   Two-fold Screen, "*Hana* (flower)." *Kirikane* (gold-leaf cutwork).   1971.

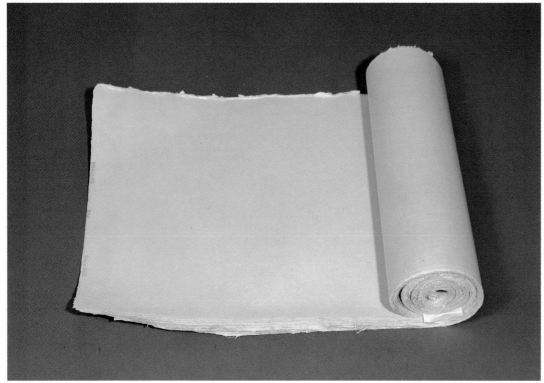

237 — Eishirô ABE *Gampi* Paper, made of *wikstroemia gampi*. 1982.

238 — Ichibei IWANO *Echizen Hôsho*, paper made of mulberry. 1975.

239 — *Sekishû Hanshi*, paper made of mulberry.   1982.

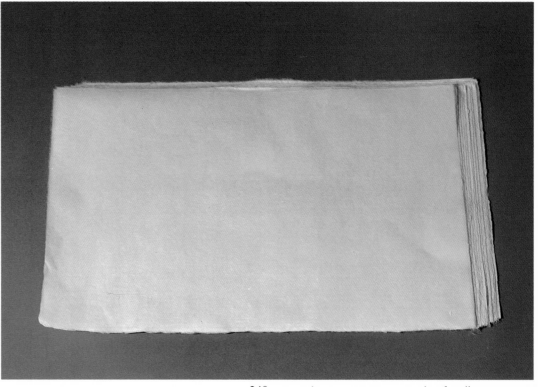

240 — Authentic *Mino* Paper, made of mulberry.   1982.

241 — *Hosokawa* Paper, made of mulberry.   1982.

1	6	11
2	7	12
3	8	13
4	9	
5	10	

Shishiai-Togidashi Makie

In producing this type of *makie* two techniques are used: raised or relief (*taka*) *makie* and polished (*togidashi*) *makie*. It is said to be the most difficult *makie* process.

Steps in the process:

1   *Okime:* stencil the basic design on a base-coat lacquered surface.
2   Put on powdered charcoal to raise the design on the left hill.
3   Add lacquer to raise this part higher.
4   Outline the entire basic design with powdered silver.
5   Add *makie* to the background and metal flakes to the left hill. Stencil on the design of the stream.
6   Apply black (*roiro*) lacquer over the upper design to fix the preceeding layers.
7   Polish the *roiro* lacquered parts.
8   Put on powdered charcoal to raise the hills in the foreground.
9   Add lacquer further to the hills. Place metal flakes on the hills.
10   Apply lacquer to the foreground hills and complete the *makie* with powdered gold of three different grain sizes.
11   Polish the lacquered hills, raise the trunk, branches and foliage of the pine tree, add metal flakes, and inlay metal pieces on to the tree trunk.
12   Complete the *makie* on the pine tree, apply lacquer and polish.
13   Paint on the final details of pine needles and grasses with gold (*keuchi*). Complete the final polishing.

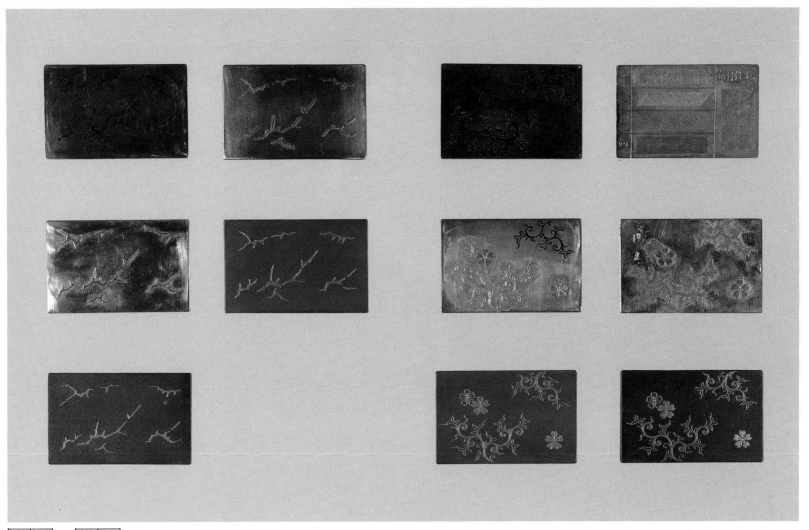

1	2			6	7
3	4			8	9
5				10	11

The Production Process and Designs of *Higo-zôgan* (*Higo*-style Inlay)

Plates 1—5 are the samples showing the carving and inlay of a *Koboku* (withering tree) design.

1 The preliminary drawing of withered tree branches on the iron ground.
2 Grooves being chiseled following the sketch lines. They are open wider inside than on the surface.
3 Gold being inlaid into the grooves to be hammered in tight from both sides.
4 Patination done to make the design stand out.
5 The patina being fixed fast on the iron.

Plate 6-11 represent the average processing steps in executing *nunome-zôgan* (fablic-texture-like inlay).

6 The preliminary drawing of the design on a thoroughly polished iron ground.
7 The *nunome*-like fine fissures executed by scratching or chiseling the metal surface vertically, horizontally and finally diagonally downwards starting from both sides.
8 The design covered with a thin gold sheet which with the use of deer horn is to be hammered into the fissures in the iron surface.
9 Part of the *nunome* fissures unwanted in the design after inlay execution is being completely deleted by chisels so that the gold stands out raised on the iron surface.
10 The patinating process to make the design in gold more distinct and outstanding.
11 The final art of fixing patina fast or keeping it from furthering on the iron surface.

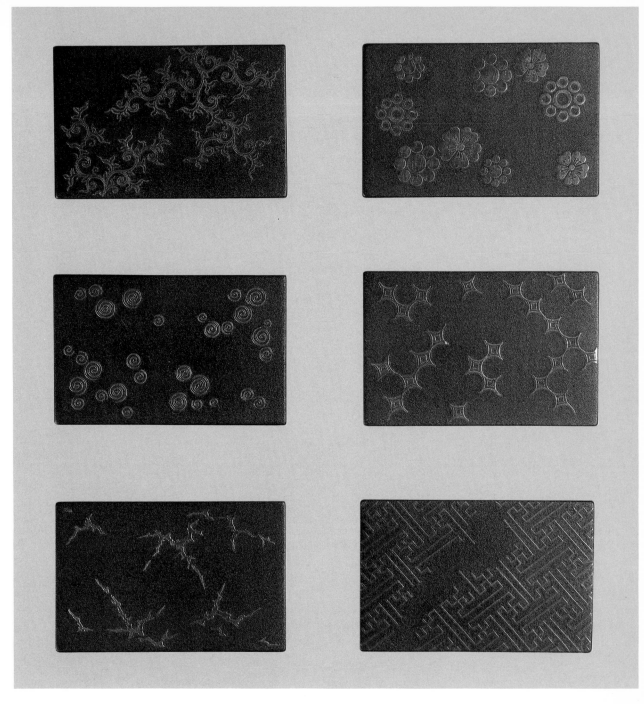

1	2
3	4
5	6

Plates 1—6 are representative traditional *Higo-zôgan* designs.

1 A design developed from a *Karakusa* pattern (Chinese herbs or arabesque), which is a basic motif in the *Higo-zôgan* tradition.

2 A design called *monchirashi* incorporating various *Kamon* (family crests).

3 Spirals called *Uzu*.

4 Stylized diamond shapes in ivy-berrylike clumps called *Tsuta-hishi*.

5 A *Koboku* design.

6 A pattern called *Rinzu* taken from a typical design associated with *Rinzu* fabric (figured silk for *kimono*).

1	2	
3	4	5
6	7	8

The Production Process of *Sukashi*-work on *Higo-tsuba* (Higo-style Openwork)

1 The basic metal having been prepared by a swordsmith following exactly the same forging operation as the material for a sword is formed into a roundel as illustrated.

2 The surface is first smoothed with a rough chisel and then a pattern cut out in a brass plate is placed on top of it to trace the outline of the *tsuba* shape with a very fine chisel.

3 With the use of a drill and fretsaw the holes and the circumference have been cut out and roughly fitted with files.

4 The roughly shaped *tsuba* is being filed step by step to take a more refined shape. When the form is finished, the center hole is adjusted and finished with files. The signature is incised at the end of this process.

5 Here the steel surface is polished with whetstones with precaution to make one side just as equally substantial or curved as the other so that the *tsuba* takes its final form.

6 When the modelling is over, thorough polishing is executed to remove every single filemark to make a smoothest possible surface. Then patination is executed. If the *tsuba* is to be inlaid the *zôgan* execution sets in before patination.

7 When the *zôgan* is over, the superfluous *nunome* is deleted before patinating the iron surface.

8 A finished *tsuba* decorated with exquisite *zôgan* work depicting peony flowers and Chinese herbs.

LIST OF EXHIBITS

notes

Some pieces rotate display for respecting their delicate condition. Mark **B** stands for those shown at the Museum of Fine Arts, Boston, mark **C** for those at Chicago Art Institute, and mark **LA** for those at Los Angeles County Museum. Roman figure **I** or **II** indicates respectively the first or the second half of the exhibition term at each museum. No mark means those to be displayed during the entire period throughout the three museums.

CERAMICS

Toyozô ARAKAWA (1894—   )

1 Tea Bowl, *Shino* ware. 1953.
   H.9.cm, D.13.2cm.
   National Museum of Modern Art, Tokyo.

2 Covered Water Jar, with a pair of loops,
   Nezumi ("mouse gray") *Shino* ware. Around 1950.
   H.14.2cm, D.25.0cm.
   Aichi Prefectural Ceramic Museum, Seto.

3 Tea Bowl, *Seto-guro* ("black *Seto*") ware. 1959.
   H.9.2cm, D.13.2cm.
   National Museum of Modern Art, Tokyo.

4 Bamboo-shaped Vase, *Ki-Seto* ("yellow *Seto*")
   ware. 1960.
   H.23.0cm, D.12.0cm.
   National Museum of Modern Art, Tokyo.

Munemaro ISHIGURO (1896—1968)

5 Tea Bowl, *Konoha* ("tree-leaf") *Temmoku*
   ware. Around 1955.
   H.5.5cm, D.15.5cm.
   Private Collection, Japan.

6 Vase, *kaki* (persimmon color) glaze. Around 1940.
   H.17.2cm, D.16.5cm.
   Private Collection, Japan.

7 Bowl, black glaze with a design of birds in
   brown dots. 1958.
   H.8.4cm, D.33.5cm.
   National Museum of Modern Art, Tokyo.

8 Vase, white glaze with a colored design of
   persimmons. 1959.
   H.18.4cm, D.17.5cm.
   National Museum of Modern Art, Tokyo.

Kenkichi TOMIMOTO (1886—1963)

9 Large Bowl, enameled porcelain with red
   Sarasa (printed textile) pattern. 1949.
   H.8.2cm, D.30.3cm.
   Private Collection, Japan.

10 Vase, enameled porcelain with gold and silver
    colors framing panels of *sometsuke* (blue-and-
    white) landscapes. 1957.
    H.22.8cm, D.28.5cm.
    National Museum of Modern Art, Tokyo.

11 Covered Vase, red-enameled porcelain with
    gold and silver fern-leaf pattern. 1958.
    H.18.0cm, D.24.0cm.
    Agency for Cultural Affairs, Tokyo.

12 Five Dishes, porcelain with different *sometsuke*
    (blue-and-white) designs. 1960.
    H.3.5cm, D.25.5cm.
    National Museum of Modern Art, Tokyo.

13 Two Wine Bottles, enameled porcelain with
    Sarasa (printed textile) pattern. 1939.
    H.11.5cm, D.10.0cm.
    National Museum of Modern Art, Kyoto.

14 Octagonal Box, enameled porcelain with gold
    and silver fern-leaf pattern. 1958.
    H.11.8cm, D.26.5cm. B.
    National Museum of Modern Art, Tokyo.

Hajime KATÔ (1900—1968)

15 Dodecagonal Bowl, enameled porcelain with a
    design of *kumagaiso* (Lady's Slipper). 1944.
    H.10.5cm, D.32.5cm.
    Private collection, Japan.

16 Covered Round Box, green-enameled
    porcelain with *kinrande* (gold color) design
    of *hôsôge* (Heavenly Flowers). 1958.
    H.11.5cm, D.21.0cm.
    National Museum of Modern Art, Tokyo.

17 Covered Jar, enameled porcelain with red and
    kinrande (gold color) floral pattern on yellowish
    ground. 1960.
    H.21.5cm, D.25.0cm.
    Private collection, Japan.

18 Large Plate, enameled porcelain with heron and
    willow design. 1961.

    H.9.1cm, D.46.2cm.
    Private Collection, Japan.

19 Five Dishes, enameled porcelain with floral
    pattern. 1961.
    H.2.1cm, D.20.0cm.
    National Museum of Modern Art, Tokyo.

20 Six Stemmed Wine Cups, enameled porcelain
    with *kinrande* (gold color) chrysanthemum
    design. 1967.
    H.8.5cm, D.7.0—7.5cm.
    Private collection, Japan.

Shôji HAMADA (1894—1978)

21 Large Bowl, *ame* (black candy) glaze with a
    white and blue cross. 1957.
    H.13.5cm, D.55.5cm.
    Private collection, Japan.

22 Large Bowl, white glaze with cursive drawing
    in black. 1960.
    H.13.4cm, D.52.2cm.
    Ôhara Museum, Kurashiki.

23 Large Bowl, *kaki* (persimmon color) glaze with
    iron-colored circular design. 1962.
    H.15.0cm, D.58.1cm.
    National Museum of Modern Art, Kyoto.

24 Large Bowl, *namako* ("trepang's gray") glaze
    with black cursive drawing. 1962.
    H.15.2cm, D.57.0cm.
    National Museum of Modern Art, Kyoto.

25 Square Plate, *kaki* (persimmon color) glaze with
    reddish design. 1972.
    H.8.0cm, 33.5 x 34.5cm.
    Tochigi Prefectural Museum of Fine Arts,
    Utsunomiya.

26 Square Bottle, salt glaze with white
    splashes. 1971.
    H.23.5cm, 10.0 x 10.0cm.
    Private collection, Japan.

Tôyô KANASHIGE (1896—1967)

27 Large Bowl, *Bizen* ware with *hidasuki* (fire
    marks). 1960.
    H.9.2cm, D.45.5cm.
    National Museum of Modern Art, Tokyo.

28 Covered Water Pot, *Bizen* ware. 1963.
    H.18.6cm, D.24.0cm.
    Private collection, Japan.

29 Square Plate, *Bizen* ware. 1953.
    H.6.0cm, 28.6 x 29.1cm.
    Private collection, Japan.

30 Set of Five *Mukôzuke* (servind dishes),
    Bizen ware. 1964.
    H.8.4cm, D.13.5cm.
    National Museum of Modern Art, Tokyo.

Kei FUJIWARA (1899—   )

31 Cylindrical Flower Vase, *Bizen* ware. 1963.
    H.26.5cm, D.11.8cm.
    National Museum of Modern Art, Kyoto.

32 Large Bottle-Shaped Vase, *Bizen* ware. 1971.
    H.38.1cm, D.27.5cm.
    National Museum of Modern Art, Tokyo.

Kyûwa MIWA (1895—1981)

33 Tea Bowl, *Hagi* ware. 1966.
    H.9.5cm, D.11.7cm.
    Agency for Cultural Affairs, Tokyo.

34 *Mizusashi* (water container), *Hagi* ware. 1972.
    H.14.5cm, D.23.5cm.
    National Museum of Modern Art, Tokyo.

Muan NAKAZATO (1895—   )

35 Jar, *Ki-Garatsu* ("yellow *Karatsu*") ware. 1967.
    H.32.0cm, D.34.0cm.
    National Museum of Modern Art, Tokyo.

36 Tea Bowl, *Karatsu* ware. 1968.
    H.8.0cm, D.14.7cm.
    National Museum of Modern Art, Tokyo.

Yûzô KONDÔ (1902—   )

37 Jar, porcelain with *sometsuke* (blue-and-white)
    pomegranate design. 1957.
    H.31.0cm, D.36.8cm.
    National Museum of Modern Art, Tokyo.

38 Jar, porcelain with *sometsuke* (blue-and-white)
    grapevine design. 1964.
    H.32.0cm, D.39.0cm.
    National Museum of Modern Art, Kyoto.

Society for Preservation of Iro-Nabeshima
Imaemon Porcelain, Arita, Saga Prefecture

39 Large Plate, *Iro-Nabeshima* porcelain with *utsugi*
    (deutzia) design. By Imaemon IMAIZUMI XII
    (1897—1975). 1965.
    H.5.4cm, D.42.8cm.
    National Museum of Modern Art, Tokyo.

40 Large Bowl, *Iro-Nabeshima* porcelain with
    karukaya (Japanese pampas grass) design. By
    Imaemon IMAIZUMI XIII (1926—   ) 1969.
    H.7.0cm, D.42.0cm.
    National Museum of Modern Art, Tokyo.

Society for Preservation of Kakiemon
Ceramic Tradition, Arita, Saga Prefecture

41 Covered Container, *nigoshide* (milk white)
    porcelain with floral design. By Kakiemon
    SAKAIDA XII (1878—1963). 1957.
    H.21.4cm, D.36.0cm.
    National Museum of Modern Art, Tokyo.

42 Large Bowl, *nigoshide* (milk white) porcelain
    with floral design. By Kakiemon SAKAIDA XIII
    (1906—   ). 1975.
    H.9.5cm, D.44.5cm.
    Agency for Cultural Affairs, Tokyo.

TEXTILES

Kihachi TABATA (1877—1956)

43 *Kimono, tomesode* (short sleeve) type "Pine Trees
    on a Beach in Winter" *Yûzen* dyeing on crepe
    silk. 1952.
    H.193cm, W.126cm. Bɪ.
    Private collection, Japan.

44 *Kimono*, with silver-colored floral design.
    Yûzen dyeing on crepe silk. 1954.
    H.157cm, W.134cm. Bɪɪ.
    Private collection, Japan.

45 *Kimono, furisode* (broad sleeve) type, "Cranes and
    Pine Trees." *Yûzen* dyeing on crepe silk.   1953.
    H.171cm, W.129.2cm. Cɪ.
    Private collection, Japan.

46 *Kimono, furisode* (broad sleeve) type, with fret-
    work ceiling design. *Yûzen* dyeing on
    crepe silk. 1946.
    H.169cm, W.138cm. Cɪɪ.
    Private collection, Japan.

47 *Kimono*, with wave design. *Yûzen* dyeing on
    crepe silk. 1952
    H.152cm, W.125.4cm. LA.
    Private collection, Japan.

Tameji UENO (1901—1960)

48 *Kimono*, "Dawn at Mt. Kotobuki." *Yûzen* dyeing
    on crepe silk. 1958.
    H.159cm, W.132cm. Bɪ.
    National Museum of Modern Art, Tokyo.

49 *Kimono*, copying *Chayazome* dyeing "Flowers of
    Four Seasons." *Yûzen* dyeing on crepe silk. 1932.
    H.156cm, W.120cm. Bɪɪ.
    Marubeni Company, Kyoto.

50 *Kimono, tomesode* (short sleeve) type, "Small
    Chrysanthemums." *Yûzen* dyeing on crepe
    silk. 1957.
    H.150cm, W.126cm. Cɪ.
    Private collection, Japan.

51 *Kimono, "Yorokobi* (Joy)." *Yûzen* dyeing on crepe silk. 1960.
H.167cm, W.132cm. CII.
Private collection, Japan.

52 *Kimono,* "Red Persimmons on a Clear Autumn Day." *Yûzen* dyeing on crepe silk. 1936.
H.158cm, W.130cm. LA.
Marubeni Company, Kyoto.

Uzan KIMURA (1891—1977)

53 *Kimono,* "*Hana* (Flowers)." *Yûzen* dyeing on crepe silk. 1965.
H.163cm, W.128cm. BI.
National Museum of Modern Art, Tokyo.

54 *Kimono, furisode* (broad sleeve) type. "Melons." *Yûzen* dyeing on linen. 1967.
H.174cm, W.126cm. BII.
Ishikawa Prefectural Museum of Art, Kanazawa.

55 *Kimono,* "*Mure* (cluster)." *Yûzen* dyeing on crepe silk. 1963.
H.158cm, W.128cm. CI.
National Museum of Modern Art, Tokyo.

56 *Kimono, furisode* (broad sleeve) type. "*Aoi* (Hollyhocks)." *Yûzen* dyeing on crepe silk. 1971.
H.166cm, W.128cm. CII.
National Museum of Modern Art, Tokyo.

57 *Kimono,* "*Matsu* (Pine)." *Yûzen* dyeing in crepe silk. 1973.
H.168.5cm, W.125cm. LA.
Nihon Denshô Senshoku Shinkôkai, Nagoya.

Katsuma NAKAMURA (1894—1982)

58 *Kimono,* "Warp and Weft." *Yûzen* dyeing on crepe silk. 1962.
H.159cm, W.129cm. BI.
National Museum of Modern Art, Tokyo.

59 *Kimono, Kuro-tomesode* (black, short-sleeved) type, with wave design. *Yûzen* dyeing on crepe silk. 1955.
H.149cm, W.125cm. BII.

National Museum of Modern Art, Tokyo.

60 *Kimono, Kuro-tomesode* (black, short-sleeved) type, with cloud design. *Yûzen* dyeing on crepe silk. 1959.
H.156cm, W.126cm. CI.
National Museum of Modern Art, Tokyo.

61 *Kimono,* "Bamboo and Ivy." *Yûzen* dyeing on crepe silk. 1963.
166.5cm, W.132cm. CII.
Private collection, Japan.

62 *Kimono, Kuro-tomesode* (black, short-sleeved) type, with *shippô* (cloisonné) pattern. *Yûzen* dyeing on crepe silk. 1973.
H.164cm, W.130cm. LA.
Nihon Denshô Senshoku Shinkôkai, Tokyo.

Kakô MORIGUCHI (1909—   )

63 *Kimono,* "New Wave." *Yûzen* dyeing on crepe silk. 1964.
H.171cm, W.133cm. BI.
Private collection, Japan.

64 *Kimono,* "Plum Orchard." *Yûzen* dyeing on crepe silk. 1965.
H.171cm, W.133cm. BI.
Private collection, Japan.

65 *Kimono,* "Chrysanthemums." *Yûzen* dyeing on crepe silk. 1975.
H.171cm, W.133cm. BI.
Private collection, Japan.

66 *Kimono,* "Fragrant Garden." *Yûzen* dyeing on crepe silk. 1968.
H.171cm, W.133cm. BII.
Private collection, Japan.

67 *Kimono,* "Plum Blossoms." *Yûzen* dyeing on crepe silk. 1972.
H.171cm, W.133cm. BII.
Private collection, Japan.

68 *Kimono, furisode* (broad sleeve) type, "Plum Orchard." *Yûzen* dyeing on crepe silk. 1964.

H.195cm, W.128cm. CI.
National Museum of Modern Art, Kyoto.

69 *Kimono,* "Chrysanthemum Flower." *Yûzen* dyeing on crepe silk. 1960.
H.161cm, W.125cm. CI.
National Museum of Modern Art, Tokyo.

70 *Kimono,* "Fragrance of Four Seasons." *Yûzen* dyeing on crepe silk. 1959.
H. 155cm, 128cm. CII.
National Museum of Modern Art, Tokyo.

71 *Kimono,* "Image of Fragrance." *Yûzen* dyeing on crepe silk. 1959.
H.162cm, W.130cm. CII.
National Museum of Modern Art, Tokyo.

72 *Kimono,* "Plum Blossoms." *Yûzen* dyeing on crepe silk. 1973.
H.157cm, W.132cm. LA.
National Museum of Modern Art, Tokyo.

73 *Kimono,* "Last Snow." *Yûzen* dyeing on crepe silk. 1969.
H.169cm, W.128cm. LA.
National Museum of Modern Art, Tokyo.

Kôsuke KOMIYA (1882—1961)

74 *Kimono, Edo komon* "*Yorokejima* (tottering stripes)." Stencil dyeing on crepe silk. 1958.
H.152cm, W.122cm. B.
National Museum of Modern Art, Tokyo.

75 *Kimono, Edo komon* "*Goku Ichimatsu* (fine checkered pattern)." Stencil dyeing on crepe silk. 1958.
H.153cm, W.126cm. C.
National Museum of Modern Art, Tokyo.

76 *Kimono* material, *Edo komon* "*Waridakejima* (split bamboo stripes)." Stencil dyeing on crepe silk. 1958.
W.36.3cm. LA.
Private collection, Japan.

Yasutaka KOMIYA (1925—)

77 *Kimono, Edo-komon "Daishô Shimazu (Shimazu's Large and Small Dots)."* Stencil dyeing on crepe silk. 1982.
H.157.5cm,, W.130cm. B.
Private collection, Japan.

78 *Kimono, Edo-komon "Karamatsu (Chinese pine)."* Stencil dyeing on crepe silk. 1982.
H.157.5cm, W.130cm. C.
Private collection, Japan.

79 *Kimono, Edo-komon "Series of Fans."* Stencil dyeing on crepe silk. 1969.
H.158cm, W.124cm. LA.
National Museum of Modern Art, Tokyo.

Sadakichi MATSUBARA (1893—1955)

80 *Yukata* garment, with stripe design. Stencil dyeing on cotton. 1954.
H.150.5cm, W.125cm. B.
Agency for Cultural Affairs, Tokyo

81 *Yukata* material, with design of bamboo and checkered pattern. Stencil dyeing on cotton. 1955.
W.35.6cm. C.
Private collection, Japan.

82 *Yukata* garment, with stripe design. Stencil dyeing on cotton. 1954
H.146.6cm, W.138cm. LA.
Private collection, Japan.

Kôtarô SHIMIZU (1897—)

83 *Yukata* garment, "Bamboo." Stencil dyeing on cotton. 1965.
H.153cm, W.128cm. B.
National Museum of Modern Art, Tokyo.

84 *Yukata* garment, "Clamshells." Stencil dyeing on cotton. 1952.
H.149cm, W.125cm. C.
Agency for Cultural Affairs, Tokyo.

85 *Yukata* garment, "Chrysanthemums." Stencil dyeing on cotton. 1952.
H.149cm, W.125cm. LA.
Agency for Cultural Affairs, Tokyo

Hidekichi NAKAJIMA (1883—1968)

86 *Ise* stencil, *"Goku Ichimatsu (fine checkered pattern)."* 1956.
26.8 x 48cm.
Private collection, Japan.

Baiken ROKUTANI (1907—1973)

87 *Ise* stencil, *"Daishô Shimazu (Shimazu's Large and Small Dots)."* 1958.
26 x 45cm. B.
Private collection, Japan.

88 *Ise* stencil, *"Karamatsu (Chinese pine)."* 1958.
26 x 45cm. C. LA.
Private collection, Japan.

Yoshimatsu NANBU (1894—1976)

89 *Ise* stencil, "Dragon." 1960.
26.5 x 44cm
Private collection, Japan.

Yûjirô NAKAMURA (1902—)

90 *Ise* stencil, fine lattice pattern. 1965.
42.5 x 53.5 cm.
Private collection, Japan.

Hiroshi KODAMA (1909—)

91 *Ise* stencil, *"Waridakejima (split bamboo stripes)."* 1957.
27 x 46.5 cm.
Private collection, Japan.

92 *Ise* stencil, ruled triple lines. Threaded by Mie Jônoguchi. 1982.
32.7 x 48cm.
Private collection, Japan

Keisuke SERIZAWA (1895—)

93 Six-fold Screen, Japanese syllabary, each graph framed by a circle. Stencil dyeing on *tsumugi* weave silk. 1963.
H.177cm, W.300cm. Bɪ.
National Museum of Modern Art, Tokyo.

94 *Noren* (doorway curtain), with design of *nawa-noren* (rope curtain). Stencil dyeing on cotton. 1955.
H.143.5cm, W.85cm. Bɪ.
Serizawa Keisuke Museum of Art, Shizuoka.

95 *Kimono*, with design of Japanese syllabary. Stencil dyeing on cotton. 1961.
H.151cm, W.122cm. Bɪ.
National Museum of Modern Art, Tokyo.

96 Two-fold Screen, with design of Japanese Stencil dyeing on linen. 1973.
H.176cm, W.164cm. Bɪɪ.
Sunagawa Museum of Arts and Crafts, Kashiwa.

97 *Noren* (doorway curtain), with design of the character *"Kaze* (wind)". Stencil dyeing on cotton. 1957.
H.101.5cm, W.74.5cm. Bɪɪ.
Sunagawa Museum of Arts and Crafts, Kashiwa.

98 *Kimono*, with design of diagonal lattice and gold hand drawing. Stencil dyeing on *tsumugi* weave silk. 1972.
H.163cm, W.121cm. Bɪɪ.
Ôhara Museum, Kurashiki.

99 Two-fold Screen, with design of Japanese syllabary in six columns. Stencil dyeing on cotton. 1973.
H.168cm, W.182cm. C.
National Museum of Modern Art, Tokyo.

100 *Noren* (doorway curtain), with design of the character *"Hana* (flower)". Stencil dyeing on *tsumugi* weave silk. 1960.
H.129cm, W.73cm. C.
National Museum of Modern Art, Tokyo.

101 *Kimono*, with design of fishes. Stencil dyeing on *tsumugi* weave silk. 1964.
H.157cm, W.127cm. Cɪ.
Serizawa Keisuke Museum of Art, Shizuoka.

102 *Kimono*, "Ogawa Paper Mills Village." Stencil dyeing on crepe silk. 1943.
H.165cm, W.129cm. Cɪɪ.
Serizawa Keisuke Museum of Art, Shizuoka.

103 Two-fold Screen, with design of the four seasons. Stencil dyeing of *tsumugi* weave silk. 1960.
H.157cm, W.175cm. LA.
National Museum of Modern Art, Tokyo.

104 *Noren* (doorway curtain), with design of waterfall. Stencil dyeing on *tsumugi* weave silk. 1962.
H.135cm, W.115cm. LA.
National Museum of Modern Art, Tokyo.

105 *Kimono*, with design of wood-grain. Stencil dyeing on *tsumugi* weave silk. 1968.
H.151cm, W.130cm. LA.
National Museum of Modern Art, Kyoto.

Toshijirô INAGAKI (1902—1980)

106 Two-fold Screen, with design of wild grasses. Stencil dyeing on *tsumugi* weave silk. 1959.
H.153.5cm, W.144cm. Bɪ.
National Museum of Modern Art, Tokyo.

107 Wall-hanging, "Waving Heads of Wheat Plants." Stencil dyeing on cotton. 1961.
H.188cm, W.162cm. Bɪ.
National Museum of Modern Art, Tokyo.

108 Wall-hanging, with design of the festival scene at Tôji Temple, Kyoto. Stencil dyeing on cotton. 1952.
H.180cm, W.180cm. Bɪɪ.
National Museum of Modern Art, Kyoto.

109 *Kimono*, with design of wild grasses, bamboo and *hitta* (knot-dyeing) pattern. Stencil dyeing on crepe silk. 1955.

H.159cm, W.134cm. Bɪɪ.
National Museum of Modern Art, Kyoto.

110 Two-fold Screen, "Interior of Sanjûsangendô Temple." Stencil dyeing on paper. 1953.
H.52cm, W.177cm. Cɪ.
Kyoto Municipal Museum of Art.

111 *Kimono*, with design of maple-leaves, and autumnal grasses. Stencil dyeing on crepe silk. 1958.
H.152cm, W.125.4cm. Cɪ.
Private collection Japan.

112 Wall-hanging, "Standing Tiger." Stencil dyeing on cotton. 1960.
H.160cm, W.86cm. Cɪɪ.
National Museum of Modern Art, Tokyo.

113 *Kimono*, with design of iris flowers and water. Stencil dyeing on crepe silk. 1958.
H.152cm, W.125.4cm. Cɪɪ.
Private collection, Japan.

114 Wall-hanging, "Crouching Tiger." Stencil dyeing on cotton. 1960
H.156cm, W.87cm. LA.
National Museum of Modern Art, Tokyo.

115 *Kimono*, "Moss Garden." Stencil dyeing on *ro* (gauze) silk. 1956.
H.154cm, W.121cm. LA.
Private collection, Japan.

Yoshitarô KAMAKURA (1902—)

116 *Kimono*, with design of mountain landscape. Stencil dyeing on linen. 1975.
H.157.5cm, W.128cm. Bɪ.
Kagawa Prefectural Culture Hall, Takamatsu.

117 *Kimono*, with design of bamboo leaves. Stencil dyeing on linen. 1968.
H.168cm, W.132cm. Bɪɪ.
National Museum of Modern Art, Kyoto

118 *Kimono*, with design of dragonflies and reeds. 1980.
H.169cm, W.134cm. Cɪ.
Private collection, Japan.

119 *Kimono*, "Pine, Bamboo and Plum-blossoms." Stencil dyeing on *tsumugi* weave silk. 1981.
H.170cm, W.134cm. Cɪɪ.
Private collection, Japan.

120 *Kimono*, with stripe design. Stencil dyeing on linen. 1969.
H.157cm, W.130cm. LA.
National Museum of Modern Art, Tokyo.

Ayano CHIBA (1890—1980)

121 *Kimono* material, indigo-dyed linen. 1956.
W.36cm. B.
Agency for Cultural Affairs, Tokyo.

122 *Kimono* material, indigo-dyed linen. 1960.
W.33cm. C.LA.
Private collection, Japan.

Heirô KITAGAWA (1898—)

123 *Futae-orimono* (double-woven) type silk, with circular butterfly and hollyhock motifs on yellow ground. 1979.
W.45cm, L.1592cm. Bɪ.
Private Collection, Japan.

124 *Jôdai ra* (ancient gauze) type silk, with vine-scroll on *hanada* (pale blue) ground. 1959.
W.45cm, L.920cm. B.
National Museum of Modern Art, Tokyo.

125 *Rakin* (gauze with gold weft) type silk, with motifs of peony scroll and mushroom-shaped cloud. 1959.
W.45cm, L.640cm. Bɪɪ.
National Museum of Modern Art, Tokyo.

126 *Nishiki* (brocade) type silk, with butterfly and bird motifs on reddish ground. 1959.
W.60cm, L.898cm. C.
National Museum of Modern Art, Tokyo.

127 Green *Jôdai Horara* (ancient gauze) type
silk. 1959.
W.45cm, L.936cm. C.
National Museum of Modern Art, Tokyo.

128 *Nishiki* (brocade) type silk, with motif of *karabana ungen* (Chinese flowers in gradations of color) 1959.
W.62cm, L.462cm. LA.
National Museum of Modern Art, Tokyo.

129 Black *Ra* (gauze) type silk. 1959.
W.39cm, L.1064cm. LA.
National Museum of Modern Art, Tokyo

Jûsuke FUKAMI (1885—1974)

130 Sword Belt, *kumihimo* (braid) plaited in
different colors. 1956.
W.10cm, L.255cm. B.
National Museum of Modern Art, Tokyo.

131 *Obijime* (sash band), light green *kumihimo* (braid) plaited in eight-fold. 1972
D.0.9cm, L.153.5cm. B.
Private collection, Japan.

132 Belt, *kumihimo* (braid) as reproduction of 8th
century piece kept in the Imperial Repository
Shôsô-in. 1930
W.8.7cm, L.320cm. CI.
Private collection, Japan.

133—134 *Obijime* (sash band) and *Haorihimo* (braid
for *haori* coat), reproduction of armor braid from
Sanage Jinja Shrine. 1955.
Obijime, W.1.3cm, L.142cm; *haorihimo*,
W.1.2cm, L.19cm. CII.
Private collection, Japan.

135 Sword Belt, *kumihimo* (braid) plaited in different
colors. 1972.
W.10cm, L.136cm; W.9.5cm, L.201cm. LA.
Nihon Denshô Senshoku Shinkôkai, Tokyo.

Eisuke KÔDA (1902—1970)

136 *Hakama* (kimono trousers) material, "Phoenix's
Elegance." *Seigô Sendai-hira* type. 1958.

W.41cm, L.1039cm. C.
National Museum of Modern Art, Tokyo.

137 *Hakama* (Kimono thousers) Seigô *Sendai-hira* type. 1968.
H.100cm, W.61cm. B.
Agency for Cultural Affairs, Tokyo.

138 *Hakama* (kimono trousers) material,
"Immortal's Waterfall." *Seigô Sendai-hira*
type. 1958.
W41cm, L1037cm. LA.
National Museum of Modern Art, Tokyo.

Zenzaburô OGAWA (1900—   )

139 *Kenjô Hakata-obi, Hakata* type sash of tough
silk. 1964.
W.32.0cm. B.
Private collection, Japan.

140 *Kenjô Hakata-obi, Hakata* type sash of tough
silk. 1973.
W.31.2cm. C.
Agency for Cultural Affairs, Tokyo.

141 *Kenjô Hakata-obi, Hakata* type sash of tough
silk. 1982.
W.32.5cm. LA.
Private collection, Japan.

Rikizô MUNEHIRO (1914—   )

142 *Kimono*, with design of lattice and red circular
patterns. *Tsumugi* weave silk. 1976.
H.173cm, W.128cm. BI.
Agency for Cultural Affairs, Tokyo.

143 *Kimono*, with design of gradating indigo-dyed
bamboo plait pattern. *Tsumugi* weave silk. 1981.
H.168.5cm, W.126.5cm. BII.
Private collection, Japan.

144 *Kimono*, with indigo-dyed bamboo pattern.
Tsumugi weave silk. 1979.
H.181cm, W128cm. CI.
National Museum of Modern Art, Tokyo.

145 *Kimono*, with gradating brown-dyed vertical
wave pattern. *Tsumugi* weave silk. 1980.
H.168.5cm, W.126.5cm. CII.
Private collection, Japan.

146 *Kimono*, "Awaiting Spring." *Tsumugi* weave
silk. 1968.
H.158cm, W.124cm. LA.
National Museum of Modern Art, Tokyo.

Society for Preservation of Echigo-Jôfu and Ojiya-Chijimi, Ojiya, Niigata Prefecture

147 *Kimono*, with chrysanthemum cross pattern on
indigo ground. *Echigo-jôfu* linen. 1958.
H.140.5cm, W.128cm. B.
National Museum of Modern Art, Tokyo.

148 *Kimono*, with brown and indigo lattice pattern
on white and brown ground. *Ojiya-chijimi* crepe
linen. 1958.
H.163cm, W.128cm. C.
National Museum of Modern Art, Tokyo.

149 *Kimono*, with gray stripes on indigo ground.
Echigo-jôfu linen. 1958.
H.159cm, W.128cm. LA.
National Museum of Modern Art, Tokyo.

Society for Preservation of Honba-Yûki-Tsumugi, Yûki, Ibaraki Prefecture

150 *Kimono*, with *daimyôjima* ("*daimyô* stripe") pattern,
Yûki-tsumugi silk. 1957.
H.151cm, W.122cm. B.
National Museum of Modern Art, Tokyo.

151 *Kimono*, with *ka-gasuri* ("mosquito splashes") in
tortoise shell pattern. *Yûki-tsumugi* silk. 1957.
H.144cm, W.121cm. C.
National Museum of Modern Art, Tokyo.

152 *Kimono*, "Pine Trees and Fence." *Yûki-tsumugi*
silk. 1976.
H. 162cm, W.128cm. LA.
Private collection, Japan.

Association of Kurume-Gasuri Weaving Experts, Kurume, Fukuoka Prefecture.

153 *Kimono, Kurume-gasuri* cotton. 1958.
H.153cm, W.125cm. B.
National Museum of Modern Art, Tokyo.

154 *Kimono, Kurume-gasuri* cotton. 1958.
H.153cm, W.125cm. C.LA.
National Museum of Modern Art, Tokyo.

Society for Preservation of Kijoka-no-Bashôfu, Kijoka, Okinawa.

155 *Kimono, "Kwaiya Banjô." Bashôfu* (banana-leaf fiber cloth). 1970.
H.150cm, W.124cm. B.
National Museum of Modern Art, Tokyo.

156 *Kimono, "Sotetsu* (cycad) Leaves." *Bashôfu* (banana-leaf fiber cloth). 1978.
H.153.5cm, W.128cm. C.
Society for Preservation of Kijoka-no-bashôfu, Kijoka.

157 *Kimono, Bashôfu* (banana-leaf fiber cloth). 1980
H.158cm, W.129cm. LA.
Society for Preservation of Kijoka-no-bashôfu, Kijoka.

Association of Miyako-Jôfu Experts, Okinawa.

158 *Kimono* Material, with floral *ka-gasuri* ("mosquito splashes") pattern. *Miyako-jôfu* linen. 1977.
W.37.5cm. B.
Agency for Cultural Affairs, Tokyo.

159 *Kimono* Material, with *ka-gasuri* ("mosquito splashes") pattern. 1977.
W.37.3cm. C.LA.
Agency for Cultural Affairs, Tokyo.

DOLLS

Gôyô HIRATA (1903—1971)

160 Dressed Doll, "Clear Fountain." 1961.
H.33cm. B.
National Museum of Modern Art, Tokyo.

161 Dressed Doll, "Leisurely Time." 1959.
H.34cm, W.17.5cm. C.LA.
National Museum of Modern Art, Tokyo.

Ryûjo HORI (1897—   )

162 Dressed Doll, "Serenty." 1957.
H.50.2cm. B.
National Museum of Modern Art, Tokyo.

163 Dressed Doll, "Sign." 1954.
H.15cm. C.
National Museum of Modern Art, Tokyo.

164 Dressed Doll, "Pledge." Around 1980.
H.23.3cm; pedestal H.2.0cm, D.24.3cm. LA.
Private collection, Japan.

Juzô KAGOSHIMA (1898—1982)

165 Doll, "Souvenir Ômori." Papier maché. 1958.
H.23.3cm; pedestal 10.5 x 16.0cm.
National Museum of Modern Art, Tokyo.

166 Doll, "Enju-bina (Longevity Couple)". Papier maché. 1959.
H.18.6cm; pedestal 21.0 x 18.3cm.
National Museum of Modern Art, Tokyo.

167 Doll, "Playing with a Top." Papier maché. 1954.
H.18.7cm; pedestal 8.8 x 11.9cm.
National Museum of Modern Art, Tokyo.

LACQUER WARE

Shôzan TAKANO (1889—1977)

168 Box for Calligraphy Paper, with a design of a lion. *Makie* (gold lacquer). 1927.
H.5.7cm, 22.8 x 20.0cm. C.LA.
Eisei Bunko Foundation, Tokyo.

169 Incense Case, with design of Paulownia emblem. *Makie* (gold lacquer). Around 1940.
H.1.8cm, D.7.6cm. B.
Eisei Bunko Foundation, Tokyo.

170 Incense Case, with wave design. *Makie* (gold lacquer). Around 1940.
H.1.5cm, D.6.9cm. B.
Eisei Bunko Foundation, Tokyo.

171 Incense Case, with peony design. *Makie* (gold lacquer). Around 1940.
H.1.6cm, D.7.6cm. B.
Eisei Bunko Foundation, Tokyo.

172 Portable Book Case, with animal and bird design. *Makie* (gold lacquer). 1931.
H.31.5cm, 28.0 x 48.7cm. B.
Private collection, Japan.

173 Box for Cosmetics, with design of squirrels and Japanese medlar. *Makie* (add lacquer) on plain wood. 1940.
H.16.5cm, 34.5 x 34.5cm. C.
National Museum of Modern Art, Kyoto.

174 Box for Cosmetics, with quail design. *Makie* (gold lacquer) on *kanshitsu* (dry-lacquer). 1965.
H.17.7cm, D22.3cm. B.C.
Kumamoto Prefectural Museum of Art.

Gonroku MATSUDA (1896—   )

175 Box for Cosmetics, with design of animals, birds and flowers. *Makie* (gold lacquer). 1919.
H.16.0cm, 21.8 x 25.1cm. C.
Tokyo University of Arts Museum.

176 Box for Inkstone, with a crane design. *Makie*
(gold lacquer) and eggshell. 1950.
H.5.1cm, 22.5 x 22.5cm. B.
Tokyo University of Arts Museum.

177 Box for Cosmetics, with design of black pine
and oak leaves. *Makie* (gold lacquer). 1956.
H.16.6cm, 22.6 x 29.0cm.
National Museum of Modern Art, Tokyo

178 Decorative Box, with design of bamboo grove.
Makie (gold lacquer). 1965.
H.11.0cm, 14.5 x 25.0cm. B.
National Museum of Modern Art, Tokyo.

179 Six Covered Bowls, with design of plum
blossoms. *Makie* (gold lacquer). 1967.
H.10.8cm, D.12.8cm.
National Museum of Modern Art, Tokyo.

180 Tea Caddy, with design of crane and tortoise.
Makie (gold lacquer). 1944.
H.7.1cm, D.7.8cm. C.
Idemitsu Museum, Tokyo.

181 Tea Caddy, with design of wave and cherry
blossoms. *Raden* (motor-of-pearl) inlaid *makie*
(gold lacquer) on zelkova wood. 1977.
H.7.8cm, D.7.8cm. B.
Ishikawa Prefectural Museum, Kanazawa.

Shôgyo ÔBA (1916—   )

182 Decorative Box, with design of melon and bird.
Hyômon. 1981.
H.14.6cm, 15.8 x 26.4cm.
Agency for Cultural Affairs, Tokyo.

Taihô MAE (1890—1977)

183 Small Container, with design of a cat.
Chinkin. 1962.
H.5.8cm, 14.0 x 27.0cm.
National Museum of Modern Art, Tokyo.

Joshin ISOI (1883—1964)

184 Octagonal Incense Tray, with design of dragon
and phoenix. *Kimma*. 1955.
H.5.2cm, D.46.5cm.
National Museum of Modern Art, Tokyo.

185 Circular Incendse Tray, with design of flowers
and butterflies. *Kimma*. 1956.
H.3.2cm, D.36.5cm. C.
Kagawa Prefectural Institute of Lacquer Craft.

186 Box for Brushes, with acacia design. *Kimma*. 1957.
H.4.5cm, 12.5 x 37.0cm. B.
Private collection, Japan.

Kôdô OTOMARU (1898—   )

187 Box for Cosmetics, with design of the moon
and rabbit. Carved lacquer on wood. 1953.
H.11.0cm, 35.1 x 27.0cm. B.
Private collection, Japan.

188 Octagonal Candy Box, carved lacquer
on wood. 1955.
H.10.5cm, D.26.0cm. B.
Private collection, Japan.

189 Box for Calligraphy Paper and Box for
Tanzaku (poetry paper). Box, with design
of intertwining wild thyme.
Carved lacquer on wood. 1955.
H.11.5cm, 30.5 x 27.5cm. B.
Private collection, Japan.

190 Candy Box, with flower design.
Carved lacquer on wood. 1960.
H.13.7cm, 15.5 x 15.5cm. C.LA.
National Museum of Modern Art, Tokyo.

191 Incense Case, carved lacquer on wood with
silver inlay. 1963.
H.6.0cm, D.10.0cm. C.
National Museum of Modern Art, Tokyo.

Yûsai AKAJI (1906—   )

192 Tray. *Magewa* (bent chip) work.
Red and black lacquer on wood. 1960.
H.5.1cm, D.37.0cm. B.C.
National Museum of Modern Art, Tokyo.

193 *Jikirô* (covered food container). Green and black
lacquer on *magewa* (bent chip) work. 1975.
H.16.2cm, D.27.3cm.
Agency for Cultural Affairs, Tokyo.

Mashiki MASUMURA (1910—   )

194 Covered Box. *Kanshitsu* (dry-lacquer). 1978.
H.15.5cm, D.25.0cm.
Agency for Cultural Affairs, Tokyo.

195 Tray in lobed Shape. *Kanshitsu* (dry-lacquer). 1981.
H.6.5cm, D.35.6cm. B.C.
National Museum of Modern Art, Tokyo.

Society for Preservation of Wajima-Nuri Craft, Wajima, Ishikawa Prefecture.

196 Dinner Set, *Wajima-nuri* lacquer ware.
Red lacquer on wood. Around 1925.
Serving table, H.26.0cm, 43.5 x 43.5cm;
Agency for Cultural Affairs, Tokyo.

WOOD & BAMBOO CRAFTS

Kôdô HIMI (1906—1977)

197 Tea Box. Sand-polished larch wood. 1964.
H.13.0cm, 14.5 x 21.5cm. B.C.
National Museum of Modern Art, Tokyo.

198 Low Table. Mulberry wood. 1974.
H.14.2cm. 31.0 x 60.5cm.
Agency for Cultural Affairs, Tokyo.

Tatsuaki KURODA (1904—1982)

199 Box for cosmetics. Lacquer on Japanese horse
chestnut. 1970.

H.15.0cm, 12.2 x 26.7cm.
National Museum of Modern Art, Tokyo.

Shôunsai SHÔNO (1901—1974)

200 Flower Basket. Purple bamboo. 1968.
H.32.0cm, 31.0 x 44.0cm. B.C.
National Museum of Modern Art, Tokyo.

201 Flower Basket, "*Kusudama* (Decoration ball)."
Largely plaited purple bamboo. 1970.
H.42.0cm, D.43.0cm. B.C.
National Museum of Modern Art, Tokyo.

202 Flower Basket, copying an old type. *Matsuba-ami* (pine-needle plait) type. 1974.
H.15.8cm, D.35.0cm.
Agency for Cultural Affairs, Tokyo.

Shôkansai IIZUKA (1919—)

203 Decorative Box, with lozenge pattern. *Sashiami*-type plait. 1974.
H.13,0 15.0 x 25.0cm.
Agency for Cultural Affairs, Tokyo.

204 Octagonal Basket, with lozenge pattern. *Sashiami*-type plait. 1980.
H.12.0cm, 15.6 x 15.6cm. B.C.
Agency for Cultural Affairs, Tokyo.

205 Flower Basket. Double plaited. 1977.
H.35.0cm, 21.0 x 23.5cm. B.C.
Private collection, Japan.

METALWORK

Iraku UOZUMI (1886—1964)

206 *Dora* (gong). *Sahari* (brass) ware. 1952.
Dora, H.10.5cm, D. 39.5cm;
Stand, H.81.5cm, W.63.5cm, D.30.0cm.
Agency for Cultural Affairs, Tokyo.

Shôdô SASAKI (1884—1961)

207 *Hiten* (flying angel). Bronze, lost wax casting.
1934.

H.20.0cm, 38.0 x 10.0cm.
Private collection, Japan.

208 Deer. Bronze, lost wax casting. 1959.
H.47.4cm, 34.5 x 12.0cm. B.C.
National Museum of Modern Art, Tokyo.

Tetsushi NAGANO (1900—1977)

209 Tea Kettle, with wave pattern. 1965.
H.19.0cm, D.26.0cm.
National Museum of Modern Art, Kyoto.

Ikkei KAKUTANI (1904—)

210 Tea Kettle, with fan design. 1979.
H.16.0cm, D.29.0cm.
Agency for Cultural Affairs, Tokyo.

Toyochika TAKAMURA (1890—1972)

211 Flower Vase, with cloth-thread pattern. *Oborogin* (silver and copper alloy). 1962.
H.35.1cm, D.11.6cm. B.C.
National Museum of Modern Art, Tokyo.

212 Vase, with design of horizontal lines. Reddish bronze. 1965.
H.20.2cm, D.26.0cm.
National Museum of Modern Art, Tokyo.

Masahiko KATORI (1899—)

213 Bell. Bronze. 1982.
H.72.0cm, D.45.0cm.
Private collection, Japan.

214 Bell, with design of *hiten* (flying angles). 1982.
H.34.0cm, D.21.0cm. B.
Private collection, Japan.

Kiyoshi UNNO (1884—1956)

215 Covered Box, with design of parrots and grape-vine. Carved metalwork. 1928.
H.7.8cm, D.13.4cm.
Tokyo National Museum

216 Box, with design of two birds. 1931.
H.6.3cm, D.29.3cm. B.C.
Tokyo University of Arts Museum.

Shirô NAITÔ (1907—)

217 Silver Vase, with design of willow-tree. 1964.
H. 19.0cm, D.17.0cm. B.C.
Tokyo University of Arts Museum.

218 Silver Plate of Hexagonal Shape, with open-work. 1981.
H.5.0cm, D.26.0-24.0cm.
Agency for Cultural Affairs, Tokyo.

Ikkoku KASHIMA(1898—)

219 *Mizusashi* (water jar), with design of flowers. *Zôgan* (inlay) work. 1977.
H.12.0cm, D.21.0cm.
Agency for Cultural Affairs, Tokyo.

220 Flower Vase, with design of willow and stream. *Oborogin* (silver and copper alloy) ware. 1979.
H.10.1cm, D.9.0 x 17.0cm. B.C.
Agency for Cultural Affairs, Tokyo.

Shirô SEKIYA (1909—)

221 Plate, Marbleized *shakudô* (gold and copper alloy) ware. 1972.
H.3.5cm, 29.0 x 29.0cm.
National Museum of Modern Art, Tokyo.

222 Bottle, with design of hammered lines. Silver and *shakudô*. 1974.
H.30.0cm, D.12.0cm. B.C.
Agency for Cultural Affairs, Tokyo.

Mitsumasa YONEMITSU (1888—1982)

223 *Tsuba* (sword-guard) of Octagonal Melon Shape,
with inlaid floral scroll. 1963.
T.0.2cm, D.8.4cm.
Agency for Cultural Affairs, Tokyo.

224 *Tsuba* (sword-guard) Octagonal Flower Shape,
with openwork and gold inlay. 1969.
T.0.2cm, D.8.4cm.
National Museum of Modern Art, Tokyo.

SWORDS

Sadatsugu TAKAHASHI (1902—1968)

225 *Tachi* (long sword). Inscription signed
and dated 1960.
L.101.9cm; blade, L.80.5cm, curve 3.3cm. B.C.
Agency for Cultural Affairs, Tokyo.

226 *Tantô* (short sword). Inscription signed and dated
1962.
L.31.8cm; blade, L.21.8cm, curve 0.2cm.
Agency for Cultural Affairs, Tokyo.

Yukihira MIYAIRI (1913—1977)

227 *Tachi* (long sword). Inscription signed
"Miyairi Shôhei," and dated 1965.
L.91.2cm; blade L.71.0cm, curve 1.9cm.
Agency for Cultural Affairs, Tokyo.

228 *Wakizashi* (middle-size sword). Inscription signed
"Miyairi Shôhei," and dated 1965.
L.42.5cm; blade 31.0cm, curve 0.0cm. B.C.
Agency for Cultural Affairs, Tokyo.

Sadaichi GASSAN (1907—   )

229 *Yari* (spear). *Yamato* style. Inscription signed and
dated 1966.
L.169.2cm; blade L.79.2cm.
Private collection, Japan.

230 *Katana* (sword). *Sôshû* style. Inscription signed
and dated 1977.

L.99.6cm; blade L.76.5cm, curve 2.4cm. B.C.
Private collection, Japan.

231 *Katana* (sword). *Ayasugi* style. Inscription signed
and dated 1979.
L.92.2cm; blade L.70.9cm, curve 2.1cm.
Private collection, Japan.

Masamine SUMITANI (1921—   )

232 *Yari* (spear). Inscription signed and dated 1973.
L.169.2cm; blade L.79.2cm. B.C.
Private collection, Japan

233 *Tachi* (long sword). Inscription signed and
dated 1974.
L.96.6cm; blade L.74.5cm, curve 2.8cm.
Private collection, Japan.

234 *Chôkutô* (straight sword). Inscription signed and
dated 1981.
L.81.2cm; blade L.62.1cm. B.C.
Sano Museum.

KIRIKANE

Baitei SAIDA (1900—1981)

235 Decorative Box, with design of overlapping
lozenge pattern. *Kirikane.* (gold-leaf cutwork) 1965.
H.11.0cm, 16.5 x 26.5cm.
Kyoto Prefectural Documentation Center

236 Two-fold Screen, "*Hana* (flower)." *Kirikane.*
(gold-leaf cutwork) 1971.
H.80cm, W.100cm. B.C.
Kyoto Municipal Museum of Art.

HANDMADE RICE PAPER

Eishirô ABE (1902—   )

237 *Gampi* Paper, made of *wikstroemia gampi*. 1982.
100 sheets; 42 x 132cm each.
Private collection, Japan.

Ichibei IWANO (1901—1976)

238 *Echizen-hôsho*, paper made of mulberry. 1975.
100 sheets, 39 x 53cm each.
Private collection, Japan.

Association of Sekishû-Hanshi Papermaking
Experts, Shimane Prefecture

239 *Sekishû-hanshi*, paper made of mulberry. 1982.
50 sheets, 25 x 35cm each.
50 sheets, 53 x 75cm each.
Association of Sekishû Hanshi Papermaking
Experts.

Society for Preservation of Authentic
Mino Paper, Gifu Prefecture

240 Authentic *Mino* Paper, made of mulberry. 1982.
50 sheets, 28 x 40cm each.
50 sheets, 63 x 93cm each.
Society for Preservation of Authentic
Mino Paper.

Association of Hosokawashi Papermaking
Experts, Saitama Prefecture

241 *Hosokawa* Paper, made of mulberry. 1982.
50 sheets, 30 x 42cm each.
50 sheets, 60 x 84cm each.
Association of Hosokawashi Papermaking
Experts.

SAMPLES OF MANUFACTURING PROCESS

Shôzan TAKANO (1889—1977)

242 Record of *makie* technique. 1952.
3 sheets of paper 25.0x100.0cm each.
Agency for Cultural Affairs, Tokyo.

Mitsumasa YONEMITSU (1888—1982)

243 Record of Higo *Zôgan* (metal inlay) technique.
1964. 4 sheets of paper, 40.0 x 60.0cm each.
Agency for Cultural Affairs, Tokyo.

CERAMICS

Toyozô ARAKAWA (1894-   )

Holder of an Important Intangible Cultural Property technique for "Shino" and "Seto-guro" (1955). Born in Toki City, Gifu Prefecture. 1921, studied at Tôzan MIYANAGA factory in Kyoto, where he served as manager. 1927, upon invitation by Rosanjin KITAÔJI, assisted him at his Hoshigaoka kiln in Kamakura. 1930, discovered the old kiln site of Shino ware at Okaya in Gifu Prefecture; after 1933, reconstructed on the spot a semi-underground single-chamber climbing kiln and endeavored to reproduce Shino, Ki-seto (Yellow Seto) and Seto-guro (Seto Black) wares of the Momoyama period. 1955, at the first registering of Important Intangible Cultural Properties, designated Holder of Important Intangible Cultural Properties "Shino" and "Seto-guro." 1971, recipient of the Order of Cultural Merits.

Munemaro ISHIGURO (1893—1968)

Holder of the designated technique for "Iron-glazed Pottery" (1955). Born to a medical doctor in Shinminato City, Toyama Prefecture. 1917, experimented in Raku ware; thereafter studied by himself in Tokyo, Saitama, Kanazawa and Kyoto. 1935, built his kiln at Yase in Kyoto, where he devoted himself to the study of old Chinese ceramics of the T'ang and Sung dynasties; he rediscoverd the glaze techniques of Black Ting, Kaki (reddish brown) Temmoku, Konoha (leaf) Temmoku, etc., of the Sung dynasty and established a unique style of his own by adding a modernistic touch to the dignity of Sung ceramics.

Kenkichi TOMIMOTO (1886—1963)

Holder of the designated technique for "Enameled Porcelain" (1955). Born at Ando Village, Nara Prefecture. 1909, graduated from the Design Department of the Tokyo Fine Arts School; while at the school, studied in England. 1915, built a kiln at his native village and began ceramic work. 1927, built a kiln at Soshigaya in Tokyo. Showed white porcelain, blue and white, and subsequently enameled wares of distinctive forms and designs at Kokugakai, Teiten and Bunten exhibitions. 1937, member of the Imperial Art Academy; 1944, professor at Tokyo Fine Arts School; retired from both in 1946. Thereafter moved to Kyoto and organized the Shinshô Bijutsu Kôgeikai in 1947. 1950, professor at Kyoto Municipal Art College (1958, principal of the same). In his late years he established a florid style of enameled porcelain decorated further with gold and silver. 1961, honored with the Order of Cultural Merits.

Hajime KATÔ (1900—1968)

Holder of the technique for "Enameled Porcelain" (1961). Born in Seto City, Aichi Prefecture. 1926, employed at Gifu Prefectural Institute of Ceramic Industry, where he made extensive researches in ceramic crafts. 1927, since the establishment of the Applied Arts Department in the Teiten exhibition, participated in governmental art exhibitions. 1940, became independent at the kiln which he built at Hiyoshi, Yokohama City. Studied and revived Chinese enameled porcelain techniques of the Ming dynasty such as the ôji kôsai (red against yellow enamels) and the kinrande (enameled and gilded) ware. Besides these, he mastered seihakuji (ch'ing-pai, shadowy blue), underglaze copper red, underglaze gold, and various other techniques. 1955, professor at Tokyo University of Arts.

Shôji HAMADA (1894—1978)

Holder of the technique for "Folk Art Pottery" (1955). Born at Mizonokuchi in Kanagawa Prefecture. After graduating in 1916 from the Ceramic Department of the Tokyo High School of Technology, studied at Kyoto Municipal Institute of Ceramic Industry. 1920, went to England and worked with Bernard Leach at Saint Ives. 1924, came back to Japan and settled at Mashiko, Tochigi Prefecture. Promoted folk-art movement together with Muneyoshi YANAGI, Kanjirô KAWAI, and others. He established a powerful, robust style based on that of traditional local wares of Korea, Okinawa, and Japan. Frequently visited Europe and America where he exhibited his ceramic art. 1962, succeeded to Muneyoshi YANAGI's position of Director of Folk Art Museum. 1963, recipient of the Order of Cultural Merits.

Tôyô KANASHIGE (1896—1967)

Holder of the technique for "Bizen Ware" (1956). Born in Bizen City, Okayama Prefecture. Studied the ceramic technique of Bizen ware with his father Baiyô. Until about 1925, chiefly made such sculptural pieces as figures of lions and Hotei. Later switched to wheel work pieces. By choice of the clay and improvement of the kiln as well as study of yôhen (kiln transmutation), hidasuki (fire mark), and other techniques, he eventually revived the style of Old Bizen ware of the Momoyama period (1573—1615) and laid the foundation for its present prosperity.

Kei FUJIWARA (1899-—   )

Holder of the technique for "Bizen Ware" (1970). Born in Bizen City, Okayama Prefecture. 1919, went to Tokyo. His first purpose was literature, and he published poems and novels. 1937, returned to his native place and began making Bizen ware; under guidance of Tôyô KANASHIGE, Handeishi KAWAKITA and others, created a distinctive new style in the traditional Bizen ware. Since 1955, participated in exhibitions of Traditional Japanese Crafts. 1974, held exhibition of "Old Bizen and Fujiwara Kei Senior & Junior" in France and Belgium.

Kyûwa MIWA (1895—1981)

Holder of the technique for "Hagi Ware" (1970). Born in Hagi City, Yamaguchi Prefecture to the keeper of the Miwa factory, which is honored to have been the official kiln of the former Mori clan during the feudal age. Mastered the hereditary Hagi ware technique; 1927, succeeded to the name Kyûsetsu MIWA in the tenth generation. Good at warm, graceful style and white glaze technique in which the effect of Korean Yi-dynasty tea bowls is harmonized with Japanese style. 1967, retired and assumed the name Kyûwa.

Muan NAKAZATO (1895—   )

Holder of the technique for "Karatsu Ware" (1976). Born in Karatsu City, Saga Prefecture. Was engaged with his family in the manufacture of Karatsu ware. 1927, succeeded to the name of Tarôemon NAKAZATO, becoming Tarôemon XII. Made field researches at the kiln sites of Karatsu ware existing in Saga Prefecture, and studied the paste and techniques. 1955, chosen as Holder of "Karatsu Ware" technique, an Important Intangible Cultural Property for Which Records Should Be Taken; the same year, began participating in the exhibitions of Japanese Traditional Crafts. His specialities are jars and pitchers fabricated by the "paddling" method. 1969, gave the name Tarôemon over to his eldest son Tadao (Tarôemon XIII) and assumed the name Muan.

Yûzô KONDÔ (1902—   )

Holder of the technique for "Sometsuke" (blue and white porcelain) (1977). Born in Kyoto City. 1917, graduated from the trainees' school attached to the Kyoto Municipal Institute of Ceramic Industry. 1921—23, apprenticed to Kenkichi TOMIMOTO and educated by the latter. After his first success in the Teiten exhibition in 1928, showed his blue and white and underglaze copper red wares at governmental art exhibitions. After 1955, member of the Japan Crafts Association. Good at blue and white jars decorated with pomegranate, plum blossom, or landscape designs, or inscribed in powerful brushwork with Chinese-style poems or prose. 1958, professor at Kyoto Municipal Art College; 1965-71, principal of the same college.

SOCIETY FOR PRESERVATION OF IRO-NABESHIMA IMAEMON PORCELAIN

Group holder of award for "Iro (Enameled) Nabeshima." Representative: Imaemon IMAIZUMI XIII. During the feudal age, when Nabeshima ware was the official ware of the Nabeshima clan, the Imaizumi Imaemon family boasted of its high standing as a family of official decorators specializing in overglaze enamel decoration. After the feudal clans were abolished at the Meiji Restoration (1868), the family was engaged, as a non-official project, in the manufacture of Iro Nabeshima porcelain in traditional techniques. The Institute for Preservation of Iro Nabeshima Techniques was organized in 1970 by fifteen leading members of the Imaizumi Imaemon Studio. It is in charge of the preservation and improvement of "Iro Nabeshima" (registered as an Important Intangible Cultural Property) in the system of divided labor, from preparing the body, fashioning, underglaze blue decoration, overglaze enamel decoration, to firing.

Imaemon IMAIZUMI XII (1897—1975)

During the feudal age when Nabeshima ware was the official ware of the Nabeshima clan, the Imaemon lineage boasted of its high standing as a hereditary family of official decorators specializing exclusively in overglaze enamel decoration. After the feudal clans were abolished at the Meiji Restoration (1868), however, the family had to endure great hardships in order to carry out the thorough manufacturing process from fashioning the shapes to overglaze enameling. Imaemon XII together with his predecessor made diligent efforts to restore the traditional Iro (enameled) Nabeshima in which underglaze blue and overglaze enamel decorations complement each other, and to establish Nabeshima ceramic art that would meet the requirements of modern society. He furthermore created new *sarasa* (chintz) patterns based upon old Nabeshima *sarasa* works, while he also experimented in new effective uses of traditional designs and their compositions, creating many fine pieces. The Iro Nabeshima, thus, was brought to revival, and the Institute for Preservation of Enameled Nabeshima Techniques, of which he was the president, was designated in 1971 as a Group Holder of Important Intangible Cultural Property "Iro Nabeshima".

Imaemon IMAIZUMI XIII (1926—   )

After graduating from the Decorative Design Department of the Tokyo Fine Arts School, he helped Imaemon XII to restore enameled Nabeshima techniques, and became Imaemon XIII in 1975 at forty-nine.

His ability for distinctive designs characterized by dynamic compositions, contrasting with the static style of Imaemon XII, must have been nurtured in a relatively free environment after his Tokyo Fine Arts Schoool period. He looks for the basic principle of composition in classical designs and creates modern enameled Nabeshima ware by fitting original motifs in classical frames, reshaping classic motifs into new designs, and employing such distinctive techniques as *fukizumi* and *sumihajiki*.

He established in 1975 the Imaemon Institute for Preservation of Enameled Nabeshima Techniques. As the leader of the Institute he, in succession to Imaemon XII, was designated a Holder of Important Intangible Cultural Property.

SOCIETY FOR PRESERVATION OF KAKIEMON CERAMIC TRADITION

Group holder of award for "Kakiemon" (*nigoshi-de*). Representative: Tadashi SAKAIDA. The Kakiemon family, from the time of Kakiemon I in the seventeenth century to the present day, has succeeded to the craft of the "Kakiemon" enameled porcelain. Kakiemon XIII, during the lifetime of his father XII, endeavored jointly with his father to revive the *nigoshi-de* (milk-white body) which had been in decline after the late Edo period, and succeeded in 1953. The Institute for Preservation of Kakiemon Ceramic Techniques was organized in the Kakiemon studio in 1971 with eleven leading experts as its members. It is in charge of the preservation and improvement of "Kakiemon" (*nigoshi-de*) in the system of divided labor, from preparation of the body, fashioning, overglaze enamel decoration, to firing.

Kakiemon SAKAIDA XII (1878—1963)

After graduation from the ceramic training school in Arita, he was engaged in ceramic manufacture under Kakiemon XI and became Kakiemon XII in 1917 at thirty-nine. Because of the depression that prevailed in Japan shortly after, and

also difficulties incurred by the artisan's lack of business sense, he was driven to such extremities that he had to think of changing his occupation. His pride as the successor of the Kakiemon family, and his zeal for revival of the Kakiemon style, eventually prevailed and he, assisted by Kakiemon XIII, succeeded in reconstructing the *nigoshi-de* (milk-white base) which had been lost sight of after the later Edo period. The "Kakiemon *nigoshi-de*" was selected in 1955 by the National Commission for Protection of Cultural Properties as a Recorded Intangible Cultural Property.

Kakiemon SAKAIDA XIII (1906—1982)

Having succeeded, jointly with Kakiemon XII, in reviving the *nigoshi-de* (milk-white porcelain) technique and reproducing the traditional Kakiemon style, he became Kakiemon XIII in 1963 at the age of fifty-seven. Eager as such to establish a new Kakiemon style, he has experimented with and realized new designs based upon his own sketches of nature, in contrast to the conservative trend of Kakiemon XII who used mainly traditional designs. His style is one of the characteristics of the contemporary Kakiemon ware.
He organized in 1971 the Institute for Preservation of Kakiemon Ceramic Techniques, whose "Kakiemon *nigoshi-de*" has been designated an Important Intangible Cultural Property.

TEXTILES

Kihachi TABATA (1877—1956) *Yûzen*

In 1895, at the age of eighteen, he succeeded to the name Kihachi TABATA III. The Tabata family were famous *yûzen* artists of Kyoto who were patronized by the imperial family. After first studying Japanese painting of the Shijô school in Bairyô KÔND's studio, Kihachi studied under the artist Seihô TAKEUCHI. Even when he had become a *yûzen* specialist, he continued to make sketches and to copy the paintings of the masters. He created painterly masterpieces that displayed his superb command of *sekidashi* (resist-outlined) *yûzen*. In 1955 his skill in *yûzen* was recognized as an Important Intangible Cultural Property. Apart from his own outstanding work, he has a collection of antique *kimono* which in itself is invaluable.

Tameji UENO (1901—1960) *Yûzen*

Tameji UENO was the eldest son of one of Kyoto's outstanding *yûzen* artists, Seikô UENO. When he was thirteen, he started to take lessons in Japanese painting under Gôun NISHIMURA and later broadened his study by entering an art school where he learned western style painting. In 1925 he began training in *yûzen* under his father. Five years later he took up *Kaga-yûzen* and held his first exhibition in which he displayed his talent with delicately painted and sumptuously designed *kimono* in a style called *Kyô-Kaga*. In 1955 he was designated Holder of an Important Intangible Cultural Property in *yûzen* techniques. During his later years he experimented with abstract designs in a pointillistic style.

Uzan KIMURA (1881—1977) *Yûzen*

Uzan KIMURA was born in Kanazawa. While learning the traditional style of *Kaga-yûzen* under Unshô WADA from *1905* to *1923,* he also studied *nanga* painting under Kinyô ÔNISHI. *Kaga-yûzen* is characterized by a painterly style with softly-shaded colors. Combining wax resist with the traditional rice paste resist techniques, Uzan skillfully worked with his brush to create exquisite tonal variations, and his experimentations opened up new possibilities in the art of *yûzen*. In 1928 at the ninth annual Teiten Exhibition his work was displayed for the first time; thereafter he exhibited regularly with the Bunten and Nitten art groups. After being designated the Holder of an Important Intangible Cultural Property technique in *yûzen* in 1955, he exhibited predominately with the The Exhibition of Traditional Japanese Crafts.

Katsuma NAKAMURA (1894—1982) *Yûzen*

Born in Hakodate in Hokkaidô, Katsuma NAKAMURA went to Tokyo in 1912 to study painting, but in 1913 he took up the study of textile design and dyeing. In 1924 he established himself as a *yûzen kimono* artist. He became a judge of the handicraft section of the Nikakai art group in 1947, and in 1955 was designated Holder of an Important Intangible Cultural Property in *yûzen*. His creative designs on the skirts of black *kimono* expressed the style prevalent in Tokyo and opened up new ideas in *kimono* design.

Kakô MORIGUCHI (1909—   ) *Yûzen*

Born in Shiga Prefecture, Kakô MORIGUCHI went to Kyoto in 1921 to study Kyoto style *yûzen* under Katon NAKAGAWA. At the same time he studied in the Shijô school of Japanese painting. In 1939 he established himself as a *yûzen* artist. In 1955 and 1956 his work received prizes at the annual Exhibition of Traditional Japanese Crafts, and every year thereafter he has entered his *kimono* and has been on the judging panel. In 1960 he became a director of the Japan Crafts Association, and in 1967 his skill in *yûzen* was recognized as an Intangible cultural Property. He is known for his bold designs employing the *yûzen* techniques of *itome* (resist line drawing), *sekidashi* (resist outlining), and *makinori* (scattered resist). Since 1970 he has been assistant director of the Japan Crafts Association.

Kôsuke KOMIYA (1882—1961) *Edo-Komon*

Kôsuke KOMIYA was born the son of a farmer in Katsushika, Tokyo. At the age of thirteen he began an eight-year apprenticeship under Mojûro WAKAMATSUYA, a stencil dyer of Tokyo's Asakusa district. Afterwards he spent several years perfecting his skill by working at various other shops until in 1907 he set up his own studio.
Although this was a time when the dyeing establishments were having difficulty coping with the revolution in techniques brought about by the introduction of chemical dyes, KOMIYA continued to produce the traditional minute *komon* stencil patterns that originally had been created for use on *kamishimo,* the samurai formal attire consisting of a vest and skirt worn over the *kimono*. These patterns are often made up of a multitude of tiny dots, as in

gokusame, which resembles sharkskin (*same*). A master craftsman of *komon* stencil work, KOMIYA was designated a Holder of an Important Intangible Cultural Property in *Edo-Komon* in 1955.

Yasutaka KOMIYA (1925—   ) Edo-Komon

The second son of master stencil craftsman Kôsuke KOMIYA, Yasutaka KOMIYA began his training at the age of fourteen under the strict discipline of his father. In 1947, in Tokyo's Shinkoiwa he took over the management of his father's studio that had been closed during the war. His work was accepted for entry in 1960 in the seventh annual Exhibition of Traditional Japanese Crafts and in 1964 at the eleventh Exhibition of Traditional Japanese Crafts it brought him a prize. Devoting himself to the study of *komon* dyes and rice paste resist, he has worked also toward the improvement of stencil paper and has encouraged young people to take up the vocation of stencil carving. In 1978, at the age of fifty-two, he followed in his father's footsteps when he was designated a Holder of an Important Intangible Cultural Property.

Sadakichi MATSUBARA (1893—1955) Nagaita Chûgata

At the age of ten Sadakichi MATSUBARA left his home in Toyama Prefecture to become an apprentice of Tokyo's *chûgata* stenciler Shôzaburô KURI. At twenty-two he established himself as an independent artisan and set up a small studio in Edogawa Ward in the outskirts of Tokyo.
Chûgata are small-to-fairly-large patterns used for summer cotton *kimono*. MATSUBARA applied himself to the art of using two stencils in order to produce an indigo pattern on a white background, the white area being formed by the resist. At that time the craft of applying the resists, which is what MATSUBARA had learned, was separate from that of dyeing, but in 1954, after overcoming the difficulties of indigo dyeing, he managed to combine the two. In 1955, just before his death, he was designated a Holder of an Important Intangible Cultural Property in *chûgata* stencil patterns.

Kôtarô SHIMIZU (1897—   ) Nagaita Chûgata

Born in Tokyo, Kôtarô SHIMIZU at the age of fourteen learned from his father the trade of applying *chûgata* stencils to white cotton *yukata* fabric. *Yukata* are indigo-dyed *kimono* worn in the summer. The patterns range in size from small designs to the more common large designs. The fabric is pasted on long boards (*nagaita*) about 6.37 m. in length, and the resist is applied to the back of the cloth as well as to the front. The cloth is then dyed in indigo, and if the resist does not match precisely on both sides, the resulting pattern will be fuzzy.
Upon his father's death in 1936, SHIMIZU took over the family's trade and showed exceptional ability in producing complex patterns that require special skill. In 1955 he received both the gold and silver prizes in a competition sponsored by the Tokyo Nagaita Honzome Chûgata Association. In 1955 he was designated a Holder of an Important Intangible Cultural Property for *Nagaita Chûgata*.

Hidekichi NAKAJIMA (1883—1968)
Ise Paper Stencils: Punched-Out Patterns

Small, repetitive stencil motifs such as flower petals or dots or squares are made with steel punches. This technique is called *dôgubori*. So that the stencil paper will not shrink or expand during the carving, it is made of several layers of mulberry paper pasted together with persimmon tannin, smoked, and dried thoroughly. Because about five of these stencil papers are carved at one time, the punch soon becomes dull and has to be taken apart to sharpen the cutting edges. Testing the limits of human skill and patience, *dôgubori* requires extensive training and a steady hand.
Born in Jikemachi, Suzuka, in Mie Prefecture, Hidekichi NAKAJIMA served his apprenticeship under Yûkichi TOYODA, a stencil maker in his neighborhood. Although he worked some time in Osaka, he returned in 1916 to the stencil-making center of Suzuka, where he was eminent among the many other outstanding stencil carvers of the town. In 1955 he was declared a Holder of an Important Intangible Cultural Property for his skill in *dôgubori*.

Baiken ROKUTANI (1907—1973)
Ise Paper Stencils: Dotted Patterns

Called *kiribori*, the technique of producing stencil patterns composed entirely of small dots is done with a crescent-shaped punching tool that is given a 180-degree turn when pressed into the stencil paper. With dots alone an innumerable variety of delicate patterns can be created, but as simple as dots may seem, the work is far from easy. If the *kiribori* tool is turned too much or not enough, the hole will differ in size. In order to produce one stencil without any variation in the size of the dots, some twenty days of keen concentration are needed.
Baiken ROKUTANI was born in Jikemachi, Suzuka City. Upon graduation from elementary school, which at that time extended to the eigth grade, he studied *kiribori* under his father and then went to work in Tokyo as a stencil maker. Returning to Jikemachi in 1942, he devoted himself to the carving of the most tedious of patterns, *same-komon* and *tôshi-komon*. Although these patterns appear uncomplicated, they are particularly difficult to carve because any unevenness is conspicuous. An extremely fine example of this type of pattern may have nine hundred dots within three square centimeters. In 1955 ROKUTANI's skill in *kiribori* was designated an Important Intangible Cultural Property.

Yoshimatsu NANBU (1894—1976)
Ise Paper Stencils: Freestyle Patterns

Freestyle patterns are designed primarily for *nagaita chûgata* dyeing and are carved out with a razor-sharp double-edged knife. This technique is called *tsukibori*.
As the knife is pushed through the stencil, it produces clean, rhythmical lines which show up as a white pattern when the fabric is dyed. A rice paste resist is spread through the stencil with a wooden spatula, and this paste repels the indigo in which *nagaita chûgata* are dyed. This kind of stencil is usually employed

on cotton fabric; stencils made in small patterns with *dôgubori* and *kiribori* are mainly used on silk to produce *Edo-komon*.

Yoshimatsu NANBU was born in Jikemachi in Suzuka, and like so many of the sons of this town of stencil makers learned at an early age to cut out *tsukibori* stencils with his father as teacher. He then studied various types of stencil carving in Tokyo, Kyoto, and Yamanashi Prefecture. In 1946 he was instrumental in organizing the Ise Paper Stencil Guild and went on to become its active leader. He also contributed to the craft of stencil making through his instruction and his collection of old stencils and research materials. In 1955 his skill in *tsukibori* was designated an Important Intangible Cultural Property.

Yujiro Nakamura (1902—   )
Ise Paper Stencils: Punched-Out Patterns

Born in Jikemachi, Suzuka City, Yûjirô NAKAMURA began to learn the trade of stencil carving at the age of twelve, following in the footsteps of his father who gave him a strict, thorough training. NAKAMURA has over three thousand punches he has made himself in a multitude of shapes and sizes. In 1955 his skill in this kind of stencil cutting, called *dôgubori*, was recognized as an Important Intangible Cultural Property.

Hiroshi KODAMA (1909—   )
Ise Paper Stencils: Carving of Striped Patterns

The carving of striped patterns is the most difficult of all of the various types of stencils used in *kimono* dyeing. Only the most skillful artisan can cut out the patterns, which may have as many as thirty-three stripes in a three-centimeter space. To enable the artisan to carry out his exacting work, the double-bladed knife he uses must be of the finest steel and made by a swordsmith, for it must be as sharp as a samurai's sword. The stencil paper, too, must be hand-made of pure *kôzo* (mulberry), and must meet the highest standards.

Born in Shirakomachi in the city of Suzuka, Mie Prefecture, Hiroshi KODAMA began at the age of ten the rigorous training a stencil maker must undergo. His instructor was his father. When he was seventeen, he began to work as a maker of striped stencils in Tokyo, the center of the stencil dyeing industry. There he met Kôsuke KOMIYA, whose skill in *Edo-komon* stencil dyeing had been designated an Intangible Cultural Property. With KOMIYA's guidance and advice KODAMA made great advances in his own work. In 1942 he returned to Suzuka where he has been living since. In 1955 the title of Holder of an Important Intangible Cultural Property was conferred on him for his ability to carve striped stencils.

Mie JÔNOGUCHI (1917—   )
Ise Stencil Paper: Reinforcement

Stencils with large open spaces or those carved in stripes require reinforcement. This is achieved by separating the sheet of stencil paper into two layers, inserting fine thread between the two, and then pasting the two together again with persimmon tannin. Fitting the pattern together is exacting work that is further complicated if the design is minutely carved. At present the time-saving method of pasting gauze on the back of the stencil has become more common, but as the gauze interferes with the smooth application of the resist, especially in striped patterns, the old method of reinforcement is still preferred and in many cases essential.

Born in Shirakomachi in Suzuka, Mie Prefecture, Mie JO⁹NOGUCHI while still a child was taught by her mother and grandmother the traditional method of reinforcing the stencils. Even after marrying and herself becoming a mother, she has continued her work. In 1955 her skill in this craft was designated an Important Intangible Cultural Property.

Keisuke SERIZAWA (1895—   ) Stencil Dyeing

Born the son of a *kimono* fabric dealer of Shizuoka, Keisuke SERIZAWA studied design at the Tokyo Higher School of Industrial Arts. He was first involved in such work as poster design, but after becoming acquainted with the *bingata* stencil work of Okinawa he decided to devote himself to traditional stencil work and returned to Shizuoka to study with a local dyer.

In 1929 he began to exhibit with the Nihon Mingeiten (a folk art group) and the Kokugakai, and allowed his genius to play with prolific work in stenciled designs for book covers. He also contributed to the folk art movement with Muneyoshi YANAGI and most of his work was connected with the movement. His skill in stencil dyeing was designated an Important Intangible Cultural Property in 1956. His influence extended overseas as well: in 1968 he was invited to a summer seminar at San Diego State University, and he also held one-man exhibitions at Los Angeles and Vancouver. In 1976, the year he held a one-man exhibition in Paris, he was awarded the Order of Cultural Merits.

Toshijirô INAGAKI (1902—1980) Stencil Dyeing

Born in Kyoto, Toshijirô INAGAKI graduated from the Kyoto Municipal School of Art where he majored in design. After working as a textile designer for nine years at the Kyoto branch of Matsuzakaya Department Store he began work on his own, and his entries in exhibitions of the Kokugakai and Bunten were awarded prizes. His meeting the great ceramic artist Kenkichi TOMIMOTO in 1940 had a deep influence on his philosophy and work. In 1946 TOMIMOTO set up a new art group called the Shinshô-kôgeikai in which INAGAKI played a leading role. From 1948 he began to concentrate on stencil work, and the following year he was appointed to the faculty of Kyoto Municipal College of Art. In 1956 his work was exhibited with the Exhibition of Traditional Japanese Crafts and he became a permanent member of the Japan Crafts Association. His skill in stencil work was recognized as an Important Intangible Cultural Property in 1962. He died the next year, and an exhibition of his life's work was held at the National Museum of Modern Art in Kyoto.

Yoshitarô KAMAKURA (1902—   ) Stencil Dyeing

Graduating from the Tokyo School of Art in 1921, Yoshitarô KAMAKURA went to Okinawa to teach at the Prefectural Women's School of Education. During his five years there he researched Okinawan crafts and became particularly interested in the *bingata* form of stencil art that had developed

through the patronage of Ryûkuan nobility. This led him to study the art of *bingata* stencil dyeing and to start a collection of old *bingata* stencils.

Upon returning to Tokyo he took a position on the faculty of his alma mater, where he taught the history of Japanese painting. In 1945 he resumed his study of *bingata*.

As a Japanese-style painter in his own right, he began to produce creative compositions in the *bingata* technique which he exhibited for the first time in 1958 at the age of sixty. His boldness of expression combined with the traditional *bingata* forms is admired for its vitality and vibrant use of color. In 1962 his skill was designated an Important Intangible Cultural Property.

Ayano CHIBA (1890—1980) *True Indigo Dyeing*

Born in the town of Kurikoma in Miyagi Prefecture, Ayano CHIBA was a unique person who continued the peasant tradition of producing indigo dyed hemp cloth. From the growing of the indigo and hemp to the spinning of the yarn and the weaving and dyeing, she did all the work herself, having learned the techniques by watching her mother. In 1955 she was designated the Holder of an Important Intangible Cultural Property title for her skill in the original form of indigo dyeing.

The dye was produced in a wooden tub with the help of wood ash and the natural heat of the summer months. No artificial ingredients or means were employed. This primitive but effective method of dyeing, which dates back to ancient times, disappeared at the beginning of the twentieth century except for the small amount that Ayano CHIBA was able to produce.

Heirô KITAGAWA (1898—) *Silk Gauze and Damask*

Born into a family of Nishijin weavers of Kyoto who specialized in the aristocratic patterns of the Heian period, Heirô KITAGAWA studied Japanese painting before succeeding to the family's business, a firm called Tawaraya, in 1927. While continuing his work of designing and weaving, he has dedicated himself to the research of ancient textiles preserved in the Shôsô-in and various museums and to the reconstruction of their lost dyeing and weaving techniques. His greatest achievement has been to unlock the mysteries of complex gauze weaves called *sha*. At the same time, he is unique in his extensive knowledge of and exceptional skill in producing the patterns of the ceremonial costumes worn at court since the Heian period.

In 1956 he was designated the Holder of an Important Intangible Cultural Property title in silk gauze weaving and in 1960 in silk damask weaving.

Jûsuke FUKAMI (1885—1974) *Karakumi (Braided Sashes)*

Jûsuke FUKAMI came from a Kyoto family that produced the braided cords called *kumihimo*. The *karakumi* technique of braiding flat sashes was introduced to Japan from China in the Nara period. During the Heian period the braiding techniques reached perfection, and *karakumi* was employed for the sash used to attach the sword to the waist when a nobleman was attired in the formal *sokutai* dress worn on ceremonial occasions.

FUKAMI devoted himself to the study of ancient braiding and dyeing

techniques and was able to produce sashes using more than three hundred bobbins of naturally dyed yarn braided tightly into various diamond shaped patterns. In 1956 his skill was recognized as an Important Intangible Cultural Property.

Eisuke KÔDA (1902—1970) *Seigô Sendai-hira*

Born in Sendai, Miyagi Prefecture, Eisuke KÔDA learned the art of weaving from his father and was the third generation in the KÔDA family to follow the weaving profession. *Sendai-hira* is made of a weft of raw silk dampened and beaten tightly into a warp of glossed silk. Famous for its closely woven texture, it is used for the skirts called *hakama* that are worn over the *kimono*, particularly men's formal *kimonos*.

Dedicating himself to the study of traditional techniques and the use of natural vegetable dyes, KÔDA displayed an exceptional skill in creating extremely fine weaves. In 1956 he was designated the Holder of an Important Intangible Cultural Property title for *Seigô Sendai-hira*.

Zenzaburô OGAWA (1900—) *Kenjô Hakata-ori*

Zenzaburô OGAWA began his apprenticeship in weaving at the age of twelve in the city of his birth, Fukuoka. This city of northern Kyûshû has been famous for its stiff silk *obi* since the early days of the Edo period when the *obi* were given as tribute (*kenjô*) to the shogun. The weaving techniques, however, date back to the Muromachi period when they were probably introduced from China. The Kuroda clan who controlled the Fukuoka area were responsible for the refinement of the weave that came to be called *hakata-ori* from the Hakata section of the town where the fabric was made. The weave is characterized by zigzag motifs which originally represented *dokko*, spear-shaped implements held in the hand by Buddhist priests during esoteric ceremonies to symbolize magical power. In 1962 OGAWA established his own weaving studio and showed great talent and skill in producing this complex weave. In 1966 he was declared the Holder of an Important Intangible Cultural Property title.

Rikizô MUNEHIRO (1914—)
Tsumugi in Striped and Kasuri Patterns

Born in the Gujô district of Gifu Prefecture, Rikizô MUNEHIRO headed an agricultural development center after the war while devoting himself to the revival of a silk floss (*tsumugi*) fabric that had formerly been produced in Gujô. Incorporating the striped and *kasuri* (ikat) patterns that characterized the old fabric, he has developed difficult techniques such as finely gradated tones, circles, and wavy lines in soft *tsumugi* weaves which retain the quiet, rustic characteristics of the fabrics of long ago. His work has received the highest awards at exhibitions of the Japan Folk Art Museum and the Exhibition of Traditional Japanese Crafts. In 1982 his skill was declared an Important Intangible Cultural Property.

SOCIETY FOR PRESERVATION OF ECHIGO-JÔFU AND OJIYA-CHIJIMI

The ramie cloth produced in the Echigo region of Niigata is of such excellent quality that during the Edo period it was given as tribute to the shogun. Made of ramie grown in the neighboring Aizu district of Fukushima Prefecture, the fine cloth is woven in plain tabby called *jôfu* and a crepe called *chijimi*. The area's heavy snow (that is used to bleach the cloth) and high humidity (that provides the ramie yarn with needed moisture) create the perfect environment for producing the cloth.

In 1955 both *Echigo-jôfu* and *Ojiya-chijimi* were registered as Important Intangible Cultural Properties.

The industry is characterized by a division of labor with the various skills grouped as follows:

1. *oumi*: hand spinning of the ramie fiber
2. *kasuri*, or ikat, design
3. *kasuri* tying
4. dyeing
5. weaving on the *izaribata*, a low backstrap loom
6. *yumomi*: treading on the finished cloth in a tub of hot water
7. *yukizarashi*: bleaching in the snow

The preservation of these skills rests with associations of crafts people in the groups listed. Overall production, however, is controlled by large weaving establishments which get in touch with the individual association member. In each association there are members who give instruction or do research as well as perform their special skills. At present the leader is Eizô ENDÔ.

SOCIETY FOR PRESERVATION OF HONBA-YÛKI-TSUMUGI

Made of an exceedingly fine handspun silk floss yarn (*tsumugi*), the fabric woven at Yûki in Ibaraki Prefecture has been produced since the Keichô period (1596—1614), originally as a supplementary income by the local farmers. It was at that time also known by the name of the region, Hitachi.

Today *Yûki-tsumugi* is still produced from local silk in the time-honored manner and is of surpassing beauty. It was accorded the status of an Important Intangible Cultural Property in 1956. The *Yûki-tsumugi* Important Intangible Cultural Property Foundation works with the locally established Association for the Preservation of *Yûki-tsumugi*, which had been organized earlier, to improve production methods, hold annual exhibitions, and provide opportunities for young people to train directly under the guidance of people skilled in the craft. Members of the Society for the Preservation must have over twenty-fie years of experience in the craft and show outstanding ability in the hand spinning and *kasuri* techniques which characterize the *Yûki* fabric, as well as in weaving on the backstrap loom. Members include both researchers and skilled instructors. The leader is Kanetoshi KOBAYASHI.

ASSOCIATION OF KURUME-GASURI WEAVING EXPERTS

The ikat weave known as *Kurume-gasuri* is believed to have been invented in the latter half of the Edo period by a young woman by the name of Den INOUE. A cotton fabric used for *kimono*, work clothes, and quilt covers, it was originally produced for a supplementary income by farmers in the villages around Kurume City in Kyûshû. Although hand weaving used to be a flourishing industry, the fabric is now manufactured mainly on power looms.

The traditional process entails the use of cotton yarn tied in *kasuri* patterns with bindings made of hemp. Dyed in indigo from Tokushima Prefecture, the yarn is woven on a flying shuttle loom in bold patterns of white and light blue on a dark blue background. In 1957 *Kurume-gasuri* was declared an Important Intangible Cultural Property, and an association for its preservation was formed. The association works toward improvement in the techniques and educates young followers of the craft. Grouped according to age and experience, the members comprise 23 instructors and 30 crafts people skilled in the traditional techniques. The head is Yûjirô SAKURAI.

SOCIETY FOR PRESERVATION OF KIJOKA-NO-BASHÔFU

Like the abaca cloth of the Philippines, *bashôfu* is made from the fiber of a plant of the banana family, *ito-bashô* (*Musa Balbisiana;* Thread Musa). Undyed or woven in stripes and *kasuri*, the fabric has been produced among the peasants of Okinawa and the Amami islands for countless centuries.

At present a group of women in the village of Kijoka in northern Okinawa still produce *bashôfu* using the traditional methods. Dyed brown with the wood of *tekachi*, an indigenous tree, or blue with local indigo, the *kasuri* patterns are unique to the Ryûkyûs. In 1974 *Kijoka-no-bashôfu* was designated an Important Intangible Cultural Property. All the members of the association are women who have undergone extensive training and who are capable of passing on their skills. Toshiko Taira, whose dedicated efforts have kept the craft alive, is the leader.

Skill	No. of People
spinning	2
kasuri tying	2
dyeing	2
weaving	2
finishing	1
all skills	1

ASSOCIATION OF MIYAKO-JÔFU EXPERTS

An exceptionally thin fabric made of ramie, *Miyako-jôfu*, was declared an Important Intangible Cultural Property in 1978, then an association for its preservation was formed and recognized as possessing the Important Cultural Property skill.

Having at least thirty years of experience and outstanding ability, these people are essential for passing on the traditional techniques of *Miyako-jôfu* to succeeding generations.

The members are grouped according to the division of skills that characterize the craft.

Skill	No. of People
spinning of weft yarn	3
spinning of warp yarn	5
kasuri tying	3
dyeing	3
weaving	3
washing	3
correcting *kasuri* faults	1

Of these twenty-one people Genshin SHIMOJI is the leader.

DOLLS

Gôyô HIRATA (1903—1981)
Holder of award for "*Ishô Ningyô*." Born in Tokyo. Trained under his father, Gôyô I, in the craft of making realistic dolls. Admitted in 1924 to the Dokuritsu exhibition and in 1936 to the Teiten exhibition, whereafter he was active at Bunten and Nitten exhibitions. 1955, designated Holder of Important Intangible Cultural Property "*Ishô* Ningyô." His art is characterized by a realistic style with which he vividly represents expressions and poses of children and women. 1930, participated in the Paris International Exhibition and contributed to the international dissemination of the art of creative doll making.

Ryûjo HORI (1897—   )
Holder of award for "*Ishô Ningyô*." Born in Tokyo. At first learned oil painting with Junzaburô NISHIWAKI and Japanese painting under Yumeji TAKEHISA. Turning from the two-dimensional representation of painting to three-dimensional form, she directed herself to *ishô ningyô* dolls. Studying by herself instead of learning from any teacher, she won her first success at the 1936 Teiten exhibition and Special Selection at the 1949 Nitten exhibition.
In 1955 she was designated Holder of Important Intangible Cultural Property "*Ishô Ningyô*." Thereafter she has shown her works at the exhibitions of Traditional Japanese Crafts. She has created a new style in this field by giving visual form to the fantasy and subtle contentment of the East.

Juzô KAGOSHIMA (1898—1982)
Holder of award for "*Shiso Ningyô*" (papier mâché dolls). Born in Fukuoka City. At first learned manufacture of Hakata Dolls from Yonejirô ARIOKA. Later went to Tokyo, studied the techniques of ancient clay statues and old paper dolls, established the craft of *shiso ningyô* by inventing the method of fabricating with *kôzo* (paper mulberry) fiber and decorating by means of *washi* (Japanese paper) dyeing. 1936, admitted to Teiten exhibition; 1956, member of the Board of Directors for the Japan Crafts Association; 1964—66, assistant chairman of that Board; 1961, nominated Holder of Important Intangible Cultural Property "*Shiso Ningyô*." He is also known as a poet of the Araragi group.

LACQUER WARE

Shôzan TAKANO (1889—1977)
Holder of the technique for "*Maki-e*." Born in Kumamoto. After being initiated into the fundamentals of lacquer art at a local school, he studied in the Lacquer Art Department of Kyoto Municipal College of Arts and subsequently in the Lacquer Art Department of the Tokyo Fine Arts School. He received private lessons from Shôsai SHIRAYAMA, a professor at the Tokyo Fine Arts School, and mastered the secrets of Shirayama school *maki-e*. Shôsai SHIRAYAMA improved the technique of precise, fine *maki-e* known as "Joken-in period work," which was reserved for use by feudal lords in the Edo period. Improving his skill further at the Kiritsu Kôshô Company, which exported high quality goods early in the Meiji period and showed its products at large international exhibitions in various parts of the world, he produced extremely elaborate *maki-e* art which was almost beyond human achievement. People called it Shirayama school *maki-e*. TAKANO succeeded to the craft and displayed his eminent skill on *kôgô* (incense cases) and other such small pieces. He brought the technique of Shirayama school *maki-e* into contact with the modern arts; making use of his distinguished ability in *kiji maki-e* and *kanshitsu* base, he worked out pieces noteworthy for their fresh designs.

Gonroku MATSUDA (1896-   )
Holder of the technique for "*Maki-e*." Born in Kanazawa City, Ishikawa Prefecture. Trained in *maki-e* since childhood by his elder brother, at the age of fifteen he was already an able *maki-e* technician and had mastered especially the technique of the Igarashi school traditional in Kanazawa. At the Lacquer Art Department of the Tokyo Fine Arts School he assisted distinguished artists of various schools in Tokyo, thus attaining simultaneous mastery of the merits of different styles. In Tokyo at the time there were many specialists of the polished crafts of the Edo and Meiji periods. MATSUDA's study in Tokyo was very fruitful. He learned not only from persons but from experience in the repair and conservation of ancient Chinese and Japanese masterpieces; absorbing techniques and designs from them he developed a dignified, many-sided style unsurpassed by any other artist. He trained many young artists at the Tokyo Fine Art School, later renamed Tokyo University of Arts. He also contributed greatly to the administration of cultural property in Japan. He is a member of the Japan Art Academy and recipient of the Order of Cultural Merits.

Shôgyô ÔBA (1916—   )
Holder of the technique for "*Maki-e*." Born in Kanazawa City, Ishikawa Prefecture to a distinguished specialist of lacquer varnish. After graduating from the Industrial Design Department of Ishikawa Prefectural School of Technology, went to Tokyo and studied *maki-e* under Gonroku MATSUDA. Under the latter's guidance he participated in the repair of the Golden Hall of Chûson-ji Temple (National Treasure) and made *goshimpô* (art treasures dedicated to gods) for the Ise Shrine; through such experiences he became well versed in the manufacturing techniques and designs of old masterpieces of lacquer art. He is a master in all fields of *maki-e* art, especially in that of *hyômon*,

through his study of this technique as displayed on lacquer works in the Shôsô-in Repository of Imperial Treasures. As a result, he has invented a new *hyômon* technique never before seen in the history of lacquer art, in which he cuts gold plate into fine strips reminiscent of lines drawn with the brush and as capable of expressing subtle effects, assembling them into detailed, elaborate designs. Excelling in the lacquer varnish craft, which he learned from his father, he successfully covers those areas of the surface where raised and sunken parts resulting from the assembling of gold plate cutouts tend to prevent smooth, even varnishing.

Taihô MAE (1890—1977)

Holder of the technique for "*Chinkin*." Born in Wajima City, Ishikawa Prefecture. Apprenticed himself to Sasuke HASHIMOTO, a celebrated master at *chinkin* in that city. He won Special Selection at the central Teiten exhibition in 1930, and was honored for his great achievement as a local artist.

Chinkin is a craft of Chinese origin that was developed in Japan to show flowing linear designs. *Chinkin* is used at major Japanese lacquerware centers as a means of surface decoration. The *Chinkin* on Wajima lacquerware surpasses all others in its technical level and excellent design. Lines are engraved with a carving knife designed specifically for gouging them clearly on a lacquered surface; liquid lacquer is applied to the hollowed lines and gold leaf is pressed into them to produce a beautiful design standing out in golden lines. Earlier *chinkin* was done only in lines. The design tended to be flat until MAE perfected a technique of pointillist representation that makes possible a three-dimensional effect. Employing this new craft, he skillfully produced such rounded motifs as a cat's body.

Joshin ISOI (1883—1964)

Holder of the technique for "*Kimma*." Born in Takamatsu City, Kagawa Prefecture. After graduating form the Lacquer Art Department of the Kagawa Prefectural School of Industrial Arts, was engaged for about six years in the manufacture of export lacquerware in Osaka; then returned to Takamatsu and devoted himself to creative activities.

He was a lacquer artist of inventive mind; versed in a rich variety of techniques and styles, he created new designs one after another. He was distinguished especially in *kimma*. *Kimma* was originally a lacquerware with Chiang Mai, Thailand as the major center of manufacture. It has the *kiji* (base) of plaited bamboo coated with lacquer, line-engraved with a knife with characteristic designs of flowering plants and other motifs, the engraving being filled in with red lacquer or lacquer of other colors. Zôkoku TAMAKAJI developed it into a subtle, noble, and highly artistic work. ISOI, while being distinguished in the traditional *kimma* craft, created new techniques suitable for modern expression rich in perspective and three-dimensional effect.

Kôdô OTOMARU (1898—   )

Holder of award for "*Chôshitsu*" (carved lacquer). Born in Takamatsu City, Kagawa Prefecture. At first received elementary lessons in wood carving and *chôshitsu* in his native place. At the age of about twenty, studied *chôshitsu* by himself, experimenting with copies of Zôkoku TAMAKAJI's works; later went to Tokyo and was engaged in creative activities. In lacquer art in China there were techniques called *tsuishu*, *tsuikoku*, and so on, in which cinnabar lacquer, black lacquer, etc. were applied many times over to form a thick layer, and designs were carved into it. The lacquer colors available were black, red, yellow, green, and intermediate colors obtained by blending these, altogether seven colors or so. Other colors did not come out when mixed with lacquer. However, progress in chemical science has made it possible in recent years to prepare durable and unfading lacquer of any color. OTOMARU makes effective use of this rich variety of colors, applying them one over another with the resulting effect in mind, and skillfully carving his designs into them. Seeking expression in which carving and colors echo each other, he has created an ornate, delicate style which is entirely new.

Yûsai AKAJI (1906—   )

Holder of award for "*Kyûshitsu*" (lacquer varnish). Born in Kanazawa City, Ishikawa Prefecture. Kanazawa has a long tradition of lacquer art and AKAJI first learned lacquering there. Later he studied with Zenzaburô WATANABE, a lacquer varnish specialist in Tokyo. The latter's father was a celebrated master in this field during the Meiji and Taishô eras. WATANABE the father studied the technique of old lacquer works and established the varnish craft, technically difficult but graceful in effect, of preparing the base carefully and varnishing the surface very thinly. WATANABE the son, under whom AKAJI studied, had succeeded to the craft, which he thoroughly mastered. He also invented a method of preparing the *kiji* (base) by building up many layers of narrow *magewa* (thin wood strips bent into hoops). *Magewa* in itself makes a strong base. When the hoops are placed in tiers one over another with slight interstices left between them, the shrinkage or expansion of wood caused by humidity or dryness is minimized and no warping occurs in the vessel itself. Employing this construction in his colored lacquer work, AKAJI has achieved a modern, clear, and fresh expression.

Mashiki MASUMURA (1910—   )

Holder of award for "*Kyûshitsu*" (lacquer varnish). Born in Kumamoto City, Kumamoto Prefecture. After receiving elementary lessons in lacquer art at a local school, he learned from a lacquer technician in Nara, then went to Tokyo and became a pupil of Yûsai AKAJI. The highly polished lacquer varnish technique originally established by Kisaburô WATANABE was thus transmitted to him through the intermediary AKAJI.

His speciality is preparation of *kiji* (base) for *kanshitsu* work. *Kanshitsu* is a craft earlier used for preparing the core of Buddhist statues in the Nara and Heian periods. In this craft, the desired shape is roughly modeled in clay; the shape is translated into a plaster mold; layers of hemp cloth are applied on the mold and, after dry, solidified with lacquer; the dry lacquer shell removed from the mold serves as the *kiji* of the desired object. It is characteristic of this method that any shape can be freely produced. MASUMURA's unsparing investigation into

plastic forms has resulted in shapes of simple condensed form which are all the more impressive because of his polished, glossy *roiro-nuri* varnish.

Although AKAJI and MASUMURA are teacher and pupil, AKAJI features *hana-nuri* (unpolished varnish) of moderate gloss, while Masumura specializes in *roiro-nuri*, lacquer surface polished with a piece of charcoal.

SOCIETY FOR PRESERVATION OF WAJIMA-NURI CRAFT

Group holder of award for "*Wajima-nuri*." Concerning the origin of *Wajima-nuri* thriving in Wajima City at the end of Noto peninsula in Ishikawa Prefecture, it is said that an excellent lacquerware existed as early as 1476, but it was in the Edo period that it became widely known.

The lacquer varnish technique of *Wajima-nuri* is characterized by its strong *shitaji* (priming) using *ji-no-ko* (priming powder) made from diatomite, a special product of the Wajima area. This *shitaji*, with liquid lacquer thoroughly infiltrated, is durable and retains warmth when hot soup is poured into a bowl. The finishing varnish technique is also excellent. For preparing the *kiji* (base), too, there are experts in *hiki-mono* (bowls), *sashi-mono*, and *mage-mono*, who make vessels of various kinds for various purposes. For surface decoration also, there are excellent *maki-e* and *chinkin* crafts.

Technical experts of *Wajima-nuri* are numerous; among them twenty distinguished technicians from the respective fields have been selected for the Association for Preservation of Wajima-nuri Craft, whose purpose is to conserve the traditional techniques of *Wajima-nuri*.

WOOD & BAMBOO CRAFTS

Kôdô HIMI (1906—1977)

Holder of the technique for "Wood Work." Born in Kanazawa City, Ishikawa Prefecture, he began to learn *sashi-mono* (joinery) craft as a child. At about twenty he showed his works at art exhibitions in the locality, but it was in 1946, when he was forty, that he began to participate in metropolitan exhibitions. He eagerly studied wood work objects among the Shôsô-in Imperial Treasures, under the guidance mainly of Gonroku MATSUDA from the same Ishikawa Prefecture.

Inspired by the Shôsô-in Treasures, where he first studied *mokuga* (marquetry), he aimed for florid, almost excessive surface decoration by assembling wood materials of diverse kinds. His *mokuga* technique was gradually simplified, however, and came to show the beauty of unsophisticated forms. He established the same style in his shapes of wood. In the last part of his life he revived the Shôsô-in wood work objects in a modern style characterized as intellectual, pure, and dignified.

Tatsuaki KURODA (1904—1982)

KURODA's father was the keeper of a large lacquerware studio in Kyoto, where many employees were engaged in the processes of lacquerware manufacture from preparation of wood *kiji* (base) to final varnish. Raised in such an environment, KURODA was skilled from childhood in the crafts of wood work and lacquering.

When he was about twenty, he became a close friend of Muneyoshi YANAGI, leader of the folk-art movement. In 1927 he and his colleagues rented a house in Kyoto, where they organized the Kami-gamo Folk Art Association and started creative activities. The Association was disbanded in two years or so, but KURODA continued thereafter to be active as a leader of the folk-art movement in the fields of wood work and lacquer art. Opposed to cleverness of hand and floridness of techniques, he established a style emphasizing the charm of the heavy, impressive texture of the wood itself. His art extends over such techniques as *raden*, varnish, *sashi-mono*, and *kuri-mono*, for making boxes, tables, chairs, interior ornaments, and so on, among which the most typical of his work is *kuri-mono* in strong plastic forms.

Shôunsai SHÔNO (1901—1974)

Holder of the technique for "Bamboo Work." Born in Beppu City, Ôita Prefecture, a center of traditional bamboo work where he learned the art at an early age. Recognized for his distinguished technical skill, he was employed from 1938 to 1959 by the Beppu Institute of Industrial Arts, where he offered guidance in techniques and designs of local bamboo work, at the same time showing his works at Bunten and other central exhibitions.

His early works were mainly florid, decorative designs in elaborate Chinese-style plaiting, but gradually he turned to a simple style in which technical manipulation was subdued and importance laid on the characteristic beauty of the bamboo itself. He chose his own bamboo material out of a bamboo grove, and himself carried out all the processes from treating the material to final finish. He was a great leader who brought to high artistic level bamboo objects which had tended to be scorned as everyday utility pieces.

Shôkansai IIZUKA (1919-   )

Holder of the technique for "Bamboo Work." Born second son of the famous bamboo work artist Rôkansai IIZUKA, he graduated from the Oil Painting Department of Tokyo Fine Arts School and was studying to be a painter. As his elder brother, expected to be the successor to his father, died young, Shôkansai turned to study bamboo work with his father.

A complicated bamboo plaiting craft has been handed down in the IIZUKA family, which has specialized in bamboo work for generations. Especially important was the unique method of plaiting cultivated by Rôkansai.

Shôkansai has continued the elaborate *take sashi-ami* and the powerful, dynamic *tabane-ami* which his father invented. Also, through study of the Shôsô-in Imperial Treasures and other classical works, he has designed new plaiting methods of his own for a resulting noble, elegant style.

METAL WORK

Yasutarô UOZUMI (artist's name: Iraku UOZUMI, 1886—1964)
Holder of the technique for "*Dora*" (1955). Born in Ishikawa Prefecture. After about 1904, engaged in the manufacture of Buddhist ritual objects under Tokuzô YAMAGUCHI of Osaka. While studying the casting of ritual bells made of *sawari* alloy he became interested in the manufacture of metal sounders and musical instruments. Born with an acute sensitivity to sounds, and having learned acoustics, he devoted himself to making *dora* (gongs) of excellent tone and resonance. For about ten years after 1935 he was engaged in casting *dora* of *sawari* under the technical guidance and with the support of Naohiko MASAKI, President of the Imperial Art Academy, and Hozuma KATORI, the celebrated artist of metal casting. He successfully mastered and became practiced in the difficult processes of metal compounding, casting, heat treatment, hammerwork finish, coloring, etc. and acquired outstanding technical skill in beating the fragile *sawari* alloy for the manufacture of *dora*.

Bunzô SASAKI (artist's name: Shôdô SASAKI, 1884—1961)
Holder of the technique for "*Rôgata*" Casting (1960). Born in Niigata Prefecture. At the age of seventeen he wished to be a cast metal artist and apprenticed himself to Randô MIYATA I, under whom he studied the *rôgata* (lost wax) casting technique which had been practised in Sado, Niigata Prefecture. 1913, went to Tokyo and participated in the Nihon Bijutsu Kyôkai, Noten, Teiten, Bunten and other art exhibitions with good results. Meanwhile, in 1924, organized the Kôgei Seiseikai Society jointly with the metal casting artist Hozuma KATORI and the metal carving artist Senroku KITAHARA for the purpose of studying ancient *rôgata* casting. Over many years held the position of member of the Jury for the governmental Teiten, Bunten and Nitten exhibitions, contributing much to the growth and development not only of metal casting but of applied arts in general. Until his last years he continued to create dramatic, fresh masterpieces exhibiting the best of *rôgata* art, infusing fresh air into the metal art world thereby. In 1958 he won the Award of the Chairman of the National Commission for Protection of Cultural Properties at the fifth exhibition of Traditional Japanese Crafts.

Matsuzo NAGANO (artist's name: Tetsushi NAGANO, 1900—1977)
Holder of the technique for "Tea-Ceremony Kettle" Casting (1963). Born in Aichi Prefecture. 1918, entered the Research Institute of Japanese Watercolor Painting. Later realized that drawing was fundamental to applied art works, and in 1920 entered the Hongô Institute of Western Painting under Saburôsuke OKADA. Gave up painting after the great 1923 earthquake of Kantô District. Influenced also by Hiroshi SHIDA and others, turned to metal casting, learning from Azumi YAMAMOTO the techniques of design, model, fashioning, *rogata* (lost wax) casting, and *komegata* casting. 1929, met Hozuma KATORI, who was then promoting a movement for a renewed look at old Far Eastern art and for modernization of the art. This prepared him for his later study of old kettles. The results of his researches on old kettles since 1929 were published in *Kettles of Ashiya, Kettles of Temmyô*, and *Kettles of Ashiya Style*, in which he explained the

styles, history, and techniques of old kettles. After more than thirty years of diligent studies, in recovering the technique of casting kettles with Japanese pig iron he succeeded earlier thought to be almost impossible. In this way he revived the tradition of old Ashiya and Temmyô kettles.

Tatsujiro KAKUTANI (artist' name: Ikkei KAKUTANI, 1904—   )
Holder of the technique for "Tea-ceremony Kettle" casting (1978). Born in Osaka. Learned the art from his father Minosuke, who was a tea-ceremony kettle caster. Later apprenticed to the artist of metal casting, Hozuma KATORI, under whom he studied tea-ceremony kettle casting as well as metal casting in general. Around 1925 received guidance on three-dimensional form and construction from Seiji SUGITA of the Osaka Prefectural Industry Encouragement Hall and from Kazumasa NUMATA of the Kyoto Institute of Ceramic Industry. Further inspired by the opinion of Kokôan HOSOMI, who was celebrated at the time for his study of tea-ceremony kettles. Thereafter studied the forms, ground decorations, and "taste" (texture) of old kettles of Ashiya and Temmyô iron wares, finding his ideal prototypes in masterpieces from Ashiya in Chikuzen Province. He shows at the exhibitions of Traditional Japanese Crafts the excellent works noted for tasteful ground decoration and the elegant effect of the cast surface resulting from his experience in the study and manufacture of bronze mirrors dedicated to Shintô shrines.

Toyochika TAKAMURA (1890—1972)
Holder of the technique for "Metal Casting" (1964). Born in Tokyo. His father Kôun was a wood sculptor, and his elder brother Kôtarô was a poet. He learned metal casting from Nobuo TSUDA. 1915, graduated from the Metal Casting Department, Applied Arts Faculty, Tokyo Fine Arts School. Thereafter devoted himself to metal casting art, winning Special Selection at the eighth, ninth and tenth Teiten exhibitions where he attracted notice for the creative products which reflected his distinguished technical and artistic ability. Making free use of the traditional *rogata* (lost wax) casting technique, he aimed at fresh forms and economic statement while dealing with classical subject matters. 1933, professor at Tokyo Fine Arts School; 1950, member of the Japan Art Academy; after 1961, member of Experts' Council for Cultural Properties; 1967, Advisor to Nitten Corporation. His philosophical concept, attained through the pursuit of modernistic expression, was of great influence in Japanese applied art circles.

Masahiko KATORI (1899—   )
Holder of the technique for "*Bonshô*" (1977). Born in Tokyo, eldest son of Hozuma KATORI. Graduated from the Metal Casting Department, Tokyo Fine Arts School. Interested in ancient metal work and devoted particularly to the study and manufacture of Buddhist ritual objects and *bonshô* (bronze bells used at Buddhist temples). Special Selection at Teiten exhibitions three times; 1953, Japan Art Academy Award; 1973, Special Award at the twentieth exhibition of Traditional Japanese Crafts; after 1954, as a member of Experts' Council for Cultural Properties, worked for the protection of Tangible and Intangible Cultural Properties. Currently, as a permanent member of the Board

of Directors for the Japan Crafts Association, he is furthering the guidance and education of young artists and is contributing in this way to the development of Japanese traditional crafts. While continuing his activities at exhibitions, he studies and repairs old Buddhist ritual objects and Buddhist statues; he is especially adept at designing and casting *bonshô* of excellent resonance.

Kiyoshi UNNO (1884—1956)

Holder of the technique for "Metal Carving" (1955). Born in Tokyo, the fourth son of Shômin UNNO, who was celebrated as a master of Mito metal work. Studied metal carving technique from childhood. 1919, graduated from Metal Art Department of Tokyo Fine Arts School together with Senroku KITAHARA and others, whereafter he became an independent metal artist. 1932, professor at the Tokyo Fine Arts School; in October went to France for study. Adding his new knowledge of European techniques to the foundation of traditional crafts taught by his father and Natsuo KANÔ, he exhibited works displaying a new trend of Japanese applied arts at the Teiten, Bunten, and Nitten exhibitions. During the year following the close of the war he suffered from ill health. 1947, member of the Imperial Art Academy; 1949, professor at the Tokyo University of Arts and permanent member of the Committee for Management of Nitten Exhibition; 1950, member of Experts' Council for Cultural Properties. Holding many such important positions, he was distinguished for his ability as a craftsman and as a leader in the world of applied arts.

Shirô NAITO (1907—   )

Holder of the technique for "Metal Carving" (1978). Born in Tokyo. 1931, graduated from Metal Work Department (Metal Carving) of Tokyo Fine Arts School, where he mastered traditional metal carving techniques under Kamezô SHIMIZU and Kiyoshi UNNO. 1929, first success at the Teiten exhibition, whereafter he participated in Nitten and Kokugakai exhibitions. Greatly influenced in thought and plastic artistry by the ceramic artist Kenkichi TOMIMOTO. Through many years of study established a modern, highly artistic style with rich, polished effects. 1960, professor at the Tokyo University of Arts; 1961, member of Japan Crafts Association; participated in the Association's exhibition of Traditional Japanese Crafts in the same year, and has since been its Non-examination Acceptance artist, member of the Jury, and Associate Director. His work is characterized by powerful *keri-bori* (kicking incisions) of simple, clear design on a metal base showing tasteful hammer marks, often enriched with *nanako* (granulations). For color effect he often uses gilding and embedding of colored powder of calcite.

Eiichi KASHIMA (artist's name: Ikkoku KASHIMA IV, 1898—   )

Holder of the technique for "Metal Carving" (1979). Born in Tokyo. The Kashimas were members of a family of carved metal artists of Edo (the present Tokyo), at Shitaya in Tokyo, who specialized mainly in *nunome zôgan* (fabric pattern inlay). From boyhood, Ikkoku learned the art from his father and grandfather, and further studied traditional methods under the artists Kazuya

SEKIGUCHI and Shin'ya SEKIGUCHI. Also favored with opportunities to receive direct guidance from Kiyoshi UNNO and Senroku KITAHARA, leaders of metal carving at the time, he learned about creative styles and artistic expressions. After 1954, served several times as a member of the Jury for the exhibition of Traditional Japanese Crafts. 1964, repaired the Sarira Casket (a National Treasure) and other metal works owned by the Tôshôdai-ji Temple, thus contributing to the preservation of Tangible Cultural Properties. He preserves the *togidashi zôgan* (polished inlay) technique invented by his grandfather's cousin Ippusai KASHIMA.

Shirô SEKIYA (1909—   )

Holder of the technique for *"Tankin"* (hammered metal work) (1977). Born in Akita. Went to Tokyo in 1928 and began studying *tankin* under Sômei KAWACHI, pupil of the Court Artist Sôkô HIRATA. Following the traditional techniques of metal hammerwork, he fabricates by soldering metal plates of different kinds to create fresh pieces featuring color contrasts in the metals. In 1962 first participated in the exhibition of Traditional Japanese Crafts, in 1968 he won the President of Japan Crafts Association Award at its 15th exhibition and the Special Award at its twentieth exhibition. He never uses any machinery, but fabricates his shapes from gold, silver, copper, iron, and other metals by beating with nearly a hundred kinds of wooden and metal hammers, large and small. The apparently simple surface finish and traces of elaborate hammering are attractive for a tenacious, unspoiled effect reflecting the temperament of a man from northeastern Japan.

Tahei YONEMITSU (artist's name: Mitsumasa YONEMITSU, 1888—1982)

Holder of the technique for "Higo *zôgan*" and "Higo *Sûkashi*" (1965). Born in Kumamoto Prefecture, the former Higo Province. Began at about fourteen to train in the technique of Higo *zôgan* (Higo inlay) and Higo *Sûkashi* (Higo openwork) with his grandfather Yasuhira TANABE and subsequently his uncle Kichitarô TANABE. Celebrated as a distinguished master in this field in the tradition of Matashichi HAYASHI (1613—99), who moved to Higo as a gunsmith and later achieved fame in metal work sword accessories; and of Rakuju KAMIYOSHI, who was renowned as a great master subsequent to Matashichi. YONEMITSU's speciality was Higo *tsuba* (Higo sword guards) of elaborately wrought iron with openwork designs of "nine-luminaries formation of cherry blossoms," "quadruple fern fronds," "dried trepang," and other such motifs, the solid areas being incised with fine lines and inlaid with gold wire or decorated with inlay of double tendril scrolls, double lozenge diaper, spirals, family crests, and so on. The iron rust coloring is thought to be a "secret." He was an irreplaceable expert in metal work, which was about to disappear after the 1876 decree abolishing the wearing of swords.

SWORDS

Kin'ichi TAKAHASHI (artist's name: Sadatsugu TAKAHASHI, 1907—1968)

Holder of the technique for "Japanese Swordmaking" (1981). Born in Ehime Prefecture. Charmed by Japanese swords since childhood. 1917, went to Sadakazu GASSAN and Sadakatsu GASSAN in Osaka to learn the art of swordmaking. 1920, trainee at the Central Sword Society to study old swords. With his inborn ability and fiery zeal for study he mastered various styles, particularly the Bizen style. Signed "Ryûôshi" or "Ryûsen" on his swords. Unsurpassed by any other swordsmith in his field, he was called the foremost *horimono* technician of modern times. Participated in various exhibitions and won many awards. He also made copies of celebrated old swords, notably the work of Kagemitsu (registered as a National Treasure, 14th century), and attained superb skill almost equaling that of ancient masters.

Ken'ichi MIYAIRI (artist's name: Yukihira MIYAIRI, 1913—1977)

Holder of the technique for "Japanese Swordmaking" (1963). Born in Nagano Prefecture. Wishing to be a swordsmith like his grandfather, went to Tokyo in 1937 and entered the Japanese Swordmaking Institute. The following year became a pupil of Hikosaburô KURIHARA, beginning regular study of swordmaking, and mastered the techniques of the "Five Styles" which are fundamental in Japanese sword manufacture. Good especially at using *oroshigane* steel for the material, he has made many excellent blades of *jigane* (blade steel), none surpassed by old swords. Received the Special Award at the first Exhibition of Swordmaking (1954), and won special awards in successive years until the fifth exhibition. 1963, member of the Jury for the exhibition of Masterpieces of New Swords. 1966—1977, member of Advisory Committee for the Society for Preservation of Japanese Art Swords. His style was modeled after those of the Sôshû style and the Shizu school of Mino style.

Noboru GASSAN (artist's name: Sadakazu GASSAN, 1907—   )

Holder of the technique for "Japanese Swordmaking" (1971). Born in Osaka. Learned in childhood from his father Sadakatsu, and mastered the styles of typical Japanese swords such as the Yamashiro, Yamato, Bizen, Sôshû, and Mino schools. He is distinguished in the Yamato and Sôshû styles and excels particularly in the family tradition of Gassan swords of the Kamakura and Nambokuchô periods featuring the *hamon* of *hoso-sugu-ha* and the *kitae-me* of *ayasugi-hada*; in addition, he is a master hand at *horimono* (ornament engraved on the blade). 1934, gave guidance on swordmaking at Osaka Army Armory. Since 1967, received awards of Chairman of National Commission for Protection of Cultural Properties and Masamune awards, each twice, and the award of the Director of Agency for Cultural Affairs at the exhibitions of Masterpieces of New Swords; subsequently qualified for Non-examination Acceptance for the same exhibition; 1969, member of the Jury for the same. Swordmaking circles have suffered in the recent past from a shortage of *tama-hagane*, a special type of carbon steel necessary for Japanese swords. He, with Yukihira MIYAIRI and other colleagues, settled the matter by reviving the traditional method of steel manufacture known as *tatara buki* (a type of foot bellows). Member, Society for Preservation of Japanese Art Swords.

Yoichirô SUMITANI (artist's name: Masamine SUMITANI, 1921—   )

Holder of the technique for "Japanese Swordmaking" (1981). Born in Ishikawa Prefecture. After graduating in 1941 from the Science and Engineering Department of Ritsumeikan University, became a pupil of Masayuki SAKURAI, director of the Ritsumeikan Institute of Japanese Swordmaking, and mastered the "Five Styles" of Yamashiro, Yamato, Sôshû, Mino, and in particular the Bizen style. He excels especially in the florid *hamon* of *ôchôji* and *jûka chôji* rich in *nioi* effect and the clearly-marked *utsuri* in the *ji* ("ground") which characterize Bizen swords of the middle Kamakura period. 1964, made the "Tamamatoi Sword" dedicated to the Ise Shrine at the shrine's periodical reconstruction. 1965 and 1966, won Excellence award and Masamune award at the first and second exhibitions of Masterpieces of New Swords respectively; subsequently became Non-examination Acceptance member and then member of the Jury for the exhibition. 1967, Holder of Important Intangible Cultural Property of Ishikawa Prefecture. 1969, made a sword for the Ise Shrine at the shrine's periodical reconstruction. 1974, recipient of Masamune award at the eleventh exhibition of Masterpieces of New Swords. Currently engaged in development of self-made steel by means of *kogata tatara* (small-scale foot bellows) and in the study and reproduction of *tôsu* (knives) preserved in the study and reproduction of *tôsu* (knives) preserved in the Shôsô-in Repository of Imperial Treasures.

KIRIKANE

Ugorô SAIDA (artist's name: Baitei SAIDA 1900—1981)

Holder of the technique for "*Kirikane*" (1981). Born in Kyoto City. His family specialized in *kirikane* (cut gold leaf) decoration on Buddhist paintings, and in this capacity belonged to the Nishi Hongan-ji temple. After graduating from the Kyoto Municipal School of Arts and Crafts in 1920, therefore, Baitei studied *kirikane* technique under his elder brother. 1945, after his brother's death, succeeded to the hereditary family job, for which he polished his skill while studying and making applied art works decorated with *kirikane*. He showed these at Nitten and Traditional Japanese Crafts exhibitions, winning awards at 1959 and 1961 Traditional Japanese Crafts exhibitions. Making effective use of the characteristic texture of *kirikane* he created a unique style of his own with subtle, elegant works such as ornamental boxes, tea-ceremony objects, folding-screens, and so forth. He was nominated Holder of Important Intangible Cultural Property "*Kirikane*" in 1981 but died on June 1 in the same year.

HANDMADE RICE PAPER

Eishirô ABE (1902—   )

Holder of the technique for "*Gampi-shi*" (1968). Born to a farming family at Yagumo Village, Yatsuka County in Shimane Prefecture. From his youth he frequented the Institute of Paper Manufacture Research and experimented on paper of various materials. In 1931, when asked to make paper for written records that should be transmitted to future generations, he produced thick *gampi* paper. The paper accidentally attracted the notice of Muneyoshi YANAGI, leader of the folk-art movement, who greatly admired it. Thereafter ABE intensified his study of *gampi* paper and also participated in the folk-art movement, endeavoring to bring the excellent quality of Japanese paper to wide recognition. He is active not only in the field of *gampi* paper but also of *mitsumata* paper, *kôzo* paper, sundry types of vegetable-dyed paper, paper in which fibers dyed in various colors are mixed together in the course of screening, and so on. They are well known under the collective name of "Izumo folk-art paper."

Ichibei IWANO (1901—1976)

Holder of the technique for "*Echizen Hôsho*" (1968). Born to a hereditary family of paper makers at Ôtaki, Imadate-chô, Imadate County in Fukui Prefecture. He made profound studies not only of his own *Echizen hôsho* but also all types of *washi* made in various parts of Japan. *Echizen hôsho*, like *honmino-shi*, is type of a soft, warm color, made from the *Nasu kôzo* of Ibaraki Prefecture. It is very strong, for it is prepared over a long period of time to allow sufficient intertwining of the fiber. It was used for *hôsho*, the most important official documents in the Edo period of the feudal age. It is now used for *Ukiyo-e* woodblock prints. A highquality *Ukiyo-e* print is done in colors painted hundreds of times over on one sheet of paper. The paper has to be of a quality that will bear the heavy pressure of the *baren* (rubbing pad used in printing) without shrinking or extending, without the slightest distortion of register; the colors and forms must be repeated exactly. *Echizen hôsho* satisfies all these requirements; furthermore, the colors printed on it become increasingly clear with the passage of years.

ASSOCIATION OF SEKISHÛ HANSHI PAPERMAKING EXPERTS

Group Holder of the technique for "*Sekishû Hanshi*" (1969). *Sekishû hanshi* is currently manufactured by seven families living at Misumi-chô, Naka County in Shimane Prefecture (the former Sekishû Province). The seven families have organized the Sekishû Hanshi Preservation Society. *Sekishû hanshi* is made from the excellent *sekishû kôzo* obtained in the locality. The fiber of *Sekishû kôzo* is glossy, fine and long. *Sekishû kôzo*, furthermore, has a layer termed *ama-kawa*, faintly greenish in tinge and containing short fiber, between the outer bark and the layer of bast fiber. The fiber in this *ama-kawa* layer fills the interstices of the intertwined long fiber, serving to strengthen the paper. *Sekishû hanshi* is therefore known for its strength among the strong *washi* papers. The greenish *ama-kawa* part turns slightly dark in the finished paper, but the gloss of unbleached *sekishû hanshi* is attractive for its peculiar, subdued sheen. The paper is used for a wide variety of purposes such as for permanent records, linings, and so on.

SOCIETY FOR PRESERVATION OF AUTHENTIC MINO PAPER

Group Holder of the technique for "*Honmino-shi*" (1969). *Honmino* paper was originally made from a good quality *kôzo* termed *tsubo-kusa* obtained in the Mino region. This *kôzo* has become extinct and is replaced by the *Nasu kôzo* from Ibaraki Prefecture, which is quite similar in quality of fiber. The fiber of *Nasu kôzo*, like that of the *tsubo-kusa*, is fine, short, and has warm, soft color and gloss. *Honmino* paper, otherwise called *shoin-shi*, is used for spreading on *shôji* (sliding screen), for documents, and for other purposes. Sunlight from outdoors let through *shôji* of *Honmino* paper is diffused softly and illuminates the interior with gentle light. The paper is viewed against sunshine; its fiber therefore has to be intertwined evenly and regularly. The paper maker who makes *Honmino* paper must possess especially distinguished skill.

Honmino paper is currently manufactured by five families living at Warabi, Mino City, Gifu Prefecture. The Society For Preservation Of Authentic Mino Paper is organized by the heads of the five families.

ASSOCIATION OF HOSOKAWASHI PAPERMAKING EXPERTS

Holder of the technique for "*Hosokawa-shi*" (1978). *Hosokawa-shi* is a very strong *washi*, compact in texture and virtually without nap. It is made from *kôzo* obtained in Gumma Prefecture near its first place of manufacture. *Kôzo* from Kôchi Prefecture is also used, partly because the raw materials from Gumma are hard to obtain now.

Hosokawa-shi is useful for a wide variety of purposes because of its strong quality; it has answered the needs of the great city Edo (the present Tokyo) since the Edo period. It is now manufactured by twenty families living at Ogawa-machi, Hiki County, Saitama Prefecture, and three families in the neighboring Higashi Chichibu Village, Chichibu County in the same prefecture. They and another family specializing in making bamboo screen organized the Association of Hosokawashi Papermaking Experts which works for the preservation of the traditional technique of *hosokawa-shi*.

GLOSSARY

Aburi-daki
The first stage of firing, during which the temperature in the kiln is slowly and gradually raised, the ware being exposed to low heat over a relatively long period of time, so that the heat is distributed evenly in the chamber. The temperature is up to around 900°C. Called *nerashi* at Arita.

Age-bi
Finishing firing. When, after reduction firing, the temperature rises to about 1100°C, the glaze on the ware at the central part of the chamber melts. Air is thereafter supplied to create an oxidizing fire and the final firing is done in heat increased to 1300°C.

Aka-e
Red decoration. Polychrom *iro-e* with red as the keynote, or a ceramic ware so decorated. Chinese *aka-e* had examples of Tz'u and related wares from the Chin dynasty; especially famous, however, are those from the Chia-ching (1522—66), Wan-li (1573—1619) and T'ien-ch'i (1621—27) eras of the Ming dynasty. In Japan, *aka-e* began to be made after Chinese prototypes around the middle of the seventeenth century.

Applying metal foil
Decorating fabric by applying gold or silver leaf or foil is called *suri-haku*. Many *Noh* costumes remain from the Momoyama period when this technique, used alone or in combination with embroidery (*nuihaku*), flourished.

Applying the design (katatsuke)
Katatsuke is the process, repeated down the length of the fabric, of aligning the stencil and forcing the resist paste through the stencil holes with a spatula. Another common term for this work is *norioki*, "putting down the paste resist."

Bengara
Colcothar, an iron oxide of high purity, used for the red and yellow colorants of *iro-e*. Made by heating *roha* (ferrous sulphate). It is said that at Arita, where it is called *rokuhan*, it is useds after being kept for two years or so in water to remove the sulphuric acid ingredient. Red pigment so prepared does not produce nice color unless it is pulverized and exposed to air over a long period of time. There is a legend that the red pigment used in the T'ien-chi'i period in China was ground over many years by successive generations, from parents to children and from children to grandchildren, before it was used in the third generation.

Bingata
Bingata (Okinawan stencil dyeing) is a characteristic craft of Okinawa. The special designs of this stencil dying method were developed to decorate the clothing worn by the noble society of the Ryukyu court during the period when the islands were in effect an independent kingdom. Technically *bingata* is based on the same methods of stenciling and paste resist that were developed in Japan proper. However the designs and the colors employed are distinct from those of the Japanese Honshu tradition and are uniquely Okinawan in style and feeling.

Bunten
A government-sponsored annual art exhibition first held by the Ministry of Education in 1907. This exhibition was sponsored by the Imperial Fine Art Academy from 1919 to 1936, and was called the Teiten during this period. After 1937, with a new sponsoring body, the Teikoku Geijutsu-in (Imperial Art Academy), it was called the Bunten. However, this Bunten was later called the Shin-Bunten (New Bunten). In 1946 the New Bunten was replaced by the Nitten.

Cutting a stencil of stripes
Cutting stripes involves repeatedly pulling a narrow cutting tool along a steel straightedge, down the stencil from top to bottom. Because the cutting motion of pulling towards one differs from the punching or cutting out of regular stencil making, this is an art unto itself. Craftsmen who specialize in stripe stencils are few indeed. It is necessary to stabilize the fine lines of the stencil to prevent any movement during use that would spoil the even design. To accomplish this, two sheets of stencil paper that were laid together and cut at the same time are pulled apart. Then fine threads are laid over one stencil face and the two halves realigned and glued together again as the tannin dries. A separate group of craftspeople do this process of *itoire*, "putting in the threads."

Dami
Part of the blue and white technique (cf. *sometsuke*). A method in which the outlines of a design are drawn with a brush and its interior subsequently coated with *gosu* solution, using a thick brush amply laden with the pigment. The painter who practices this process is called *dami-te*, one in apprenticeship being referred to as *dami-ko*. At Arita since the Edo period the *dami* has been a woman's job. The similar process in *aka-e* is also termed *dami*.

Dami-fude
A brush used for *dami*. Made of hair, whose tips are not worn, from the root of a deer's tail. It holds liquid well and lets liquid run easily. A design is painted with the brush amply laden with *gosu*, the butt end of hair being tied to keep the design from being mottled.

Dôgubori
The shaped blade point of a cutting tool is used with a quick, punching motion to cut out, for example, a single petal of a cherry blossom. To cut the entire design in the stencil requires not only painstaking repetition but usually the use of different tools for each component shape. The cutting tool consists of two pieces of shaped blade slightly opened upwards so that the unwanted paper areas after being cut away are forced up and out with each thrust of the blade.

Double stencils
If two stencils are used in combination there are greater compositional possibilities and the resulting design can be made more complex or beautiful. With two stencils a finished design may result where the motifs stand completely independent. This would be impossible to cut in one stencil without its falling apart.

Often the main design is cut on one stencil (*omogata*). With one application of resist paste using the *omogata*, the design is sixty per cent complete. Then the other stencil (*keshigata*, or "canceling out of unwanted details" stencil) is aligned and the resist goes on a second time to complete the design. This method is sometimes called *okkakegata* or repeat stenciling, and in fact the method need not be limited to two stencils. Three or more stencils may be used for ever more detailed patterns. In a very different category from the repeat stencil dyeing of *naga-ita* chûgata is stencil *yûzen* dyeing. This requires several hundred stencils in a process of truly pictorial depiction in varied colors on silk fabric.

Dye-containing resist paste
In the *utsushinori* method chemical dyes are mixed into the resist paste, which is then applied to the fabric. Exposed to steam, the dye colorants are fixed in the fabric and the paste is later washed away. This technique came into use in places like Kyoto and Osaka at the middle of the Meiji period. In Tokyo the method was widely adopted for *komon* and other dyeing at the beginning of the century. Today *ironori*, colored paste resist, is used throughout the broadest variety of dyeing processes.

Fashioning
Ceramic objects are fashioned by various methods: *tebineri* (hand-modeling), *wazumi* (coiling), *rokuro mizubiki* (wheeling), *tatara* fashioning, *uchikomi* fashioning, as well as *ikomi* (casting) fashioning, and others. *Wazumi* is a method in which a jar, pot, etc., is fashioned by preparing the clay in the shape of a long rope and coiling it from the base upward. In *rokuro mizubiki*, the commonest method of handmade ceramics, a shape is effected by the rotation of a wheel turned by hand, by kicking, or by electricity. *Tatara* is to make a box-shaped object by combining clay boards. In the *uchikomi*, an object is fashioned roughly in the *rokuro* method, placed in a matrix, and beaten into it to make hexagonal, ocatagonal, chrysanthemum-shaped, and other forms. At Arita the last-mentioned method is called *kata-uchi zaiku*. *Ikomi* is to fashion a shape by pouring liquid clay into a plaster mold and letting it adhere to the absorbent inside wall of the mold.

The vessels thus fashioned are classified by their shapes into *ko-mono* (small pieces) such as teabowls and teacups, *hira-mono* (flat or shallow pieces) like dishes, and *fukuro-mono* such as wine bottles, teapots, and so forth.

Fukizumi
Soufflé. A technique of underglaze decoration in which *gosu* pigment is sprayed on the surface of the ware to achieve a pointillist effect. Examples are found in Chinese blue and whites of the late Ming-early Ch'ing periods, and also in Japan since the early Imari.

Fukizumi may be sprayed over the entire interior surface of a dish or bowl; applied on a vessel with its border covered with *en-gami* (hem paper), which is then removed to leave that part reserved white; or sprayed around paper cutouts (*fusegami*) placed on the surface in rabbit and other designs.

Fusube leather
This is a very old process of dye-curing leather a single color by smoking it. A design results when the smoke cannot penetrate those areas where a stencil has adhered to the leather or, in variation, where strings have been bound tightly round the leather, or the paste resist design has been directly applied to the untanned leather.

Futsugata
This is the term for a type of double stencil dyeing, used in Kyoto and extremely popular from the late 1880 until about 1920, that creates a fine, delicate pattern in color on white ground. People in the Kantô area called the same technique "Kyoto *okkake*." Unlike the usual repeat double stencil dyeing method, the pattern is created with two equally important stencils each carrying fifty per cent of the design.

Glazing
There are various methods of applying a glaze on a bisque: *nagashi-gake* (pouring), in which liquid glaze is poured on the surface from a ladle; *zubugake* or *tsukkomi* (dipping), in which the object is immersed in the glaze, and so on. To apply a glaze on a body dried sufficiently without bisque firing is termed *name-gake* (raw glazing).

Ginsai (silver painting)
A technique of overglaze silver decoration similar to *kinsai*.

Gosu (blue) and purple
The principal constituent of *gosu* is manganese, cobalt being only slight in amount. At the high temperature of glaze firing manganese evaporates and cobalt works as the colorant, resulting in indigo-blue *sometsuke*; at the low temperature of enamel firing manganese rather than cobalt works and produces a purple. *Noto gosu*, named after its place of origin is manganese, but such natural *gosu* is hardly obtainable now. The most stable purple is obtained by melting *shiratama* and manganese in a crucible into frit state and adding appropriate amounts of *to-no-tsuchi* and silica.

Gu
A green, yellow, or purple pigment made from the *kasu* obtained after the *tatewake* process.

Hakuji
White porcelain, fashioned with petuntze and kaolin, covered with a transparent or translucent white glaze, and fired. White porcelain was produced in Japan in the early Imari period and was gradually disseminated throughout the country. Due to differences in ingredients and in firing methods, the white color varies to some extent among the Imari, Kakiemon, and Kutani wares. White porcelain with a faintly bluish glaze is termed *seihaku-ji* (in Chineses *ying-ch'ing*).

Hikizome

This term is limited not only to *katazome* (stencil dyeing) but is commonly applied to hand painted dyed fabrics (such as *yûzen*), and refers to applying the dye with a brush to fabric that has been stretched over a series of flexed rods. Because only one side of the fabric receives an application of dye, resist paste is also applied only to one side.

Hon-yaki

Glaze firing. A fashioned ware, bisque fired or underglaze decorated on the bisque, is covered with a glaze and subjected to full firing. Glaze firing is done in a large-scale kiln such as a *noborigama* (climbing kiln), the firing heat rising to almost 1300°C. In *iro-e*, the ware is decorated with overglaze enamels after this glaze firing and subsequently fired again at a lower temperature.

Hori or -bori

Taka-bori: Carving in high relief where the pattern is raised.
Sukidashi-bori: A kind of carving in low relief. The flat background is furrowed so that the pattern shows up as in relief.
Ke-bori: (hairline carving): The pattern consists of thin lines engraved by a V-shaped chisel.
Katakiri-bori: Unevenly V-shaped carving lines; one side of the line is carved into the metal surface at a sharper angle (almost vertical) than the other.
Sukashi-bori: Perforation carving.
Kata-bori (*Katachi-bori*): Carving of details of designs on the rough shapes and outlines that have been hammered out on the metal plate from the back side; almost all *menuki* are made according to this method.
Maru-bori (carved in the round): Figure carved from a solid piece of metal.

Important intangible Cultural Property

The Law for Protection of Cultural Properties, enacted in 1950 under the jurisdiction of the National Commission for Protection of Cultural Properties (now the Agency for Cultural Affairs) provides that in addition to such tangible cultural properties as pictures, sculptures, and buildings, intangible cultural properties should also be protected by the State. By definition, "intangible cultural properties" are intangible cultural products realized through such human endeavors as drama, music, dance, and applied arts which have a high historical or artistic value in and for this country. The State protects the techniques by designating as Important Intangible Cultural Properties the arts which it recognizes as specially valuable and also by recognizing as their Holders those who represent the high standard of such properties. In order to provide a standard for the reservation of intagible cultural properties, records are taken by various means such as photographs, films, technical samples, scores, long-playing records, etc.; in the field of applied arts, similar efforts are made to create a sound basis for the preservation of traditional techniques by making models or taking records of manufacturing processes.

Iro (enameled) Nabeshima

An elaborate enameled porcelain ware originated at the offical ceramic factory of the Nabeshima clan, ruler of Saga fief during the feudal age, located at Okochi, Nishi Matsuura County, Hizen Province (the present Okochi-machi, Nishi Matsuura County, Saga Prefecture), featuring a peculiar style and technique of decorationon a white porcelain body in underglaze blue and overglaze colors in which red, yellow, and green are dominant. The Imaizumi Imaemon family which served as official *aka-e* decorators during the feudal age have inherited its traditional technique and continue it to the present day.

Iro-e

Overglaze enamel decoration, executed by painting a design on the glaze of white porcelain or pottery in red, yellow, green, dark blue, purple, and other pigments and firing at a temperature lower than that of glaze firing.

Iro-e (in metal work for sword fittings)

Thin gold and silver or other alloy sheet metal fixed on the ground metal by means of soldering to provide a varicolored pattern.

Iro-mi

Test pieces to be withdrawn from the kiln during firing to examine the state of melting of the glaze. Called *agete-mi* at Arita.

Itogiri

A ceramic vessel of square, rectangular, oval or other non-circular form has a *kodai* (foot) matching the shape of the vessel. In this case board-shaped flat pieces of even thickness are cut out from the mass of paste with thread (*itogiri* means thread-cutting) and are worked into the designed shape to form a *tsuke* (applied) *kodai*.

Itoire

In order to keep the design (of stritpes, etc.) from shifting in the stencil face, very fine silk threads form a mesh between two thin sheets of stencils that are perfectly aligned and glued together as one stencil. The direction and density of the threads are determined by the design. Often the threads run in one direction across the main design, for example, perpendicular to the stripes. The two halves of the stencil, which have been cut as one sheet and pulled apart, are glued back together as part of the process of gluing in the threads with tannin. To prevent the tannin from clumping or filling up the fine spaces between the threads and the design, the thread inserter, traditionally a woman, often the wife of the stencil cutter, blows vigorously as she goes along.
Since the early 1920s the craft of *itoire* has been widely replaced by the use of a layer of gauze glued to one side of the stencil sheet with lacquer. The inserted thread stencil is still required, however, for fine stripe patterns and other designs.

Ji (Finished surface of the metal gorund)

Migaki-ji: Polished and smooth surface.

Ishime-ji: Finely roughened or stippled metal surface appearing like a stone surface.

Tsuchime-ji (hammer-mark ground): Slightly uneven or finely dented metal surface hammered for the purpose of smoothening.

Jiki (porcelain)

Jiki is a hard ceramic ware made by fashioning a paste of pulverized petuntze into shapes, glazing, and firing at a high temperature. The major material for handmade porcelain currently used in Japan is pulverized and refined quartz dolerite, with the addition of certain amounts of effloresced kaolin, a type of clay known as *gairome,* or other such clay of more viscous quality.

The porcelain body to be decorated with overglaze enamels is covered with a glaze composed of feldspar, silica, lime, and a small amount of petuntze, to which wood ash, preferably with no iron ingredients, is added, causing a fine foam to appear on the glaze surface. The body so prepared is the most suitable for hard-color *iro-e.*

Jishiro

In *chûgata* when the fabric ground which is protected by the resist paste during dyeing is left white, it is called *jishiro.* When the proportion of ground to colored motifis is large it is *o-jishiro,* and when the ground in reserve is divided up by a fine colored pattern it is termed *ko-jishiro.* In the opposite case, when the design motifs are reserved in white and the ground is dyed, the term is *jizomari* (colored ground).

Kamishimo komon (komon for kamishimo—old ceremonial dress)

This expression referes to the *komon* patterns dyed for *kamishimo* worn by the Bushi (soldiers) in the Edo period.

The technique consists of dyeing a small minute pattern in one color, the *komon.* Throughout the Edo period a tremendous variety of patterns were produced. There were some *komon* patterns, used by the Daimyô families, which were called *tomegara* (forbidden patterns). In modern times (from the beginning of the twentieth century), the patterns have been made available for general dress. Today these traditional *komon* patterns are used for women's clothes (kimonos).

Kannyu (crackle)

Cracks occurring on the glaze surface due to the different rates at which the body and the glaze contract after firing. At Arita it is termed *kan* or *hiki.*

Kappazuri (kappa rubbing)

The method of rubbing the dye materials onto the stencil with a brush. It is also called *surikomi* (rubbing in).

Kata-e-zome

Kata-e-zome refers to the work done by individual artists to create original pieces of dyed art using the traditional techniques of stencil dyeing (*katazome*). The term was coined originally to describe the art of Keisuke SERIZAWA when he was designated the Holder of an Important Intangible Cultural Property or skill, in other words, a "National Living Treasure," according to the law about Important Intangible Cultural Properties established in 1954. Since that time artists working in *kata-e-zome* have come to prominence one after another.

Katazome

In general usage *katazome* is the technique of applying resist paste through a paper stencil on which the desired motif has been cut, and then dyeing the fabric to color those areas not protected by the paste. In the broader definition, however, the term is not limited to paper stencil dyeing, but includes all methods of dyeing such as using wood, metal, or other materials as stencils or even printing plates, thus eliminating or varying the resist step. One method used from early times, *nassen* dyeing, applies the dye colorant directly through the stencil — as in silk screen printing. Another traditional technique, *mokuhan-zuri,* stamps the design directly on the cloth with a printing block of wood, again omitting the resist paste step. Other methods of *katazome* include printing the design in resist wax or paste using a plate, or *kata* (which in Japanese means both plate and stencil) and jamming or compressing parts of the cloth between wood or metal boards so tightly that the dye cannot flow and is absored by those areas caught between the boards.

Keiseki

Silica. Also termed *hinooka-ishi* after a locality in Kyoto. The vitreous component of enamel colors. Added to *shiratama* to make it less easily meltable or to add viscosity.

Ki (yellow)

Produced by mixing a slight amount of *bengara* in *shiratama.* *To-shirome,* an oxide of antimony, can also be used as a material for yellow.

Kin-gama (or nishiki-gama)

A wood fuel kiln for overglaze enamel firing. It is a direct flame kiln, but contains an *uchi-gama* (muffler) in the chamber to prevent the flame from working directly on the objects being fired. The flame rises along the outside of the muffler, heating the objects to a temperature of about 900°C. An electric kiln is sometimes used.

Kinrande

The technique of applying gold leaf with lacquer and fusing it on a glaze fired body or on a body previously decorated in overglaze enamels (*aka-e*), which developed in China during the Ming dynasty.

There are two varieties: one in which gold leaf cut out in desired designs is

applied on the surface, and the other in which the design is drawn on the surface in lacquer and gold leaf is applied over it. The piece so decorated is placed within a sagger in the kiln and fired at about 100°C so that the lacquer is not completely carbonized.

Interior lines on the gold leaf, for example the veins of a tree leaf, are scratched with the point of a metal needle, bamboo, or wood while the lacquer is half dry.

Kinsai (gold painting)

A technique of overglaze gold decoration, effected by painting a design in gold paint on a bisque fired body or on a red-enamel fired body and firing the piece again to fuse it. After fusing, the gold part is burnished with scouring brush, an agate bar, sea-bream tooth, etc. *Iro-e* with *kinsai* added is often termed *nishikide*.

Kiribori

The method of cutting a stencil where tiny circular holes are repeatedly punched out to produce a fine stipple pattern. *Same-komon*, "sharkskinlike stipple," is one classic version of this technique. The head of the awl (*kiri*) used for *kiribori* is shaped in a half-moon like a narrow cylinder cut in cross section. Pushed and twisted in a half revolution it bores a neat circular hole. The most minute *komon* patterns require such extremely fine workmanship that they are labeled with the prefix *goku* ("ultimate"), as in *gokusame, gokudoshi*, or *gokugyogi*. A *kiribori* pattern with slightly larger dots that on first glance could be mistaken for a *goku* pattern is called *nitari* ("close resemblance").

Ko-Kutani

Among the early styles of enameled porcelain in Japan is the *Ko* (Old) *Kutani*, said by tradition to have been made during the Edo period at Kutani in Kaga Province (now Ishikawa Prefecture). The existing examples of Ko-Kutani are *densei-hin* (preserved, not unearthed pieces). Much remains unclear about its origin, history of its manufacture, and reasons for its abolishment. The characteristics of Ko-Kutani are thought to lie in painterly designs in which purple, green, and yellow are dominant, and in the powerful brush work with which the designs are painted. The impressive effect of broad, heavy color spaces covering *gosu* outlines is quite unique in Japanese enameled porcelain.

After Ko-Kutani factories were abandoned new official factories were established at Kaga, Daishoji, and other places during the Bunka-Bunsei eras (1804—29). Their products are termed Saiko (restored) Kutani. The present Kutani ware derives from them.

Komon

Today the term *komon* is defined so broadly as to include any kimono fabric of repeated small motifs aligned in one direction and done in *katazome*. Originally *komon* fabric (*kamishimo*) was used only by the warrior upper class, but the traditional distinction between *komon* and *chugata* has disappeared in common usage. In order to make it clear, the Commission for Protection of Cultural Properties, since 1954 when it designated the technique as an Important Intangible Cultural Property, officially uses the term "*Edo-komon*" for contemporary pieces.

The board on which *komon* dyeing traditionally is done resembles that for *chugata* (stencil dyeing of cotton *yukata* cloth) but it is slightly larger, 7.5 m. in length by 45 cm. in width. The fabric is stretched out on the board and the paste resist applied through a stencil down the length on one side. The fact that Edo period examples of *komon* are usually dyed on only one side leads to the conclusion that the *hikizome* method (applying the dye with a brush) was used in most cases. During the second half of the Meiji era, the method changed with the development of new chemical dyes that could be mixed and applied with the paste resist. In place of the dye that had been applied with a brush, *komon* dyeing was done by using a spatula to apply the dye-containing paste to the material and then exposing the material to steam. In steaming the chemical dye is fixed in the fabric.

Kon (deep blue)

Cobalt oxide is used for *kon* in overglaze enameling. Natural cobalt was formerly used.

Kôsai (hard color) and nansai (soft color)

Terms to denote the quality of pigments used on *ito-e* porcelain.

The hard color—also termed *gosai* (in Chinese *wu-ts'ai*, "five colors") as the basic colors are red, yellow, green, dark blue, and purple:— is made by adding a small amount of powdered metal oxide as coloring agent to the powder of lead glass known as *shiratama* (frit).

The red, lacking both thickness and transparency, is similar in quality to the soft color known as *funsai* (in Chinese *fen-ts'ai*).

The *funsai* (powdery, opaque, colors) created in China during the Yung-cheng period (1723—35) in the Ch'ing dynasty, are opaque pigments of cloisonne enamel quality. While they permit free brush work as in ordinary painting, they are considered to be lacking in thickness and in "texture," so that they are seldom used by Japanese ceramic artists. They are used abundantly, however, for mass-produced Western-style table ware and are therefore known more com-monly as *yo-enogu* (Western pigments) or *hira* (flat) *enogu*, as contrasted with the hard color which is termed *wa* (Japanese) *enogu*.

Mokuhan-zuri (wood block printing)

A method of dyeing on cloth using a wood block of relief carving and applying the dye materials or colored pastes directly to the block. Depending on the sizes of the wood blocks, the cloth is placed on the relief surface of the block and pressed or rubbed to transfer the pattern to the cloth. Other similar methods used are called wood block dyeing (*mokunazome*) or block printing.

Mushikui (worm-eaten)

The worm-eaten appearance of the glaze that has peeled to expose the body because of different shrinkage of the glaze and the body; frequently used on Chinese blue and white wares of the late Ming and early Ch'ing periods, and often on Ko (Old) Imari. At Arita it is termed *fuchigasa*.

Naga-ita chûgata

Chûgata refers to the stencil (and the technique) used for dyeing the light cotton kimono fabric for *yukata,* or informal summer wear. Traditionally the cotton fabric was stretched on a long board, or *naga-ita,* and the stencil repeatedly laid down the length to apply the design in resist paste. A board of *momi* (a type of fir) wood, cut to traditional measurements that translate to about 7 m. long, 45 cm. wide, and 2.5 cm. thick, was considered the most suitable. The term *naga-ita chûgata* came into use in the 1920s to distinguish this traditional method that continued despite the growing popularity of the *tenugui* dyeing method. This simpler method of folding the cloth over after each application of resist was developed for thin cotton towel fabric (for *tenugui* towels) and did not require a long board. It was soon used for *yukata* too. Because the cotton fabric of traditional *naga-ita chugata* is vat dyed, the design must be applied in resist paste on both sides of the fabric in order for the motif to come out clearly and distinctly. To produce a more complex or free-floating design two stencils (*okkake* stencils) are used one after the other over the same area, a process which requires exactly matching the pattern four separate times (twice on each side) for each application of resist.

Before the mid-nineteenth century *chugata* stencils, like those for silk kimono *komon* fabric, with a small or fine pattern exactly repeated down the whole length, were cut within a field of 12 cm. from top to bottom. After this period as design motifs became larger and were positioned over wider space, the cutout area of the stencil became wider, but the length, which matches the width of kimono fabric, has remained unchanged.

Nakadachi-shi (transmission paper)

A traditional method used at Arita for repeating a design by drawing it on a sheet of *mino-gami* paper in a carbon ink called *hyotanzumi* ("gourd ink," formerly made from charcoal of gourd, now from that of paulownia wood) and pressing it reversed against the surface of a vessel to leave an ink impression there. A design can be repeated twenty or thirty times by this method. The impression is then traced in *gosu* pigment. The carbon ink burns and disappears during firing.

Nigoshi-de

A body of warm milk-white color peculiar to the Kakiemon ware, which Kakiemon SAKAIDA XII, assisted by Kakiemon XIII, succeeded in reconstructing. The *nigoshi-de* body, thought to have been originally created by Kakiemon I in his last years, was inherited through the successive generations of the Kakiemon family as one which makes the *aka-e* decoration over it stand out more clearly and beautifully. The art was lost with the decline of the family at the end of the Edo period. Kakiemons XII and XIII, after consulting the *Tsuchi-awase-cho* (Recipes of Clays) of 1690 and after many experiments (for example, adding the peculiar porcelain clay of Iwayagochi), finally succeeded in reviving the technique in 1953. In the dialect of the Saga district the milk-white water remaining after washing rice is called *nigoshi.* The term *nigoshi-de* (nigoshi type) probably derives from it.

Nitten

This exhibition was first called the Nihon Bijutsu Tenrankai (Japan Fine Art Exhibition) and the first exhibition was held in 1946. However, it can be traced back to the Monbusho Bijutsu Tenrankai (Bunten) started in 1907. The sponsoring body of the Nitten was the Ministry of Education at first, but after 1949 the Nihon Geijutsu-in (Japan Art Academy) and the Nitten Unei-kai (Nitten Administration Office) jointly sponsored it, and it was half-governmental, half-private. Since 1958 it has been a non-governmental exhibition sponsored by the Nitten Corporation.

Pinholes

Tiny holes often occur on the surface of slip or glaze. They are cavities left by the combustion of particles of organic substances that existed in the clay. At Arita they are called *subosashi.*

Processes of Painting a Design in Overglaze Colors

The surface of the body is first wiped with a thin solution of gelatin or glue to form a film to prevent the pigments from running or being repelled by oil. Black lines are drawn with manganese or *gosu* powdered carefully in water to which tea has been added. Red pigment is also ground in a tea solution. This is because tannin in the tea helps to fix the painted ornament. After the red and black decoration is finished and is dried thoroughly, colors are added with yellow, green, purple, and dark blue pigments mixed with a solution of *funori* (a glue plant). Because manganese and *gose* used for the preliminary drawing do not fuse at lower than 800°C, they should be covered with enamel colors other than red.

Enamel colors prepared for the painting of the design are entirely different from the colors resulting after firing. They should be used with the finish colors in mind.

Reduction fire and oxidizing fire

When insufficient oxygen is in the kiln, carbon monoxide (CO) in the firing chamber takes on oxygen from a metal oxide existing in the glaze and settles as carbon dioxide (CO_2), thus reducing the metal oxide. For example, ferric oxide (Fe_2O_3) becomes ferrous oxide (FeO), resulting in a bluish glaze. With oxidizing fire, in which a sufficient supply of air promotes oxidization, the opposite is the case. An excessive amount of air in reduction firing causes the glaze to be yellowish in part; in the opposite case it turns grayish. At Arita these hues are termed *kinami* (yellowish) and *kuromi* (grayish). When the result of firing is the finest grade, that kiln is called *tonbo-gama.*

Resist paste

Resist paste, or starch, prevents the fabric from absorbing the dye in those areas where it has been applied. In *katazome* dyeing it is usually applied through a stencil. This paste, sometimes called "stencil-applied" paste, varies slightly in composition according to the particular type of stencil dyeing, but the main constituents are high gluten rice flour, rice bran (*nuka*), and lime.

Rôkechi

Rôkechi is the term used for dyed pieces from the Nara period where wax was used as the resist medium. In most extant cases the wax was stamped on with several different small stamps. The technique is known both for repetition over and over of the same simple shapes and for the grouping together of a variety of component shapes to achieve a paintinglike composition.

Rokushô

A type of copper oxide, the green colorant in *iro-e*, obtained by keeping brass powder, copper plate, bits of copper wire, etc. immersed in salt water. Before use these are washed in water to remove the salt completely and then dried.

Saya (saggers)

Fire clay boxes, capable of being piled one over another, for containing the ware during firing and to prevent flame or ash from falling directly on the ware. Called *engoro* at Seto and *boshi* in Kyûshû.

Seme-daki

Reduction firing covering the inside of the kiln with flame and cutting off the air supply after the glaze near the fire has begun to melt at about 950°C. Called *kubekomi* at Arita.

Shakudô

Copper bronze alloy mixed with gold (6—7%) and finished by chemical means to a glossy dark bluish black color (the alloy itself looks like red copper).

Shibuichi

Copper and silver alloy usually in the proportion of three (copper) to one (silver); dark gray.

Shinchû

Brass; copper and zinc alloy yellow in color.

Shippô

Closionne or colored fused on the surface in a pattern.

Suaka

Red copper.

Shiratama

Frit. Basic flux for enamel colors; a sort of glass powder made by melting in a crucible a mixture of silica, borax, and red lead and then cooling it quickly. Different melting points of the materials produce various types of frit meltable at any desired temperature between about 800° and 600°C, thus causing changes in the quality and hue of the enamel colors.

Shita-etsuke (underglaze decoration)

Effected by painting a design in *gosu* or other pigment directly on a bisque, covering it with a transparent glaze, and firing; blue and white (*sometsuke*) is typical.

Some-nishiki

A combination of underglaze blue and overglaze colors; that is, a porcelain ware fired after *sometsuke* decoration, then decorated on the glaze in red, yellow, green, purple, black and other colors, often with the addition of gold or gold and silver, and fired again. *Some-nishiki* began to be manufactured at Arita in the seventeenth century and was exported to Europe through the Dutch East India Company.

Sometsuke

Blue and white. A white porcelain ware bisque fired, decorated in *gosu* (cobalt oxide), covered with a transparent glaze, and glaze fired, the *gosu* producing an indigo blue color. In China, where it is termed *ch'ing-hua* (blue decoration), it originated during the Yüan dynasty with Ching-tê-chên as the major center. The technique was introduced to Japan by visiting Korean potters and has been used since the early Imari period.

Stencil paper

Stencil paper ready to be cut is called *katajigami*. It is made from sheets of a handmade *kôzo* (a type of mulberry that produces long, strong fibers) paper glued together with persimmon tannin, or *kakishibu*. For *komon* design stencils two thin sheets of paper are joined together. Stripe stencils require two slightly thicker sheets. And *chûgata* stencils are even thicker, so that three sheets are glued together in the usual practice today. A stencil of the desired thickness of sheets glued together with tannin is called *namagami* ("unaged paper"). In the past, several years of drying were required before the stencil was ready to cut, but the stencil paper used at present is cured in a smoke treatment (*muro-karashi*) and can soon be put to use.

Stencils (katagami)

From the Edo period to the modern day, families of craftsmen in Shiroko and Jike villages have made what has become Suzuka City, Mie Prefecture, famous as the production center of stencils. These stencils are often called Ise stencils or Shiroko stencils from the old name of the areas. The traditional stencil-making methods of *kiribori*, *tsukibori*, *shimabori*, and *dôgubori* have been handed down and continued. For delicate motifs such as stripes, the stencils are still firmly fixed with inserted threads, in a separate process of *itoire*. Craftspeople specialize in each of these methods, each person possessing the painstaking skill and training necessary for making one of the various types of stencils, the most important of which are *komon*, *chûgata*, and stencil *yûzen*.

Stencil spatula (hera)

In early seventeenth to nineteenth century paintings of, for example, "Various

Craftsmen at Their Work" (*shokuninzukushie*), we can find representations of a long, narrow bamboo spatula (*hera*) being used by the dyers to force resist paste through the stencil. From the late nineteenth century on a convex spatula made of *hinoki* (cypress) wood, called a *debabera*, was used in the Kanto area. Still used in Tokyo today are a similar, convex *debabera* or *yokoppaki*, employed in a back-and-forth motion across the narrow width of the fabric, and a *tategaki*, a blade moved down the length of the fabric. In Kyoto or Kanazawa, on the other hand, a rectangular *komabera* is most often used.

Stencil yûzen

Stencil dyeing to produce *yûzen* designs is a separate method called stencil *yûzen*. Many (even hundreds) of stencils are used in combination over a single area to apply a design in colored resist paste (*utsushinori*), or else to apply the dyes directly through the stencils. This precisely repeated process results in the very pictorial designs for which *yûzen* is famous.

Suemon

Sheet metal cut in the shape of a pattern is placed on the surface of the guard and fixed in place.

Sumihajiki (or suminuki, ink reserve)

A technique of *sometsuke* used frequently for *komon* (tiny pattern) decoration on Nabeshima ware. A design is drawn in carbon ink lines on a bisque fired surface, a *gosu* pigment is applied thinly over it, and the piece is fired again, whereupon the carbon ink burns and disappears leaving the drawing reserved in white against the *gosu* blue. The resulting decoration features a soft effect.

Suribitta

This is a stencil dyeing technique that results in a pattern closely resembling *hitta-shibori*, the painstaking traditional tie-dyeing of Japan. Not merely a simple substitute for tie-dyeing, however, *suribitta* requires a stencil of extremely intricate handiwork. The stencil is laid on one side of the fabric and the dye applied through it with a brush.

Suyaki (bisque firing)

The raw ware is dried thoroughly after fashioning and bisque fired prior to glaze firing in order to harden the body and prepare it for decoration and glazing. Bisque firing may be omitted for mass-production. The body shrinks to some extent in bisque firing.

Sword (parts of the Japanese sword)
Bôshi: Patterns of tempering on the point.
Kissaki: Point of the blade.
Yokote: Dividing line (transverse ridge) between the surface of the blade and the point.
Shinogi: Longitudinal ridge line tetween the edge and the back, usually closer to the back.

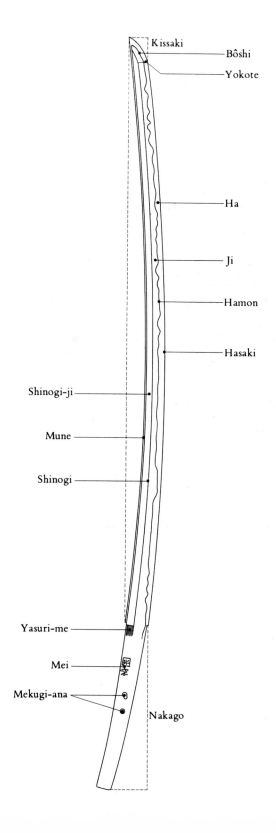

Ha: Sharp edge of the blade.

Hamon (ha-mon, edge pattern): tempering pattern along the edge of the blade.

Mune: Back of the blade, opposite the cutting dege.

Ji: Blade surface between the tempering pattern (*hamon*) and the ridge line (*shinogi*).

Jigane (Ji-gane): Steel structure of the blade surface.

Shinogi-ji: Blade surface between the ridge line (*shinogi*) and the back (*mune*).

Nakago: Tang of the blade.

Yasuri-me: File-marks on the tang.

Mei: Signature and inscription chiseled on the tang.

Mekugi-ana: Rive hole in the tang (may beseveral, done at different times).

Mihaba: Width at the center of the length of blade.

Yaki-haba: Width of tempered surface of blade.

Nanako-ji: Tiny fish-roe shaped dots all over the metal surface made with a round punch with a hollowed recess in the tip to produce a minute circular shape (raised dots).

Tatewake
Pigment classified by the grade of particles. In the case of overglaze enamel materials, the finest particles are termed *hana-uki*, next *naka-uki*, and the rest, *kasu*. Green vitriol (ferrous sulphate) is also classified into *hana-dami* and *kasu*. *Gosu* for blue and white is likewise classified into fine particles and *kasu*, the former being used for *dami*.

Tokin
Coating in gold or mercury.

Tokyo Fine Arts School
The present Tokyo University of Arts at Ueno, Tokyo.

Tô-no-tsuchi
White lead. Also called *tô-seki* in Arita. A flux used for lowering the melting temperature of enamels.

Tsukibori
In this technique a narrow, small knife is used to cut out the stencil. The blade point always faces away from the stencil cutter as he works with a boring or scooping motion. The method is particularly suited for cutting very fine patterns. Designs in older stencils, even of stripes, were invariably cut either by this process or *kiribori*.

Usu-ao
A bluish green pigment made from cuprous oxide and *kasu* (cf. *tatewake*).

Usu-ruri
Faint blue. A technique of *sometsuke* peculiar to Nabeshima, in which the decorated areas are coated with carbon ink and the other side of the vessel is dipped in a thin solution of *sometsuke* pigment, thus covering the surface without using a brush.

Uttori
Similar to *iro-e* method in metal work, but done in a more primitive way; used in the Muromachi period.

Uwa-etsuke (overglaze decoration)
A design in pigments painted on the glazed surface of a ceramic object. *Iro-e jiki* (enameled porcelain) is a typical example.

Vat Dyeing
Tsukezome is dyeing by completely submerging or soaking the fabric in a bath of indigo or other liquid dye. With this method both sides of the fabric are dyed so that when a stencil or printed motif is desired the design in resist paste must exactly match on both sides of the cloth. If the resist were applied to only one side, the dye would seep through, muddying or destroying the motif.

Yamagane
Copper incompletely refined.

Zôgan (Various kinds of Craftsmanship including Inlay)
Hira-zogan: The surface of the ground metal was first carved in the shape of the pattern to be inlaid, and the pattern cut from other metalic material was inlaid in the carving to make a flat surface; flat inlay.

Nunome-zogan: The metal surface (usually iron) was first chiseled in textured or roughened surface, and thin gold or silver sheet or wire was hammered into the fissures of the surface (a type of inlay but much less durable than true inlay).

Sen-zogan: This is very similar to *hira-zogan* but the inlay is done in very thin lines instead of a flat plane.